Sex & Chocolate

Edited by

Richard Peabody & Lucinda Ebersole

"A Cup of Chocolate: Letter to the Fan Maker from Sade" from *The Fan Maker's Inquisition* by Ducornet, © 1999 by Rikki Ducornet. Reprinted by permission of Henry Holt and Company, LLC. Moira Egan's "Lady Godiva" was first published in *Literal Latte*, and appeared in her book *Cleave* (Washington Writers' Publishing House, 2004) and is reprinted here by her permission. The excerpt from Enid Futterman's *Bittersweet Journey: A Modestly Erotic Novel of Love, Longing, and Chocolate* (Viking, 1998) appears by permission of the author, © 1998. "Her Affair" is reprinted from *A Chapter from Her Upbringing* by Ivy Goodman. © 2001 by Ivy Goodman. Reprinted by permission of Carnegie Mellon University Press. The excerpt from Jaimy Gordon's novel *Bogeywoman* first appeared in the *Notre Dame Review* (premiere issue) and in the book published by Sun & Moon, 1999. Reprinted here by her permission. The chapter from *Chocolat* by Joanne Harris, © 1999 by Joanne Harris. Used by permission of Viking Penguin, a division of Penguin Group (USA) Inc. "The First of Your Last Chances" by John McNally. Reprinted from *Troublemakers* by John McNally by permission of the University of Iowa Press. © 2000 by John McNally. Susan Smith Nash's "A Good Éclair Is Hard to Find" appeared in her collection *Channel-Surfing the Apocalypse* (Avec Books, 1996) and is reprinted here by permission of the author.

R R Angell's "French Twist" was first published in *WordWrights!* (Argonne Hotel Press, 2000). Jodi Bloom's "Cookies" appears in the chapbook *Teenage Vixens from the Netherworld* (Argonne Hotel Press, 1999). Jane Bradley's "A Taste of Gianni Mascarpone, Please" first appeared in *MOTA Volume 4: Integrity* (Triple Tree Publishing, 2004). Mary Ann Cain's "Wired on Chocolate in the Midget Bed," first appeared in *Abiko Quarterly Review*. Richard Grayson's "Those Old Dark, Sweet Songs," appeared in the webzine *Pug* and in his collection, *The Silicon Valley Diet* (Red Hen Press, 2000). Nancy Ludmerer's "Eavesdropping" appeared in *Night Train #2* as a Firebox Fiction prize-winner. Christy Sheffield Sanford's "Dreams of Snakes, Chocolate and Men" appeared in *Only the Nude Can Redeem the Landscape, The Exquisite Corpse, Anthology of Poetry since 1970: Up Late*, and *The Stiffest of the Corpse: An Exquisite Corpse Reader, 1983–1988*. Gregg Shapiro's "Chocolate-Dipped" was published in issue 2 of the dangerous queer fiction website, *Velvet Mafia* (www.velvetmafia.com).

ISBN: 0-931181-21-6
First Edition
Published in the USA

Book design by Nita Congress. Cover by David Paul Wyatt Perko.
Printed by Main Street Rag Publishing, Charlotte, NC.

Paycock Press, 3819 North 13th Street, Arlington, VA 22201,
www.gargoylemagazine.com

Acknowledgments

Special thanks for aiding and abetting to Nita Congress and M. Scott Douglass without whom none of our books would be possible. Tons more thanks to David Paul Wyatt Perko for the cover design. Hats off to all of the advance subscribers whose generosity helped underwrite this project. And a rain of chocolate sprinkles (plus kudos for all the tasty quips) to: Jenny Badman, Lauren Baratz-Logsted, Elizabeth Benedict, Robert Bixby, Jodi Bloom, Loretta Bryant, Brie Burkeman, Ann Burrola, Elise Carpon, Leslie Davisson, Barbara DeCesare, Denise Duhamel, Julia Duncan, Janice Eidus, Lora Engdahl, Barbara Esstman, Taryn Fageness, Jean-Marc Favreau, Amy Fries, Fiona Giles, Steve Gillis, Jeff Goldman, Ivy Goodman, Karen Elizabeth Gordon, Carl Graf, Richard Grayson, Bob Gregory, Barbara Grosh, Margaret Grosh, Caitlin Johnson, Casey Kane, Karen J. Kovacs, Peggy Kuo, Robert Lang, Mary Leary, Sara Levy, Joe McCourt, Michelle Markley, Bob Mentzinger, Julee Newberger, Mia Pardo, David Plumb, Lily Pond, Maritza Rivera, Ricky Rood, Jamie Salek, Holly Sanders, Michele Slung, Lee Smith, Laren Stover, Silvana Straw, Todd Swift, Michael Tieg, Kyla Wazana Tompkins, Jim Williamson, and the York (England) City Museum.

In memory of Beatrice Wood, fellow Pisces, who died at 105 and attributed her longevity to "chocolate and young men."

Contents

Introduction

"...every 100 grams contains 660 milligrams of phenyletylamine, a stimulant closely related to the body's own dopamine and adrenaline. It raises blood pressure and heart rate, and heightens sensation and blood glucose levels. In short it induces a high similar in kind—if not in intensity—to sexual climax."
—*New Scientist*, 1851 (Dec. 12,1992), p. 26

Why this book? Because we're the only two people who have ever poured chocolate syrup on a Barbie doll as part of their performance at a major literary festival. Said festival would be the Miami Book Fair of 1993 where we joked that we were premiering the "Karen Finley Barbie doll" as part of our song and dance to promote the *Mondo Barbie* anthology. Some of our audience walked out offended while the majority laughed and cheered. How could we follow that visual joke? And bingo another idea was born—for what could be better than sex and chocolate?

Why doesn't everything we put in our mouths taste as good? And for that matter, why doesn't everything we read massage the same sensory organs? Can chocolate be as erotic as sex? Can sex be as erotic as chocolate? We decided to find out by discovering poets and writers who wanted to examine sex in/with/for/about/ because of chocolate. Here at last we have gathered all possible manifestations of sex and chocolate—an assortment of sticky fun and games that cater to all five senses.

Since the actual language of chocolate is a triumph of the advertiser's art—it is wicked, seductive, sinful—this anthology seemed a natural. After all, Casanova preferred chocolate to champagne when it came to getting down to business. Madame Du Barry gave chocolate to all of her suitors. Montezuma drank fifty cups of chocolate a day before visiting his harem. As one writer said, "Chocolate is soul food. Body food, too." But our scavenger hunt for chocolate erotica yielded few results. Truly surprising considering that Erotica has been such a strong publishing market this past decade. Puzzled that we had encountered no chocolate love manifestos, or rapturous sonnets on the cocoa bean's power to dazzle and win love or lust, besides the bittersweet magical realism of Laura Esquivel's *Like Water for Chocolate*, we wondered if this anthology would ever fly.

How could these works be so difficult to find? Chocolate has always been a serious indulgence whose sexual message was the bottom line throughout history—from the very beginning as far back as 1000 B.C. when it was used by the Indians of Central and South America. The Aztecs worshipped the stuff, called it *xocoatl* or *chocolatl*, a gift from their Plumed Serpent god, Quetzalcoatl, who brought the cacao seeds from The Garden of Life and gave them to man. They used cacao beans as money and served cacao as a drink to the high and mighty of their court. The Toltecs and Itza used chocolate in their rituals. Chocolate was given to virgins before they were sacrificed. The Spanish brought it to Europe in 1519, thanks to Cortés, and kept it a secret. But by 1606 the secret was out, and the rest of Europe was discovering the elixir. By the 1800s, physicians advised their lovelorn patients to eat chocolate to help calm their emotions.

Today the very idea of chocolate in the bedroom can recharge some rundown motors and tired libidos. A man who brings a woman chocolate offerings expects (hopes for) a reward. Ads geared toward women have stressed additional benefits—health, delight, youth. Those geared toward men promise a boost in energy.

But you really don't care about the history of chocolate, do you? (Wink, wink.) So, after our hunt unearthed a few existing pieces (Enid Futterman's *Bittersweet Journey* and Joanne Harris's *Chocolat*, along with works by Rikki Ducornet and Susan Smith Nash), we asked writers to create something new. Only two rules were given: Every work must have both sex (any kind) and chocolate (any kind).

The results are funny, feisty, and sexy, as authors went into a collective chocolate haze and delivered the chocolatey goods. Some find sex and chocolate in Paris, some find it in Chicago, some find it at the mall. R R Angell and John McNally have fun with chocolate bondage; Jodi Bloom's teenage protagonist bites off more than he can chew (complete with recipes); sex is a defense mechanism so a writer can buy a little more time with the computer in Ann Androla's short-short; Rikki Ducornet presents an epistolary Marquis de Sade; Kevin Killian recalls a legendary and apocryphal Rolling Stones scandal; Shelley Jackson takes Willy Wonka where even Johnny Depp would never dare to go; Moira Egan channels Lady Godiva, the first lady of chocolate; Robert Bixby indulges in phone sex; Nick Carbo and Gregg Shapiro play sex games; the hooker in Denise Duhamel's story tricks for chocolate; Cynthia Hendershot's protagonist has sex with an FBI agent in a chocolate factory; Cheryl A. Townsend and Ivy Goodman fantasize, while Leslie Pietrzyk and Susan Smith Nash focus on sublimation and longing; Jane Bradley's chocolate addict falls for an old Italian sweet shop owner; Mary Ann Cain finds that Death by Chocolate gives her insomnia; as a voyeur watches, a woman in Antony Oldknow's story has a near-death chocolate experience; a teenager falls for the man whose crazy wife killed her mother in Nani Power's story, which uses chocolate as a memory device; Eugene Stein addresses sex education among sisters; Jaimy Gordon deals with anorexia and obsession in an asylum setting; Enid Futterman takes a Parisian chocolate odyssey from shop to shop; Richard Grayson's protagonist travels to Hershey Park, and Lynda Schor does too, where she enters into the politics of chocolate and chocolate people; Deirdra

McAfee's story crosses the color line and plays cancer and the unknown against a tableau of loss and longing; the sculptor in Anna Geyer's story establishes the John Thomas Candy Co., whipping up chocolate penises for the true connoisseur; Christy Sheffield Sanford riffs on the magical mystical qualities that drive sex and meaning; Patrick Chapman lampoons television space operas and revenge fucking in giving a past-it Valentino his just desserts; a Chocolate Lady breaks up an engagement in Laurence Gonzales's story, which gives "chocolate cake" a new meaning; Nancy Ludmerer introduces a baby monitor into the mix with too true frustration and hilarity; and Lee Upton sheds light on a very bitter chocolate bunny's point of view.

As the pièce de résistance, we asked friends for additional sex and chocolate quips, which we've layered between the works in this volume like swirls of chocolate in a colossal torte.

We wanted a delightful bonbon of a book that teased you, dear reader, seduced you, and ultimately pleased you. A Valentine's Day gift that even Freud could truly love. *Bon appétit.*

Richard Peabody
Lucinda Ebersole
Washington, D.C., 1998/2006

Why Chocolate Is Better Than Sex

- You can GET chocolate.
- You can have chocolate all weekend long and still walk straight on Monday.
- Chocolate satisfies even when it has gone soft.
- You can safely have chocolate while you are driving.
- You can make chocolate last as long as you want it to.
- You can have chocolate in front of your mother.
- If you bite the nuts too hard the chocolate won't mind.
- With chocolate, you don't HAVE to use a wrapper.
- You don't have to take the whole thing into your mouth at once.
- The word "commitment" doesn't scare off chocolate.
- You can have chocolate on your desk without upsetting your co-workers.
- With chocolate there's no need to fake it.
- Chocolate doesn't make you pregnant.
- You can have chocolate any time of the month.
- Good chocolate is easy to find.
- You are never too young or too old for chocolate.
- When you have chocolate it does not keep your neighbors awake.
- Having chocolate in public won't get you arrested on a morals charge.
- With chocolate size doesn't matter; it's always good.
- You don't have to tell chocolate how good it was afterwards.

JOHN McNALLY

The First of Your Last Chances

John McNally is the author of two novels, America's Report Card *(2006)
and* The Book of Ralph *(2004), and one story collection,* Troublemakers
*(2000). He was a 2005 National Magazine Award Finalist in Fiction. His
stories have appeared in over thirty magazines, including* Gargoyle, Virginia Quarterly Review, *and* New England Review. *A Chicago native, he
presently teaches writing at Wake Forest University in North Carolina.*

My girlfriend, Patrice, points at a cloud and says it looks like a
cow. Another day, it's the profile of a lumberjack. Occasionally,
the image gets more complicated: a fat man walking his poodle,
or the head of a famous statesman, Winston Churchill or Henry
Kissinger, hovering ten thousand feet above us.

"Look," she'll say. "Mousy Tongue."

"What?" And then I'll remember: it's a nickname, a pun in her
vast repertoire of puns. "Ah, yes," I'll say. "Got it! Mao Tse-tung.
Of course, of course."

"See him?"

"Nope."

Two days ago, she saw my mother holding a spatula.

"Do you see her?" she had asked. "Right there—see that dark
streak? That's her bottom lip. You know that look she gets? That's
it to a tee, Michael. It's amazing."

But I couldn't see it. Patrice's clouds are not my clouds. It's
been four weeks since we've had sex, and what I see each time I
look up is raw carnality: clouds humping clouds, or long cumulus

1

erections floating overhead, ominous as zeppelins, swallowing us with their shade.

"I'm sorry," I said, "but I don't see my mother up there."

"Really?"

"Really."

■

At work, Darren tells me he's recorded a voicemail ad for himself in the personals. He's just a kid, turned nineteen last month—a tall, skinny, hollow-eyed college dropout. His cigarette is jammed in the corner of his mouth, and each time he speaks, he fills the cab of the truck with thick, blue-gray smoke.

"They've got these different categories," he says. "*Looking for Love, Unusual Appetites, Three's Company.*"

I crank down the window, suck in a lungful of fresh air.

"So I recorded one under *All Tied Up*," Darren says. "For laughs, you understand."

"*All Tied Up*," I say. "And what was your message?"

"Oh, Christ, I don't know. 'Looking for a woman who can tame this beast.' Something like that." He's smiling and laughing, but there is genuine fear in his eyes. The reason he's telling me this is because he wants reassurance that what he's done is OK, but I won't give him any. When he realizes this, he says, "I've got my first date. Saturday afternoon." He says this quietly, almost as an afterthought.

"Hey, hey!" I say. "Congratulations."

Darren is hunched at the wheel, so I clap him on the back. My burst of enthusiasm perks him right up. "Her name's Tova," he says. "Get this—she asked if I was a dom or a sub."

"And?"

"I said, sometimes a dom, sometimes a sub. Depends on my mood."

"Good answer."

He squints through smoke and says, "You think?"

"Absolutely," I say. "When in doubt, straddle the fence."

Darren snuffs out his cigarette, and in a rare moment of self-confidence, he grins at me and says, "That ain't all I'll be straddling, pal."

■

After it gets dark, I carry a coat rack up from my truck to my apartment. I'm head of University Surplus—our job is to lug away whatever the departments don't want and offer it once a week to the public at a reasonable price—and every night for the past five years I've taken a little something home for myself, a bonus for making it through another day. Yesterday it was a file folder from the Department of Mortuary Science and Funeral Service. Today it's a coat rack from a dean's office. Tomorrow we're removing every last item from the old Student Health building, which is scheduled for demolition, and I've got my eye on a magazine rack from the waiting room. What I'd really like is a water fountain—we have three of them—but I haven't yet figured out the logistics for hooking one up inside my apartment.

After dinner, I go to Patrice's. She lives across the street from Wrigley Field on the top floor of a brownstone. Clearly, I have done something wrong—I have erred in any of a thousand ways—but Patrice won't tell me what I've done. Whatever it was, though, it happened a month ago, and this is why the sex has been cut off. Any minute now I expect Patrice to give me an ultimatum. She has a pun for this, too. *Ultimatum* becomes *old tomatoes*, as in, "They've been living together for five years, so Marcy finally gave Jack the old tomatoes: marry her or move out." Like Mousy Tongue, the old tomatoes is part of another language, a language with a past I can't quite wrap my brain around. It's another Patrice from another time in her life talking to people I've never met. Nonetheless, I see the old tomatoes coming, and I'm prepared to duck.

Outside Patrice's window is a gorgeous view of Wrigley Field. I'm in the middle of moping, staring mindlessly at the empty ballpark below, when Patrice walks over and starts mussing my hair, what's left of it. She pushes it around until the top of the fringe that surrounds my head curls up onto the bald spot like a pair of horns trying to sprout. I read this as a sign of forgiveness, but when I try to return the touch, a brush of thumb against her breast, she grabs my wrists and leans back, surveying her work. Patrice is a Classics major at Northwestern, and what she's doing is fashioning me into a famous Roman.

"So," I say. "Who am I?"

"What do you mean?"

"I mean, which Roman am I?"

Patrice opens her mouth, but the first vibrations of an approaching train stop her from speaking. It's the Evanston Express roaring up from the Belmont stop south of us. Patrice's apartment is so close to the tracks, I could lean out her window, if I felt like it, and knock on the passing train's windows. Every time a train goes by, it's an event around here. First, pots and pans rattle. Then the leaded glass of Patrice's bay window starts to shiver in its sockets, thrumming harder and harder. Then the beast itself appears—whistle blowing, metal grinding against metal, showers of sparks thrown at us from the hot rails. Eventually, the last car blasts past us, and the train snakes around another apartment building, disappearing from view. This happens several times an hour, all day long and most of the night.

"Wow," I say when it's over. "It's like friggin' Cape Canaveral around here. How do you stand it?"

"Stand it?" she asks. "How do I stand *what?*"

"Living here," I say.

Patrice lets go of my wrists and glares at me. I'm in trouble again, so I try steering us back on course. "Hey!" I say. "You never told me who I am. I'm a Roman, right? Come on, Patrice. Tell me. Who am I?"

"Nobody," she says. "You're nobody." Then she heads for the kitchen.

■

"We talked dirty on the phone last night," Darren says. Darren speaks out of the corner of his mouth, the corner without his cigarette, but the cigarette still bobs up and down with each syllable.

"Watch where you're walking," I say. "Keep your mind on work." We're carrying a gynecological examination table out of Student Health. It's the fifth one we've moved this morning, and I am now acutely aware of all the never-before-used muscles in my body, muscles which feel prodded with sharp instruments one second, then set ablaze the next. There are fifty-two rooms in Student Health—four of which are large waiting rooms—and we need every last thing cleared out of here by Monday morning before the wrecking ball strikes the east wing.

Darren says, "I've never talked dirty before. I mean *really* dirty."

"Why do you think I'm interested?" I say. "Why?"

"She asked me if I've ever done a woman in the, you know, in the *butt*."

I get a better grip on the table by looping each of my arms underneath a stirrup. I grunt, heave the table higher.

Darren wiggles his end of the table through a door frame. "Do you and Patrice ever talk dirty?"

"Patrice does. But that's just how she is. She talks dirty to everyone."

Darren and I stop when we reach Betty. Betty is the better of our two dump trucks—reliable, most days; Veronica, on the other hand, is sluggish, unpredictable, sometimes hard to start. My other two workers are loading Veronica full of cabinets with sliding glass doors, each cabinet as heavy as a pool table.

"I bet Betty here talks dirty," I say, lowering her lift. "Don't you, honey?" We scoot the exam table onto the lift, then I hit the lever so we can ride up with it. The back half of the truck is already cram-packed full of shit—waiting room furniture, upright scales, even the rubber torso of a woman, apparently for teaching breast self-examination techniques.

Darren flips the butt of his cigarette out the back of the truck, and without warning, he breaks into his impression of Tova: "*I want you to take that nice big throbbing cock of yours,*" he says, "*and I want you to stick it as far up my hairy ass as you can get it.*"

Two undergraduate girls appear just then from between Betty and Veronica. They are on their way to class, taking a shortcut across campus, thick books clutched to their chests. They glance quickly into the dark cavern of the truck, and when they see the two men inside—one hollow-eyed and talking dirty, the other sweaty and out of breath—they turn away quickly and pick up their pace.

Darren chuckles sheepishly. He fiddles with the stirrups, then stops what he's doing and says, "Just what the hell are these things for anyway? I've never seen them on any examination table *I've* been on." He wiggles the stirrups again, pushing them in and out of the table, the way a bored child would.

I reach over, take hold of Darren's chin, and playfully wag it back and forth. "You're in over your head, my friend," I say. "*Way* over."

∎

After work, I sit in the darkened office and read through the printouts of our stock. We always have more discarded items than we have room to store—too many dormitory desks, too many chairs, too many outmoded computers and achingly slow dot-matrix printers. This is the hour when I decide what I'm going to take home. Will it be an oscillator today or will it be a set of free weights? Pyrex beakers or a swing-arm lamp? *This* or *that*? I'm never at a loss for things to choose from. The fact is, enough junk passes through here in a year's time to furnish a small country.

I settle on one of the small jewels of Surplus: a Bell and How-ell sixteen-millimeter projector. The mere sound of its chugging sprockets and clicking shutters is enough to lull me back to grade school, all those long mornings spent slouching in webs of light while grainy films about photosynthesis, Stranger Danger, and reproduction danced and jerked before our eyes.

I carry the projector out to my truck, then return to Surplus. After some digging, I find a box of empty reels, two new projector lamps, and a stack of Biology films about a fictional guy named Joe.

∎

When I arrive at Patrice's apartment, she buzzes me in, but by the time I climb the stairs up to the third floor, she's already in the shower. I turn the Cubs game on and wait. The game on TV is the exact same game being played right outside Patrice's window at Wrigley Field. I hate baseball, actually, but I decide to do an experiment. I try to see if I can detect the millisecond delay in the broadcast. When the crowd outside the window roars over a nicely executed play, the crowd on TV roars as well. So here I sit: ear toward the TV, thumb on the remote control's volume, hoping to catch a moment so small it boggles the mind.

This is the sad way I occupy my time these days instead of having sex. Patrice is in the shower, and just a month ago I'd have been in there with her... *Patrice's back mashed up against the tub surround, her right leg raised and jutting out, the ball of her foot pressing down onto the tub's edge to give her some leverage while I move in and out of her, in and out.* This is how things used to be around here: *panties, still warm in the crotch, resting on the floor*, a sight that rarely fails to get me hard. But not anymore. Nope. I am reduced to watching a sport I hate and acting like a child. Another month, and I'll be outside plucking apart grasshoppers and poking sticks mindlessly into sinkholes of mud.

"Hey," I yell. "Is everything OK in there? You turned into a prune yet or what?"

No reply. Half an hour has come and gone, and Patrice is still in the shower. Then Jose Hernandez hits a home run for the Cubs, and the crowd roars louder than ever. There is no difference, I decide, between real time and TV time, so I give up my on project. I turn to the picture window, hoping to see the ball as it soars out of the park and onto Waveland Avenue, but as soon as I lean closer, the window's glass explodes into the apartment, causing me to duck and fall out of my chair. For a second I think it's Jose Hernandez's ball that has smashed the window, but when I regain my balance, I see that it's a rock the size of a golfball. I poke my head out the broken window and catch a glimpse of the culprit, a grown man. He's running down the street, looking every so often over his shoulder, making sure no one's on his heels. I'm about to yell, but he turns a corner and disappears from my sight.

Patrice steps from the bathroom wearing a robe I've never seen, an extra-fluffy salmon-colored towel wrapped swami-style around her head. She doesn't seem to notice the shattered glass all over her living room. All she notices is *me*. She stares a bit, then yawns and says, "Oh. You're still here. Well, I need to paint my toenails," she says. "So if you'll excuse me." And then she is gone again, locked in the bathroom, leaving me once more to my own devices.

I sweep up the glass, seal the rock up inside of a Ziplock baggie, and set it on the kitchen table with a note (EXHIBIT A, it reads). Then I take the El home.

■

Saturday morning, Patrice and I take a stroll through Lincoln Park while two men we don't know fix her window.

"They'll steal your CDs," I say.

Patrice shrugs.

"They'll take your TV," I say.

She shrugs again.

"OK," I say. "It's your junk, not mine. Want to go to the zoo? The monkeys are always worth the price of admission."

"Monkey shmonkey," Patrice says.

"Not in the mood to visit the relatives today? So be it," I say.

We plop down onto a park bench, deciding our next move. Patrice leans her head back, and I figure she's soaking in the sun when she says, "That big cloud? Right there?" She points.

"What is it?" I ask.

"Hairy ass," she says.

"Really!" I say. At long last, I think. Abstinence has finally taken its toll on Patrice. We are riding the same wave. We are both seeing sex where there is no sex.

Patrice squints, shades her eyes, and says, "Hairy Ass Truman."

"Ah," I say. "Of course." First, Mousy Tongue; now, Hairy Ass.

"The cloud next to it?"

"Yes?" I say, but I am tired of her antics, tired of funny names and pointless cloud gazing.

Patrice turns to me and says, "It looks like you." She says this like an accusation.

I look up, and for once I see what she sees. The cloud does *look* like me. But it also looks like I'm wearing a fedora, and it would appear that I have a hard-on that's roughly twice as long as I am tall.

"And look," Patrice says. "Gerald Ford's over there. Sort of hovering behind you."

But now I'm lost again, unable to see anything other than myself.

"Gerald Ford," I say. "Now, *there's* a fascinating man, if you ask me. Here's a guy who forgave Nixon for his crimes. Nixon! Of all people! Ford found it in his heart to forgive this awful, evil man." I say all of this without any pretense of subtlety. The man who broke Patrice's window, I've decided, is her new lover, and what I need from Patrice is forgiveness, even if it means forgiveness for crimes I can't remember committing.

"It's called a pardon," Patrice says. "Ford *pardoned* Nixon, and I'm sure it was agreed upon before Nixon resigned. Part of the deal, I imagine."

I stand up from the bench. I pace back and forth, then stop in front of Patrice. "I know what this is about. The old tomatoes, right? Don't tell me it's not. You're going to give me the old tomatoes. Am I right?"

I am saying all of this louder than I mean to, and people are watching us. They are watching *me*.

"OK," I say. "OK, OK. What did I do? I can't take this anymore. Tell me, would you? Tell me what I did so you can pardon me and we can move on."

"Why should I tell you if you can't remember?"

"Why?" I say. "*Why?*" Her question is a preposterous follow-up to my question, but I store it away as evidence—*concrete evidence*—of the difference not just between Patrice and myself, but between *all* men and women, from Adam and Eve to every last couple, fat and thin, young and old, here with us today in Lincoln Park.

I soften my voice and ask one last time: "Why?"

Patrice narrows her eyes. She says, "Does the word *fudge* mean anything to you?"

"Fudge? Are you saying I *lied* to you about something? Is that it? I *fudged* the truth?"

Patrice lets out a deep, hoarse sigh. It is a sigh of disgust, a sigh of finality. She stands and gathers her belongings. "Look," she says without looking at me. "I need to get going. My paper on the Triumvirate is due on Monday."

Patrice walks away, and I yell to her back, "I have *never* lied to you. Do you hear me? Never!"

∎

Only after Patrice is gone and I have made a public spectacle of myself do I understand the fudge she means. My apartment is across the street from a shop called The Fudge Pot—they specialize in expensive fudge and chocolate—and a month ago Patrice gave me a twenty-dollar bill to buy her a brick of Turtle Deluxe. Two days later I found that same twenty-dollar bill crumpled in the front pocket of my jeans, and I had thought, *A windfall…Too good to be true!* Here was twenty dollars I couldn't remember—a miracle, it had seemed, since I had less than ten bucks left to my name and payday was still a week away.

"Jesus Christ," I say. "*Fudge!*"

But it's not the fudge that's gotten to her. I realize that now. Fudge was merely a clue, a fingerprint attached to the larger issue at stake, and the only reason Patrice even brought it up was so that I might figure everything out for myself.

On the day that Patrice had given me the money to buy fudge, she had also broached the subject of me moving in with her. "It just makes sense," she'd said, and she started to tell me how much money I'd save in rent, but I cut her off: "Tell you what. Let's talk about this when I bring your fudge over. We'll sit right here and gorge ourselves on the most expensive chocolate in the city and hash out this moving-in-together thing once and for all. Whaddaya say?" "Deal," she said, and I said, "Deal." And then I never brought the fudge.

I had forgotten about the fudge, truly, or else I wouldn't have been so surprised at finding the twenty bucks two days later. It's possible that I subconsciously pushed the fudge aside. This was *not* the first time Patrice had suggested that I move in with her; it *was*, however, the first time I had agreed to talk about it. We had struck a deal! We may even have shook on it. But once the fudge was out of my mind, so was the deal. Until today.

"Ah, shit," I say. "Shit."

Parents move their children along. Couples look anywhere but at me.

"Shit, shit, shit," I say and throw my hands up and sigh.

There is a message on my answering machine from Darren when I get home. His afternoon date with Tova is over, and he's calling me from the emergency room at Rush-Presbyterian.

His voice, trembling, whispers from my machine: *I need a ride. And bring a soft pillow, would you?*

I am there in less than twenty minutes, watching the poor bastard limp toward my truck.

"Darren," I say, offering my hand, pulling him up into the cab.

"Ow, ow, *easy.*"

"What happened?" I ask.

"I need a drink," he says. "I need a drink to help the Darvocet go down."

"You really shouldn't mix—," I start to say, but Darren raises his hand.

We go to a bar called Smoky Joe's, and Darren sits quietly, wincing when he shifts from one haunch to the other. He shivers periodically and shakes his head as if trying to empty it—trying, I suspect, to shake off what must surely have been the horror show of his life, his date with Tova.

After an hour of silence and three shots of rail whiskey, Darren says, "It started out in good fun. I mean, hell, when she started talking dirty to me face to face, I couldn't *wait* for her to tie me to the bed. You'd have felt the same way."

"Of course," I say.

"I had one of those gags in my mouth. You know, the kind with the red ball. So I can't talk, right? And she says, 'I'm going to give you three chances to bail. I'll ask you three different times what you want me to do, and if you want me to stop, just wiggle the little toe on your right foot.' Simple enough, right? So she gives me my first chance right then and there, but since she hasn't done anything to me yet, I don't wiggle jack-shit. Then she does all sorts of, you know, *good* things to me, mostly with her tongue, so when she asks me the second time, I don't do anything again. Why would I? Hell, I was having a real bang-up time. Then she brings out the heavy artillery, and I start screaming my head off. Hot wax, whips, dildos—you name it. She even burnt me with my own cigarette." Darren opens his palm to show me, but I can't see much more than a blemish. He says, "She never asked me a third time. She never gave me my last chance."

"You're lucky she didn't kill you," I say.

"You're telling *me*," he says. "Swear to God, I thought it was check-out time."

We order more beer, more shots. Darren starts to light a cigarette, but once the lighter is in his hand, he thinks better of it, meticulously returning the cig to its pack and dropping the lighter back into his droopy shirt pocket.

"Jesus," I say. "This whole Tova experience, something like this'll probably sour you for good on dating."

"You'd think so, wouldn't you?" Darren says. "But I'm not so sure about that. I know you're not going to believe this, but it's opened my eyes. I was sitting in the emergency room and I started thinking, there's so much out there, so much shit I've never even *heard* about. It's weird, I know, but this whole experience brought that home for me. It made me realize that I haven't even scratched the surface yet. I don't know how to say this—I mean, Tova wasn't the right woman for me, but she unlocked this massive door of possibilities. *Infinite* possibilities, man."

"You're drunk," I say.

"No, no, I mean it," Darren says.

"I shouldn't have let you mix the booze and pills," I say. "Listen to yourself. A woman just rammed you with a dildo, and you're waxing philosophic on me."

"OK," Darren says. "Whatever. But I don't see what's so god-damn exciting in *your* life that you think you can criticize *mine*."

He lifts his drink and starts to lean back quickly in his chair, his cue to me that the conversation is over, but a sharp pain rockets through his ass, and Darren lets out a yelp that causes half the patrons to turn and look at us.

I'm pissed, but I don't say so. I stew instead. I can settle into silence like no one else I know. Part of why I'm pissed, though, is because Darren has unwittingly stumbled upon a few sad truths. What *is* so goddamn exciting in my life? Why *do* I think I'm in a position to criticize him?

"Excuse me," I say. On my way to the men's room, I stop at the pay phone and call Patrice. I get her answering machine, so I leave a message, telling her to meet me at my apartment at midnight, that we need to talk tonight, we need to hammer out, one way or the other, what's left of our future together. "The old tomatoes," I say and hang up.

Back at the table, I ask Darren if he can give me a hand. "I need to move a few things from Surplus to my apartment."

Darren lets out a loud stage laugh. "Are you kidding?" he asks. With much more caution this time, he leans back in his chair. Then he proceeds to wag his head at me and snort and look around the bar at the other patrons, all for dramatic effect. "Haven't you heard anything I've been saying?" he says. "I mean, look at me. I'm in pain. I can barely *walk*."

I remove four fifty-dollar bills from my wallet and slap them down in front of him.

"OK," Darren says. "All right. What the hell."

■

Darren and I haul the last heavy item up to my apartment by nine o'clock. After Darren leaves, I shower and shave, and by the time Patrice knocks at the door just shy of midnight, everything is in perfect order, so I yell for her to come in.

"What's all this?" she asks. "What's going on here?"

I'm standing behind the Check-In partition, hands clasped on the counter. I'm wearing a long, white examination coat and a stethoscope around my neck. From the *Highlights for Children* scattered about the room to the Norman Rockwell artwork on the wall, my apartment has been converted into a doctor's office, courtesy of Surplus and the old Student Health building.

Patrice reaches across the Check-In counter, lifts the stethoscope, and holds it to her mouth. "*You*," she says, "are a man with a loose screw. You realize that, don't you?"

"Do you have an appointment?" I ask.

She drops the stethoscope. She huffs and shakes her head. "Yeah; sure; why not?"

"Well then," I say. "Please have a seat." When she doesn't move, I point to the waiting room.

"This is too much," she says, but she does as she's told. She sits in the middle of a row of connected chairs. When she realizes that I'm not going to say anything right away, she crosses her legs and picks up a magazine, flipping through it once, quickly, then tossing it aside. She taps her fingers impatiently on the chrome of the chair's armrest. I open and close filing cabinet drawers, making a show of it, before flipping off the lights. "Hey!" Patrice yells, but I shush her. The old Bell and Howell sixteen-millimeter projector starts to chug, and a funnel of light shoots across the room. The shadow of Patrice's head floats on the screen behind her.

"Scoot down," I say.

Patrice looks over her shoulder, sees the eerie silhouette of her own head, then slides down onto the floor. The movie is a classic: *Joe's Heart*. It is one in a series of movies about Joe's various organs. I sit next to Patrice. I press my mouth against her ear and ask, "Are you here to see a physician?"

"I guess so," she says, playing along, seeming to get into the spirit of the night.

I loop a lock of Patrice's hair behind her ear, and while Joe's heart pounds around us, I lean in and kiss her cheek. "What do you think about Joe?" I ask softly. "He seems in pretty good shape."

Between kisses, Patrice says, "He should probably avoid strenuous activity. Too much stress on his heart—" we kiss "—might kill him."

"You think?" I ask.

"Absolutely," Patrice says.

"Here," I say. "I want you to follow me."

She hesitates. "I don't know," she says. "I don't think we should go to the bedroom."

"The bedroom!" I say. "Ha! What kind of a doctor do you think I am? That's the *examination room*. And I need to *examine* you. So *please*. Please do as I say. Let's not put up a fight."

Amazingly, she doesn't. She stands, and with one finger hooked into my collar, she tags along behind me.

"Wow," she says when I open the door. "Look at this."

The room has an examination table, pale-green cabinets, and three shiny canisters labeled for gauze, cotton, and tongue depressors. I say, "Please remove your clothes and slip into this." I hold out a thin pale-green gown with ties in the back.

The room's only window is open, the curtains are parted, and it is cooler here than in the rest of the house. Antiseptic. The lights are off, but there is moonlight to see by, moonlight and the play of light and shadow from the movie in the other room. Joe's heart thumps on, gently vibrating the floor. My own heart pounds away, beating, I realize, much harder and faster than Joe's.

"You'll feel better," I say, "once you've put this on."

Patrice takes the gown. She shrugs out of her sweater, then unlatches her bra. She uses the ball of one foot to remove the shoe of the other, then she wriggles free of her jeans. She is standing in front of me in nothing but panties and socks, and when she peels down the panties—silky fabric rubbing against thick ringlets of pubic hair—the friction creates static electricity, and blue sparks flicker and crackle between Patrice's legs. The hair on my arms lifts. In an instant, the air in the room has become dangerously alive.

"May I leave my socks on?" she asks. She is wearing white tube socks scrunched down to her ankles.

"You may not," I say. "The socks must come off as well."

She removes them using only her feet. "OK. I'm sockless now," she says.

"Sockless indeed," I say. "Now up on the table." I pat the sanitary sheet that covers the exam table. "Upsy daisy," I say. She tries being as gentle as possible, but the paper sheet still crunches beneath her. "Lean back," I say. "Relax. There you go. Now, put your feet in the stirrups." Patrice takes a deep breath. "Good, good," I say once her feet are in place. "Now, scooch forward. That's right. Scooch right up to the edge of the table."

Joe's heart suddenly quits beating. The last of the film runs through the sprocket, and a blast of hot white light illuminates the living room, brightening our room as well. Patrice's gown is wadded up around her waist. Between her legs, she is wet and thick, as open and raw as a fresh wound, and I am about to touch her, to put a finger inside of her, but then I stop. "Mousy Tongue," I say. I reach over to a box of powdered rubber gloves and pull four out. I take the first one, wrap it around her left ankle and the stirrup, and tie it in a knot. A second glove keeps her right ankle from moving. I tie her wrists to the insulated pipes above and behind her head.

"You're going to torture me," she says.

"Nope," I say. "I'm going to *cure* you." I wheel over a table of surgical instruments, on which sets a pair of scissors. Starting from the bottom hem, working my way up to her neckline, I snip away the gown. "Patrice, Patrice," I say. Patrice is completely naked now and goose-pimpled in the chilly room.

"Do something to me," she says.

"I will," I say, and I lift the lid off the top of the tin canister labeled GAUZE. I reach in and pull out the first of what I owe her.

"What's that?" she asks.

"Turtle Deluxe," I say. "See these canisters? They're full of fudge. All three of them. Sixty dollars' worth of fudge, to be precise. Interest on your twenty bucks," I say. I hold the fudge near her mouth, but not close enough for her to reach it. Patrice lifts her head off the table, opens her mouth. "C'mon," I say. "Have some." Patrice tries touching the fudge with her tongue, but she fails. When I finally give her a bite, I stand back and watch her savor it. The noises she makes—deep groans of satisfaction—are the same noises she makes when I am inside her and moving slowly. She swallows the bite, licks her lips.

"We had a deal," she finally says.

"The fudge has arrived," I say. "The deal's back on."

"I want to make something perfectly clear," she says. "I'm going to give you one more chance, but there is a finite limit to how many chances I can give." She is shivering as she speaks. The veins beneath her skin are visible, and there is evidence in every soft tissue of her body that the blood inside those veins is pumping hard and fast. "Understood?" she asks.

"It seems to me," I say, "that you're the one tied up. I'm not sure that you're in the best position to negotiate."

"Well, look at you," she says. "If it isn't my little Caligula."

She shifts her focus to the fudge again and parts her lips. She strains to reach my hand, arching her back and stretching the rubber gloves. I let her take a huge bite this time, a bite nearly too large for her mouth.

"Is that enough?" I ask.

"No," she manages to say.

I give her yet another bite, though there is barely room for any more in her mouth. "Mmmmm," she says, and while she chews and swallows, dribbles of juice running down her chin, I slip out of my clothes. I ask her if she wants more, and she nods. I am standing between her legs. I lean forward and place the last of the fudge in my hand onto her tongue. Outside it is dark, the hoots and jeers of nighttime carousers drift up to the open window, and the clouds passing the moon look like clouds.

When it comes to chocolate, everybody swallows.

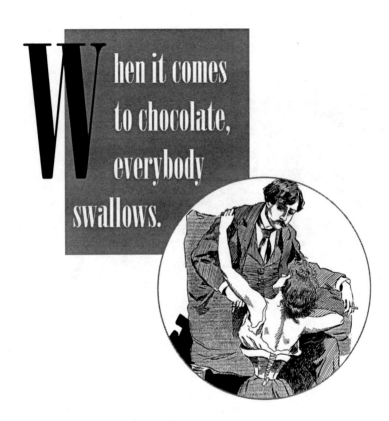

JODI BLOOM

Cookies

Jodi Bloom's short fiction has been published in many literary journals and anthologies here and abroad. Recently, her stories (www.so-charmed. com) can be found encircling the wrists of romance novelists, rock 'n' roll royalty, ex-porn stars turned blues singers, female race car drivers, and many other hip girls the world over. Jodi lives in Takoma Park, Maryland, with seven-year-old Molly.

On his very first morning reporting for Christmas season stock-boy duty at the Broward Mall, Jeremy pulled aside the curtain to the back room of *Bon Appétit Fine Cookware* and stood facing the most magnificent pair of tits he had ever seen in his entire nineteen years. Porno mags, videos, and real life, inclusive.

The rest of the cluttered back room, crammed full of poten-tially interesting things, even a few other people, receded into a blur. They were spectacular. Firm, full breasts—the kind you can't decide whether to kiss, or fuck, or just simply hold in your hands, thanking god for creating such absolute perfection.

Jeremy, although transfixed, slowly raised his eyes up from the beautiful tits, with their pink-brown nipples, to the face of their owner. Later, as he struggled to remember this important moment, he wished he'd had the whole thing on videotape, so he could rewind and replay, discovering with certainty whether the owner—a total goddess with pale skin and shoulder-length brown hair—had held his gaze with her chocolate-syrup eyes just a second longer than she should have, before bringing one delicate hand up to her mouth and exclaiming "Oh!"

"Jeremy Blazer," someone else was saying, and Jeremy watched the topless goddess tug her fuzzy white angora sweater down over her bare chest. He brought the room into focus just as the other woman shoved herself in front of him. "I'm Margie," she said, extending her hand. She wore denim from head to toe, a floppy denim hat, denim shirt, and a long skirt that looked like it had lived a former life as a regular pair of blue jeans.

"Jeremy," Jeremy said, extending his hand and hoping it wasn't too clammy. How could a person's face feel like it was on fire, his hands like he was standing on the polar ice cap in his boxer shorts?

"And this creature is Ava," Margie said, turning toward the beautiful woman. "She promises to keep her new breasts to herself for the remainder of your Christmas holiday employment, don't you Ava?" Jeremy stared at the creature. *Just say no*, he prayed silently.

"Promise," Ava said, smiling a totally killer smile. She was dressed like one of Santa's helpers, in the fuzzy white sweater and a short baby-blue figure-skater's skirt that barely covered her ass.

"I'm Dot," another woman said, easing her enormous self forward out of the blur, and squinting up at Jeremy through a large round pair of eyeglasses. A Santa Claus pin with blinking yellow lights winked at him from the front of her gigantic pink polka-dotted dress. "Guess I don't rate an introduction," she snorted. Jeremy had the thought that she was mad at him for something, although he'd only known her for about ten seconds. "Have a cookie," she demanded, holding up a plate piled high with Toll House Chocolate Chippers. The rich smell of butter and sugar wafted up Jeremy's nose. "These are just the first batch," Dot said, apologetically. "Yummy enough, but I'm not really warmed up yet." She smiled a big fat-lady smile at him. He took a cookie, glad to have something to do with his hands and afraid she might kill him otherwise.

"Well, I'm off," Margie said. "You kids stay out of trouble now. Girls, don't let the presence of this handsome young man distract you from your responsibilities," she teased, giving Jeremy a wink. "And remember, Dot's in charge." Margie whisked out of the back room, and he heard the grate at the front of the store go up.

"I thought she was the manager," Jeremy said. His mother had told him to "see Margie," when he got to *Bon Appétit*; Margie and she were aerobics-friends, and Margie had agreed to employ Mrs. Blazer's son while he was home from college for Christmas.

"She is," Dot explained. "Flu epidemic at the Miami store. She'll be down there during the holidays. So. Like the boss-lady said," she smiled, leaving the back room and heading toward the cash register, a set of keys dangling from her wrist, "I'm in charge of this joint. Grab an apron, Mister Blazer. You too, Miss November."

"*Bitch*," Ava said, when she figured Dot was out of earshot.

"I heard that," Dot hollered from somewhere in the small store.

"*I* should have been manager," Ava yelled, sticking her tongue out like a bratty kid. She turned to Jeremy. "Dot is so jealous of me," she whispered. Then she lowered her voice as though she were taking Jeremy into her deepest confidence. "And I don't think she's been laid since her divorce five years ago. Who can blame her husband? Would you want to wake up next to *that* every morning?" Jeremy didn't think the question really needed an answer. Thank god—because he was completely tongue-tied.

"Maybe they based the promotion to manager on sales of *cookware*," Dot shouted from the front of the store. "And not on back room blowjobs with the male customers."

"She's so crass, isn't she?" Ava asked. She stuck her lower lip out at Jeremy, who stood staring at her in total amazement. She didn't seem at all embarrassed over the fact that he'd just seen her half-naked. He considered running up to the front counter to interrogate Dot about the back room blowjobs; some very vivid mental pictures had started running through his head like a private film where he was both the star and the director. Ava sighed deeply and tied a canvas butcher's apron around her waist, slowly raising the bib over her chest and tying the strings behind her neck. Her nipples were erect, two tiny hard buttons on the front of the white sweater. Jeremy had the thought that she was probably one of those women who made a lot of throaty noises during sex.

"Here," Ava said, handing him a bright red apron with the words *Bon Appétit!* emblazoned across the front in white script. "It's the uniform. And our motto," she added, smiling.

■

The following morning, Jeremy ducked under the iron grate and made his way through the store, which, aside from being decorated from polished hardwood floor to fluorescent-tubed ceiling with every conceivable kitchen utensil and gadget, had also been decked out for the holidays, with tasteful strings of twinkling white lights.

"Too early," Jeremy complained out loud to no one, not a comment on the lights, although Thanksgiving had just passed and it did seem ridiculous. It was a simple remark on the time of day; even at school Jeremy never had to be awake much before noon. Oh yeah, he'd figured out optimum class scheduling the second semester of freshman year. Yet, here it was Winter Break and he was up and at 'em before nine o'fucking clock. Jeremy had just completed an elective course called "Irony and Modern Culture." The irony of his situation was not lost on him.

There were other ironies; in fact irony abounded. November, and the air in Fort Lauderdale remained steamy hot, soaring past ninety degrees most days. They could spray all the fake snow they wanted on the windows of the stores at the Broward Mall; Santa would still have to arrive in his swimming trunks, sipping a tall cool drink.

Jeremy had actually been looking forward to his holiday employment. In another twist of irony, he'd envisioned himself relaxing for a couple of weeks at some store (*Sam Goody? The Gap?*), making a few bucks, flirting with teenage mall girls and older girls who, like himself, were home from college up north. It didn't take a rocket scientist to realize that the only "girls" Jeremy was likely to meet at *Bon Appétit* were his mom's age, except for Ava, who was maybe in her late twenties, but was clearly in the OML (Out of My League) category.

Ironically, however, he still owed the elective professor at Brown a final term paper, and, if nothing, else he was gathering material. He'd managed to charm his way to an extended deadline, but in fact his status at school, not to mention his soccer scholarship money, depended on receipt of a decent grade. Jeremy had fucked around just a little too much, and his average for the first semester of sophomore year teetered just above failure.

∎

"What do they call you, Jeremy Blazer?" Dot asked, when they were all gathered at the front desk awaiting arrival of the morning's first customers. She poked her tongue around the corners of her lips, where some gooey pink lipstick had gathered in little clumps. "Got any cute nicknames?" If Jeremy hadn't known better, he would have thought the fat lady was genuinely flirting with him. Or was she just being nice?

He contemplated Dot's question. The guys on his floor at school called him Blaze. Not for being fast or anything, but because he always had a lighter or a match for the bong or pipe or joint. And a group of girls at the end of the hall had christened him Germ, when, during the debauchery of Freshman Rush Week, he'd managed to make out with a representative girl from every floor, spreading a wicked stomach virus through the entire dormitory and nearly causing Brown University's first-ever medical quarantine.

"Jer," he finally said, feeling stupid and brushing his sandy brown hair out of his eyes. He stared sleepily at a large copper kettle that hung on the wall behind the two women. "My mom calls me Jer."

"Oh, what a terrible waste," Ava said. "Jeremy is such a *poetic* name. So *romantic.*" *Jesus fucking Christ at Christmas. Were Ava's eyes roving down across his crotch?* He suddenly felt like he'd walked into some totally weird dream, one he couldn't get a grip on, but which seemed full of the potential for either major thrills or bitter disappointment. Did it qualify as a "paradox"? There was another one of those concepts from school.

"So," Dot said, "Jer. Be a good boy and bring me that box of lemon zesters from the back room. And have another cookie while you're at it. There's lots more where those came from."

■

Although he continued to have to report to the mall at the ungodly hour of nine o'clock, Jeremy's job was easy enough: lift and carry stuff, change burnt-out fluorescent tubes, lift and carry more stuff. Most days there was nothing at all for him to do for long hours at a stretch and Dot would make up projects, like moving all the impossibly heavy Le Creuset French enameled cookware to the opposite side of the store, trading places with the monstrously oversized Calphalon pots and pans. Or rearranging the rows of garlic presses and spice racks and fancy corkscrews. After which, she'd insist he eat cookies, cookies, and more cookies. The Chocolate Chips gave way to a plate of gooey Rice Krispies Treats, then a tub of Jell-O Pudding Swirlies, and later in the week a tray of simple sugar cookies—Dot's Dots she called them—some decorated with red M&M's, some with green ones.

"You know what they say about the green ones, don't you?" Dot had begun giggling like a schoolgirl, the orange polka dots on today's tent-sized dress heaving up and down with each cackle.

"What?" Jeremy said, popping a green M&M'd cookie into his mouth.

Dot looked up at him from beneath her huge glasses. "They make you *horny*," she said and broke into a cackle that turned into a death-defying cough.

An unexpected embarrassment washed over him. Dot was one of those people who was so big and fat that Jeremy couldn't tell how old she was, but he judged her to be... old enough to be his mother. "Uh, great," he said, "thanks."

■

On the fourth day of his employment, in a surprise move that earned her a permanent place in his heart—well, at least for the duration of the holiday retail season—Dot pulled rank and changed the store schedule.

"Starting tomorrow," she said to Jeremy, "you're on nights. Ava can open; you and I will close. Mornings are beat anyway; I'm sure Ava can strain her singular brain cell and handle it. You come in at three, the three of us will have two glorious hours together, then Miss Centerfold can go off to whatever it is she does with her evenings. Not that I really want to know," Dot concluded with a shudder.

"I'd like to know what Miss Centerfold does with her evenings," Jeremy joked, realizing his mistake the second the words floated out of his big stupid mouth. Dot seemed to have developed, in just four days, a bona fide crush on him. Paradox again: Although he basically wouldn't touch Dot if she were the last female on earth after a nuclear holocaust, he still liked the attention. Besides, if he played his cards right, the crush could translate itself into a raise from his pitiful hourly minimum wage. Dot glared at him. Yeah, he'd fucked up again.

"So. Jer. They're not real you know," she said.

"What's not?" Jeremy asked. Margie's comment earlier in the week had not filtered through the haze caused by Ava's little exhibitionist display.

"The boobs," Dot said, narrowing her eyes. "She bought them. Two grand a piece. Idle rich, that's our Ava. Daddy owns half of South Beach. She only works at the mall so she can conquer men, you know. Don't be a sucker, Jer; she'll only add you to her scorecard."

Well, conquer away, Jeremy thought, but he kept his mouth shut.

"On the other hand," Dot continued, "some women pride themselves on a certain natural state of voluptuousness, not to mention good old-fashioned brain power." She tapped a fat finger on her temple and lowered her eyes across her ample chest. Jeremy got the distinct impression that Dot thought she was somehow…*attractive*. Her rack was astounding, *if* you were judging solely on size. But then, so was the rest of her. Jeremy gave a weak smile that he hoped looked genuinely appreciative.

∎

"Unholy cow!" Ava hissed, when she heard about the new schedule. "Dot just wants you all to herself, doesn't she? I see right through her, you know. She thinks she's so…smart." She stared at Jeremy and wrinkled her brow in the cutest way. "Beauty doesn't always exclude brains," she added, and stomped away.

Jeremy watched her from behind and sighed. Ava was wearing a pink fuzzy sweater with a minty green skater skirt. The day before, it had been a lavender sweater with a lemony skirt. She appeared to own an endless number of sherbet-colored, tortuously sexy Santa's helper outfits. Jeremy could just picture her twirling around the North Pole, driving Santa and the elves into a frenzied state of horniness. Then Ava started baking for him, and he was totally undone.

"Here," she said, one afternoon when Dot was in the bathroom and she and Jeremy stood up at the front counter alone. She pulled a silver tray out of a bag she was holding. "I baked you some *real* Christmas cookies. I think you've had enough of that trashy excuse for baking she comes up with, Jeremy dear. Introducing Ava's Chocolate Macadamia Delights. My very own Grandmum's recipe. I added the powdered sugar," she said proudly.

He took one and bit into it. Just as he was about to swallow, the apron ties around Ava's neck slipped free and the bib fell down, revealing the pair of gorgeous bra-less tits, nipples hard beneath a peach angora sweater. Jeremy choked and coughed, sending powdered sugar flying up his nose and making him sneeze twice.

"God bless you, Jeremy," Ava said, reaching up to brush some sugar off his cheek.

"God bless us one and all," Jeremy said.

■

"**S**hut up Ava," Dot said. "He likes *mine* better than *yours*."

Jeremy stood outside the back room listening, while munching on one of Dot's Heath Bar Clusters. *Nope*, he thought, picturing himself caressing Ava's breasts from behind, his fingers gently pinching her nipples to an even more erect than usual state, *sorry Dot*.

"You know Dot, you really should stop feeding him that crap," Ava said, "haven't you noticed he's breaking out from your sugar-overloaded candy-covered cookies? The boy obviously needs a change from *quantity* to *quality*. He's going to bloat up like, like, like...*Santa Claus!*"

Jeremy raised his fingers to his face. It was true; he was basically living on cookies, at least for lunch and dinner. And ever since Ava had gotten into the act with her imported Swiss chocolate and other expensive ingredients, Jeremy had sprouted a small mountain range of zits on his forehead. Come to think of it, maybe he should wander down to CVS and pick up some Clearasil, except he figured that, given the irony he was experiencing at the Broward Mall, there would no doubt be some beautiful young girl behind the cash register, and he'd feel like a total pimple-faced idiot. Jeremy stuck a finger into the waistband of his Levis. Were his jeans getting tight?

"You're so full of it, Ava," Dot argued.

"Well why don't we let Jeremy decide," Ava said. "Tell you what. For the next week, we each bring a dozen per day, even-steven. If he gobbles up my goodies first, you turn over manager position to me for the rest of the holiday and I am forever forgiven for last year's…um…little mistake." Dot had explained to Jeremy that one week last year Margie had left Ava in charge. The ditzy bitch (as Dot put it) had forgotten to lock the grate, and they'd all come in the next morning to a thoroughly ransacked store, with thousands of dollars' worth of merchandise gone. *Daddy bought his little girl's way out of that one, too*, she'd concluded, shaking her head with disgust. Jeremy couldn't picture the sort of person who would rip off a mall cookware store. Some crazed Fort Lauderdale housewife? It made him smile to himself. Even Ava's mistakes were…way cute.

"And if I win?" Dot said, "what are you going to do, start wearing a bra?"

"Hmm," Ava said, "how about five hundred dollars?"

"You're on," Dot snapped. Ava really wasn't stupid. Dot was a gambler, and not a very good one; it was a well-known fact that she was in hock up to her eyeballs from buying lottery tickets and playing in a secret weekly bingo game that had an enormous cash kitty. "War is declared."

Jeremy fled to the front counter, a sick feeling in the pit of his already-full stomach.

■

P*op-Quiz Question:* What guy wouldn't want to live on a steady diet of homemade Christmas cookies? *Answer (and yet another irony):* a guy who was being force fed by two insane older women who he was beginning to think were fattening him up for slaughter. Forget Christmas goose; it was Stuffed Jeremy this holiday season.

And so, the sweet stuff began flowing with new passion, exactly two dozen cookies per day. Dot's Raisin Bran Crunchies were met head on by Ava's Hazelnut Alpine Lace Crispettes. Ava's

Raspberry-Filled Butter Droplets (a secret recipe handed down for three generations) faced off with Dot's elaborately decorated Gingerbread Men, complete with edible silver buttons on their jackets and gumdrops for eyes. Jeremy dutifully ate three of them, one spicy brown arm at a time.

The truth, though Jeremy dared admit it to no one, was that Ava's concoctions, complex and brilliantly executed as they were—not to mention drool-worthy since they had been shaped by her delicate hands and since she was obviously putting the rest of her glamorous life on hold to bake them for him every single night—simply were too rich for his blood. Jeremy was, if anything, your basic junk food junkie, with a diet consisting mainly of cereal, Cokes and crunchy snacks, burgers and fries. At the mall food court, he'd never felt the need to venture much beyond the Roy Rogers stand, except for one failed trip to Hong Kong Heaven, where he ate a very greasy egg roll that made him burp continuously for the duration of his shift.

Similarly, he preferred Dot's modest but effective recipes, often concocted from breakfast cereals and decorated with favorite candies. He was just waiting for her to show up with a Sugar-Pops 'n Skittles cookie. But Jeremy, in an effort that anyone would recognize as purely heroic, maintained true fairness, eating one elegant Ava creation for each unpretentious Dot.

Still, he couldn't keep up, and cookies stood in towers on every surface at *Bon Appétit*. There were fine porcelain dishes stacked high with Ava's concoctions, and pink plastic Tupperware containers filled to the brim with Dot's. Jeremy began to wonder how he might survive the remaining few weeks at his job without needing an entire new wardrobe from Big Men Tall Men, down at the obscure southern end of the mall. Besides, the acne had spread from his forehead to his left cheek, and his teeth hurt. And so, in order to while away the long evening hours without stuffing his face, Jeremy began working on his overdue term paper at the front counter. Dot read romance novels during the slow weeknights, and didn't seem to mind.

"How's it comin' Jer," she asked one particularly dead evening. Jeremy had been scribbling in his notebook for over an hour at the counter; he was actually skating down the home stretch of his essay entitled: *Irony at the Broward Mall, a Microcosm (or was that a Paradigm?) of Modern Culture.*

"Oh, all right, I guess," Jeremy said. "Although I don't know how I'm ever going to get twenty-five pages typed before I have to go back," he added. "To school, I mean."

"Typed?" Dot asked, setting down her book, the cover of which featured the usual oil painting of a damsel in distress wearing a corset that was several sizes too small and over the top of which a pair of lovely pale tits spilled, like a double scoop of vanilla ice cream. Come of think of it, the girl on this particular cover looked just like Ava. "Jer?" Dot asked. "Earth to Jer-e-my…"

He turned his gaze from the book cover to Dot. Today, her polka dots were yellow. Jeremy thought of that kid's book where the funny animal changes his spots from pink, to purple, to blue. "Oh, yeah. Typed. Yeah, I don't type too well," Jeremy said. "You know," and he did a demo for her on the counter with his two index fingers.

"Can I read it?" Dot asked, grinning like she was… *lovestruck?* "I'd just love to see what goes on in the mind of a smart young college man like yourself."

Jeremy considered. "Well, it's kinda messy," he said. "But yeah, OK." He handed her the notebook, glad he hadn't yet gotten to the irony of the Cookie War in his essay.

"Well don't just stand there fidgeting, boy," Dot said, sounding once again like someone's mom. "You're making me nervous."

Jeremy wandered off to unpack some boxes of Cuisinart mini-food processors.

■

"Typed?" Dot asked an hour later, setting down the notebook. "Jer, you know I've become quite fond of you. So I hate to tell ya this Jer, but you need a wee bit more than typing here. This paper, well, let's just say, it could use some work," she said, frowning.

"Really sucks, huh?" Jeremy said.

Dot's Santa pin was blinking away at him. She placed a plump hand firmly on his arm and squeezed. "Jer," she said, "have I got a deal for you."

Dot proceeded to spill the story of the Cookie War while Jeremy played dumb and innocent. "I just have to win this one," she concluded, "I've got to beat that rich bitch at the only game in town I stand to win. I've always been a baker Jer, it's in my blood. You like my cookies better anyway, don't you?" she asked, narrowing her eyes.

"Well…" Jeremy hesitated.

"Oh, I see. You're a nice boy and you want to play fair. Well, life just ain't fair, Jer." Dot laughed at her rhyme. "You let me win and the paper is not only typed but revised to guarantee you an A. Here's something you didn't know about Dot," she began, talking about herself in the third person. "Dot not only bakes a mean cookie, but she graduated from Broward Community with honors, so there."

"OK," Jeremy said. "Deal."

"And Jer?" Dot asked. "Listen carefully. If you ever tell Miss High and Mighty that I rigged this contest, you'll be real sorry you were born."

■

The next day (Nestlé Crunch Squares versus Irish Cream Kisses), Jeremy caused Dot to pull a nose ahead in the Cookie War. He did this with great sensitivity, by secretly burying a half-dozen of Dot's cookies in the back room trash, just enough for her to gain an advantage, but hopefully not enough for Ava to really notice.

Later, Jeremy sat at the front counter at the end of Ava's shift, like he always did, so he could watch her walk out of the store. Every day he tried to think of something clever to say. Because even though she was baking for him like she was his... *girlfriend*, he figured she still thought of him as just another dork salivating at her feet. So far he'd come up with nothing better than, "Bye Ava, see ya tomorrow," which admittedly made him feel like just another dork salivating at her feet.

And which was exactly what he was about to say, when Ava pressed a piece of paper into his hand on her way out. "Bye cutie," she said, and was gone. Jeremy gulped.

"BOO," Dot said, coming up behind him.

"Shit, Dot," Jeremy said. He was still in shock. "You scared me."

"What's that?" Dot asked, eyeing the piece of paper suspiciously. "Love note from the pin-up girl?"

"Yeah right," Jeremy said. Had he sounded wishful? "I mean it's probably like some kind of death threat," he added, hoping to cancel out anything in his tone of voice that would have made Dot mad. "She probably noticed you were winning today."

"Well never you mind, Jer," Dot said. "By the way," she added, "that term paper of yours is coming out *terrif*. And I spoke to Margie today. She asked for my holiday bonus recommendations."

In the store bathroom, with the door locked for safety, Jeremy took the note out of his pocket and unfolded it. It said (in Ava's loopy, amazingly sweet and schoolgirlish handwriting): *Meet me for dinner on your break? Tonight at Hong Kong Heaven, 7 pm. Luv, Ava.*

Jeremy broke into a sweat. It was five o'clock. Two measly hours for him to transform himself from Jeremy Jerk-off to Jeremy the Incredibly Fascinating, If Younger, Guy.

■

He sat across from Ava at a table in front of Hong Kong Heaven. Her voice sounded creamy and beige, like the fuzzy sweater du jour, which was contouring around her tits as per the usual. Was it his imagination or could he actually see her nipples through the pale-colored wool?

"Is that all you're going to eat?" Ava was saying, nodding at his tray. Her nose was perfect. He'd never noticed that before.

Jeremy eyed the soggy pair of egg rolls afloat in a puddle of grease on the Styrofoam plate. "Well, I'll probably top this off with a few cookies, you know?" he said. "A few delicious, delectable, homemade Christmas cookies." God he felt idiotic. Maybe he should just stop talking altogether.

"Jeremy," Ava said, twirling a slippery sesame noodle around and around her plastic fork. "I don't know if it's just my overstimulated imagination at work here, but I could swear that you've been gobbling up Dot's cookies like there's no tomorrow."

No tomorrow? Jeremy had determined in Philosophy 101 last semester that he was no existentialist, not by any stretch. "There's *definitely* a tomorrow," he said. Ava finally hooked the noodle between two tongs of the fork and brought it up to her mouth. He watched as she pursed her lips and sucked until the last half-inch of it disappeared.

"Jeremy?" Ava asked, "Don't you like mine better?"

Did he really care if the tits were natural or man-made? Nah. They were still the most beautiful set he'd ever seen, even in his dreams. And if he ever got his hands on them, he'd simply give a mental high-five to her surgeon instead of to god.

"Yes," Jeremy said, poking his fork into one of the fat egg rolls. An unpleasant-looking orange fluid oozed out. "Yes, Ava. Yours are definitely, I mean absolutely, way better."

Ava drew herself toward him across the table and dropped her voice to a whisper. "I know what you want, Jeremy," she said. She tucked a stray lock of dark brown hair behind her ear.

"I think you know what I want too and I think you know exactly how to help me get it. So, let's help each other out, OK?" Jeremy's thoughts began crashing together like carnival bumper cars, slamming and bouncing and circling, no single thought really getting anywhere at all in the sudden frenzy. Ava slurped another noodle or two and stood up. He hadn't even agreed to the amazing offer, but she seemed satisfied that the discussion had ended.

"Break's over Jeremy," she said. "Thanks ever so much for joining me for dinner. I'm glad we had this time to get to know each other more...intimately. Bye now. I really do like you, you know," she added, smiling and turning away.

"Bye," Jeremy called. He watched the beige sweater and chocolatey brown velvet mini-skirt disappear into the crowd as Ava made her way down the food court and out into the mall.

■

Day Five of the Great Christmas Cookie War had Jeremy in a serious panic. He sat at the front counter of *Bon Appétit*, staring off into space. It was like one of those annoying brainteaser problems, a puzzle with a piece missing. Somehow, an innocent bakeoff had turned into a major moral dilemma: *School versus Sex*.

Then again, was it a dilemma at all? Really? At night Jeremy wasn't dreaming about his professor's sourpuss face cracking into a smile when he'd read and graded the brilliant (and neatly typed) paper on irony, thanks to Dot. He wasn't dreaming about his continued soccer scholarship or even kicking the Yalies' asses. Ava, on the other hand, had slipped very nicely into his dreams—Ava the sweater girl, long-legged Ava, Ava on top, riding in perfect rhythm, those beautiful bare tits bouncing within easy reach of his tongue. Enough said.

On Day Six, Jeremy had to go into the *Bon Appétit* employee bathroom and masturbate, an activity he had, up to that point, managed to confine to the privacy of his bedroom at home. But Ava had been flirting viciously, licking and biting her lips, tossing her hair around—the entire female-in-heat routine. And the heavy canvas apron only seemed to accentuate the bulge of his embarrassing hard-on, so he really had no choice. He grabbed a handful of Ava's Chocolate Cherry Sleigh Bell cookies and headed into the tiny bathroom, setting them on the back of the toilet. He had no intention of eating them, even if each Sleigh Bell had, buried in its center, a syrupy-sweet maraschino cherry. Jeremy was utterly and totally sick of chocolate, a condition he would never have thought possible had anyone presented the idea to him a few weeks ago.

He did the deed (Ava and he locked in an endless sixty-nine position, his face buried in her sweet pussy, her face giving deep suck—*Bon Appétit!*), and he came quickly into a sizeable wad of TP. He said the Lord's Prayer, which he always said before a soccer match and after masturbating. Then he dropped the TP and the Chocolate Sleigh Bells into the toilet, laughed because they really looked like little brown turds floating in the bowl, flushed, and headed up to the front counter.

Ava and Dot were engaged in some argument that thankfully ended just as he arrived. As he stood looking at them—the gorgeous sex kitten and the motherly fat lady, both of whom seemed to want something from him, although he was confused about exactly what—the answer to the brainteaser fell right into place. *A tie.* Why the fuck hadn't he thought of it before? A god damn tie score, like the match with Cornell last year. But would the women go into overtime? Would they go to the death? If so, it would be *his* death; his sorry pathetic death by chocolate—the final irony. On the other hand, if not—*if* he could somehow convince each of them that they had something unique and special to offer, something he valued equally—he could end up with an A on his paper, his scholarship intact, and the best fuck he was likely to have in his lifetime—based on projected prospects, anyway.

"What's up?" Jeremy asked, as he approached the counter. "How are my two very favorite cooks in the whole world this evening?"

He smiled, confident that his new game strategy would turn the lose-lose into a win-win. For the next two days things would be neck and neck, so close no one would be able to figure out who was ahead. He would dump equal portions of Dot's and Ava's cookies into the trash or the toilet and by the end of Day Seven, there would be just two cookies left. Then, with a final swallow, the last pair would disappear down the hatch—*Merry Christmas to all, and to all a good night!*

■

On Day Eight, Jeremy, like any champion, expected his prizes to come rolling in, but nothing at all happened. He'd followed through brilliantly on his plan, managing to get rid of dozens upon dozens of Christmas cookies, the fancy and the plain. Then, with great drama and a big winner's smile on his face, he'd finished off the last two at the front counter, before Ava's shift ended. He was careful, he was sensitive. Oh, he was *good*, nibbling and chewing and swallowing bite for bite, crumb for crumb, while Ava and Dot watched. Then he made a show of sucking the sugar and chocolate and whatever else off of his fingers, giving one last sensuous lick of his lips for Ava's benefit. "Thanks," he said, grinning. "You're both terrific."

"Yes," Ava said.

"We sure are," Dot agreed.

■

On Day Nine, Ava grabbed Jeremy in the back room. "You want to collect, don't you?" she asked, smiling and pulling him close, so close he could smell her hair. She pressed her body into his, putting her hands on his ass and grinding against him. Jeremy thought he might faint. Then he almost did, because just as he began to kiss her, just as he brought his hand up over her glorious right tit, Ava kneed him in the groin, sending him crumpling to the floor in breathless agony.

"Trying to flush my cookies down the *commode*," she said, standing over him, looming huge and angry (but still somehow really beautiful). "We saw them floating there, Jeremy. And throwing Dot's in the trash! Did you think we wouldn't notice dozens of cookies in the store trash? Even *Dot* doesn't deserve *that*. You blew it, Jeremy. You really blew it."

"Yeah," Jeremy managed between gulps for air. "I guess you could say that."

Ava left the back room, and in another minute Dot appeared. Jeremy felt like Ebenezer Scrooge having a series of terrible Christmas nightmares. He had managed to crawl to a sitting position against the wall. Dot stood looking down, peering over her eyeglasses at him, the Santa pin blinking like crazy from the front of her massive polka-dotted chest.

"Guess you're not doing the term paper, huh?" Jeremy said.

"Term paper, Jer? What term paper would that be?"

"Can I at least have my notebook back?" Jeremy winced. His balls still felt crushed.

"Notebook, Jer? What notebook would that be?" Dot asked.

■

On his dinner break that night, Jeremy wandered down to CVS and bought a tube of Clearasil and a new spiral-bound lined-paper notebook. There was, of course, a beautiful young girl at the cash register, but he didn't really give a fuck at that point. In fact, Jeremy purchased the biggest god damn tube of Clearasil on the market. He made his way to the food court, bought a burger, and sat down at one of the little tables. Taking a pen from his pocket, he opened the notebook and turned to the first page. At the top he wrote: *Irony at the Broward Mall, a Microcosm of Modern Culture. Part I: The Great Cookie War, in Which One Man Courageously Battles the Brutal Forces of Female Nature.*

■

Dot's Dots

1½ C powdered sugar	1 C margarine or butter, softened
1 tsp vanilla	½ tsp almond extract
1 egg	2½ C all-purpose flour
1 tsp baking soda	1 tsp cream of tartar
Granulated sugar	2 lb bag M&M's candy

Mix powdered sugar, margarine, vanilla, almond extract, and egg. Stir in remaining ingredients except granulated sugar. Cover and refrigerate at least 3 hours. Heat oven to 375°, divide dough into halves. Roll each half ³⁄₁₆" thick on lightly floured, cloth-covered board. Cut into desired shapes, sprinkle with granulated sugar. Place on sheet, bake 7–8 minutes, until edges lightly brown. Separate green and red M&M's, press into cookies while still warm.

Ava's Chocolate Sleighbells

½ C honey	⅔ C butter
1 egg	1 tsp vanilla extract
2 C whole wheat flour	⅓ C cocoa powder (imported)
Shredded coconut	42 candied cherries

Melt honey in saucepan until it bubbles. Add butter, egg, and mix well. Add in other ingredients except coconut and cherries. Refrigerate 2–3 hours. Heat oven to 350°. Shape dough into balls, burying one cherry into the center of each ball. Place on cookie sheet and bake 10–15 minutes until done. Roll still-warm cookie balls in shredded coconut. *Bon appétit!*

GREGG SHAPIRO

Chocolate-Dipped

Pop culture journalist Gregg Shapiro's reviews and interviews run in a variety of regional publications including Chicago Free Press, HX, Baltimore Outloud, *and* Bay Area Reporter, *as well as online at afterelton. com. His creative work can be found in anthologies (*Poetic Voices Without Borders, Sweet Jesus, Getting It On, Mondo Barbie, Mondo Marilyn, *and* Bar Stories, *among others), literary journals (*Bloom, modern words, Gargoyle, *and* Blithe House Quarterly, *to mention a few), and textbooks (*A Multicultural Reader *and* Literature & Gender*). He lives in Chicago with his life partner Rick Karlin and their dogs Dusty and k.d.*

It's funny, don't you think, the way an accident can become a habit. Unclear, though, how a habit develops into a ritual. Then, before you know it, the ritual transforms itself into a fetish. Shoplifters, for instance, are said to get a sexual charge from quickly, discreetly slipping something unpaid for into their coat pockets or purses, boldly strutting toward the exit. But is it the thrill of the act or the threat of getting caught that can repeatedly bring the petty criminal to the brink of orgasm? Ask a fire starter or the person who follows the sound of sirens to the scene of the head-on collision in a busy intersection if they know what it is about these events that makes the tops of their heads feel as if they might become unattached.

My lover Cary and I were cleaning up our apartment after my sister, brother-in-law, and two nephews, Cruise and Willis, went home. They were the last of the stragglers from my biological family who had been in attendance at our annual friends-and-family winter holiday party. At a little after midnight, Cary and I were both on the receiving end of what amounted to a second wind. We both enjoyed entertaining, did it frequently, and weren't averse to leaving dirty glasses and dishes in the kitchen sink if we could see the sun coming up over Lake Michigan through the kitchen window, which wasn't an unusual occurrence after any one of our parties throughout the calendar year. However, the combination of the cold temperature outside, the threat of a potential Chicago snowstorm, and the presence of family members of all ages guaranteed that this party would not be one of those.

Cary was the one who had suggested that we invite our respective families to what had traditionally been a party consisting of our chosen family. Over the years, four to be exact, our "chosen" family began to include members of Cary's biological family. Initially, it had been Cary's first cousin Jon who cracked the barrier of the family, and that was only because he came out to us at Cary's parents' fortieth wedding anniversary party, and we soon began to socialize on a regular basis.

At first, I was a little jealous. I didn't have any gay cousins. As far as I knew, I didn't have any gay relatives at all. From all appearances, I was the one exception to the heterosexual rule in my clan, but, fortunately for me, I was never ostracized or treated any differently by any of my immediate family members after I came out at the age of twenty-two.

Eventually, our "all-inclusive" holiday party (Christmas, Solstice, Kwanza, Hanukkah, and any other winter holiday of note) also grew to include our blood relatives. In surveying the damage from the evening's entertainment, it would seem that we had emerged unscathed. In fact, we felt quite proud of our achievement. We threw a party consisting of some forty (including significant others) invited guests, and tossed our relatively small families (my parents, sister, brother-in-law, and nephews, Cary's recently widowed father, his two older brothers, and their wives) into the mix, and nothing was spilled that couldn't be cleaned up or broken that couldn't be fixed or discarded without too much fuss.

I'm not sure what it was then, that possessed us to do the clean up in the buff. Perhaps one or the other of us had become aware of the smoky smell that permeated our holiday finery, even though all of our smoking guests had been instructed to do so on the balcony. It was such a blustery night that the cigarette smoke managed to be blown into the room every time a smoker returned from the outside, opening and trying their best to close the balcony door as quickly as possible. Maybe it was just that it was really very warm in the apartment. The heat had been on all night, and it was as if the walls of the apartment, the furniture, and the area rugs had managed to retain some of our guests' body heat.

Whatever it was, we were suddenly scurrying about, collecting wineglasses and empty beer bottles, festive paper coffee cups and crumpled napkins, messy paper plates and plastic silverware, and filling the tall, black Hefty kitchen garbage bags, naked as the day we were born. There was already a garbage bag filled to the brim with glittery wrapping paper scraps from the grab-bag gift exchange. It was tied up tight, looking like something mummified, and leaning against a wall in the kitchen.

"There's something sticky on this table," Cary said, kneeling on his bare, lightly hairy knees before the vintage teak coffee table in front of the oversized sofa, running his fingers over something blurring the surface.

"Do you want a moist sponge or a paper towel?" I asked, heading for the kitchen, while keeping my ear cocked for his response.

"Paper towel, I think," he said, "and a couple of dry ones, too, please."

I grabbed a half-full garbage bag and collected trash on my way into the kitchen situated at the other end of the apartment. I wasn't watching where I was going, and five steps into the kitchen, I stepped on something gooey and slick, feeling it adhere to the bottom of my bare foot while it ground into a couple of the black and white checkerboard parquet squares beneath me. I righted myself before twisting my back too much, and simply said, "Shit!"

"Ira? Did you say something?" Cary called out from his watchful station in front of the sticky stain on the table.

"I said, 'Shit,'" I said, looking down to determine what it was that I had stepped in and smeared across the floor. A few inches away from where I was standing were the empty bent gold foil discs that I recognized as the covering for the large milk chocolate "coin" I had stepped on. Who knew how long it had been sitting there out of its protective wrapping? Apparently long enough to have softened up to a mushy, not crumbly, consistency.

Earlier in the evening, when Cary gave my nephews their little plastic mesh bags of chocolate Hanukkah "gelt," he had specifically told them that when they wanted to eat one, the kitchen was the place to do so. If there was one thing I could say for my older sister Ina and her husband Jim, it was that her children always did as they were told. Just as I was about to try to decipher whether it was Cruise or Willis who had done this, Cary came into the room.

"Is that your imitation of a pink flamingo?" Cary asked over my shoulder.

When he said that, I realized that I had been standing on one leg, with my right, chocolate-smudged foot crossed over my left knee.

"I stepped in something," I said, pointing to the darkened soul of my bare foot. Cary moved closer to me, his soft body hair brushing against my bare back. He stood a full head taller than I, and as I leaned back against him, I felt the crown of my head make contact with his Adam's apple.

Earlier in the evening, at the party, I became aware that I was not making as much physical contact with Cary as I usually did in social situations. We've earned a reputation among those who know us for being something of a demonstrative couple, completely at ease with ourselves and our relationship. While we never do it to shock anyone, we are, within reason, prone to public displays of affection. But for some unknown reason—the presence of both of our families, perhaps—I felt myself holding back. At one point during the party, Cary became especially animated while telling a particularly funny story. I felt this sudden urge to excuse both of us from our guests while we took to our bedroom to alleviate the unexpected hard-on I felt expanding within my khakis.

He nuzzled the back of my neck, and before I had a chance to put my chocolate-coated foot on the floor, he wrapped his arms around my waist, lifted me up, and carried me to the kitchen counter near the sink. He helped me ease my bare butt onto the cool and slightly cluttered Corian surface. For a second, I was embarrassed by our nakedness in the kitchen, but one look at his completely erect penis told me I had nothing to worry about.

I waited for him to turn on the tap so that we could rinse off my foot, and was surprised when he crouched down in front of me. He took my chocolate-splattered foot in both hands and proceeded to lick the sweetness off of my skin. I felt his tongue on my heel, then his lips, and just a tease of teeth. It tickled in a different way than fingers did. It felt like fingers wrapped in warm velvet. He dropped one of his hands between his legs and alternately pulled on and stroked his erection as his tongue and lips moved sweetly across the arch of my foot. He turned my foot sideways, stretching his mouth open wider, gripping it gently with his teeth, while he ran his tongue back and forth across the most tender part of the flesh.

I had been using my hands to support myself on the counter-top, which had warmed up enough for me to move one hand into my lap and over my boner. I reached over to the bottle of environmentally safe dish-washing liquid to lube myself with, when Cary tightened his grip on my foot. Our eyes met, and with only the slightest motion, he shook his head no, his chocolate-coated lips and tongue making their way to the ball of my foot and my toes.

"Kiss me on the mouth," I said, "I want something sweet, too."

Cary stood up, his erection not allowing him to get too close to the kitchen cabinets, and looked at me smiling. He had the look of a little boy who had just stolen all of the just-baked, still-warm, chocolate chip cookies off the rack where they had been cooling, and eaten every last one. My first urge was to find something with which to wipe off his mouth and chin, the tip of his nose. Instead, I wrapped my legs around his waist, my arms around his neck and kissed long and hard.

While we were kissing, he reached up to the cabinets behind me, where we kept the spices and the baking supplies, and pulled out an unopened bag of Nestlé's chocolate chips. He opened the cabinet below where I was sitting and retrieved a pot. He pulled away from me and tore into the bag of chocolate chips, pouring more than half the bag into the pot and putting it on the stove, a low, blue flame pulsing from the burner. He came back to where I was sitting, looking at him with eyes both dejected and curious. He kissed me quickly, jamming his still chocolatey tongue between my lips, as he retrieved a wooden spoon from the drawer below where I was sitting.

At the stove, he stirred the pot with his back to me. His shoulders were wide from years of regular workouts at the gym. His back was modestly muscular and hairless, narrowing down to his hips and his slightly furry bubble-butt. His legs were nicely defined and slightly bowed, the hair from his butt-cheeks growing darker and a little thicker on his thighs and calves, stopping where his ankles met his feet. I wanted to go to him, my erection losing a little of its hardness. I tried to move discreetly off of the counter-top, but my hairless buttocks made a squeaky sound when I moved forward.

"Stay where you are," Cary said, "I'll be right there. All the chips have almost melted."

In less than a minute, what he said was true, and I watched him pour the liquefied chocolate chips, which let off a whisper of steam as they flowed, dark and slow as proverbial molasses, into a soup bowl. Using his foot, he dragged the step stool I used to reach things on the upper shelves of the kitchen cabinets over to where he had been standing in front of me and stepped up, giving himself, and his unflagging erection, some leverage, and allowing me an unobstructed view of more of him. Without speaking, he spread my legs apart, making room on the counter for the bowl of hot chocolate. He cupped my genitals in both hands, scooping them up, while slightly tipping the bowl back toward my groin. He released me, and there was a thick, slow-motion splashing sound.

When my cock and balls made contact with the chocolate dip, it felt as warm as a mouth. My dick quickly regained its hardness, skimming the bottom of the bowl, then rising out of it, like a waterborne creature surfacing from the deep. The tips of my pubic hair, closest to the base of my dick, were frosted in chocolate, glistening briefly before drying and clumping together. He massaged the chocolate into the taut skin of my dick and balls; it felt so good, I sighed, as if close to orgasm.

"Don't you dare," he said, recognizing the familiar sound.

"I won't," I said.

He crouched down again, still on the step stool, both feet dangling off the edge of the narrow surface, and began to eat and suck my chocolate-dipped dick. His lips smacked with every motion he made, forward and back. He sucked each chocolatey ball gently into his mouth, grazing them with his teeth. And when they emerged from between his lips, the skin was only lightly veined with chocolate.

"Lay back," he said, his voice thick with chocolate, and I did.

Some of the chocolate must have streaked down below my balls into the space above my asshole, because his tongue followed a trail down there, slurping as he went. His chocolate-stained thumbs spread my ass-cheeks and I figured that Cary either found more chocolate spillage or that he wanted to personally introduce my prostate to chocolate with his tongue. Even without touching myself, I knew I was dangerously close to coming with Cary's mouth firmly planted between my buttocks and his chocolate-breath melting my defenses.

"Cary, if you don't stop that, I won't be able to hold back much longer."

He stood up and leaned over me, planting a kiss on my mouth that tasted like a mocha version of me. Our lips detached and he was back at the stove. There was a little chocolate in the bottom of the pot which only took a few seconds to heat up and turn into a sexy cocoa-based sauce, sufficient to coat the head of Cary's still rock-hard cock. He smoothed it into the head, working as methodically as a safecracker. He scooped the remaining chocolate from the pot with the index and middle fingers of his other hand. He subtly moved his head from side to side, indicating to me that he wanted my ankles on his shoulders.

I eased the lower half of my body forward, while leaning back, careful not to knock anything over. It was a surprisingly graceful move in a limited space. As soon as my heels made contact with his shoulders, his chocolate-slicked fingers were sliding gently in and out of my asshole. I had never before considered the lubricating qualities of chocolate, and was surprised by the silky texture. Just as I was beginning to enjoy the sensation of his fingers, I felt something more substantial in their place.

My eyes went wide and my head was thrown back like a Pez dispenser. He was halfway in before I let out a sweetened grunt. Such an action was completely out of character for both of us, advocates of safe sex and long lives, but we were obviously under the spell of the chocolate narcotic. Still, we both knew that the chocolate would have probably done more damage than good to a condom, and experience had taught us not to do anything foolish.

I grabbed my Tootsie Roll dick and stroked it in rhythm to Cary's thrusts. He pulled out after a few minutes: the synchronized orgasms and our cum like white chocolate pools on my chest and stomach only sweetened the deal.

While I never considered either of us creatures of habit, pretty soon, anything chocolate or chocolate-coated was stockpiled for variations on this theme. Once, after shaving Cary's chest and armpits, I slathered his upper torso in Frango mint chocolate, and spent more than an hour licking him clean. We tried Belgian chocolate and Hershey's Syrup. We pelted our fannies in Fannie May and Fannie Farmer. We'll never look at a Whitman's Sampler in quite the same way again. You can only imagine what happened to the five-pound, red-satin, chocolate-filled, heart-shaped boxes of candy we exchanged on Valentine's Day, can't you?

I'm just thankful I didn't step in peanut butter or raw liver.

The average American bathtub can be filled with chocolate pudding, leaving room for two adults, for $158. If adding a third adult, use half as much.

What Girls Want

Leslie Pietrzyk is the author of two novels: A Year and a Day *(William Morrow, 2004) and* Pears on a Willow Tree *(Avon Books, 1998). Her short fiction has appeared in many journals, including* TriQuarterly, Shenandoah, Iowa Review, Gargoyle, Gettysburg Review, *and* The Sun, *and her work has been nominated several times for the Pushcart Prize. She has been awarded fellowships from the Bread Loaf and Sewanee Writers' Conferences.*

You'd never made fudge before, but it was his favorite food. You were young, you did things like find out a boy's favorite food and then cook it for him. You were earnest and enthusiastic and you listened to your mother when she talked about dating and boys and hairstyles and life.

The boy's name was Mark, and he was awfully cute. All your friends thought so. He had the kind of looks that you'd find in a catalogue of fishing equipment, outdoorsy and capable, a boy who was actually going to turn into a man. Mothers liked Mark and even the toughest fathers liked Mark. Brothers wanted to be Mark. Sisters were impressed that he remembered their names. Dogs came when he whistled. That's how you thought of him, anyway, as that kind of boy. Or perhaps that's how he thought of himself, and so, of course, you had no choice but to think that way, too.

He went to the high school on the other side of the river, the one with the air-conditioned classrooms and the new football field where his team always beat your team. Someone said that in the yearbook, there were more pictures of him than anyone else. Or maybe he'd told you that. His father was a surgeon which was different from being a doctor, though you weren't sure how.

At a party he'd decided he liked you—was it your smile? Your perfectly straight blonde hair? Your pretty hazel eyes? Or was it the tight jeans; that too-small tank top, damp with sweat from dancing on the patio; a bottle of beer loose in one hand; flipping your hair back every time you laughed, laughing a lot? He'd wanted to dance with you, but you'd promised someone else the next dance, and he watched you from inside, through the glass picture window in the kitchen; you saw his thoughts: *No one makes me wait*, and you heard your mother's voice: *yes, make him wait, boys want to fight for something*. The song you finally danced to was slow and long and he barely spoke, but he held you closer than anyone else had, and the muggy smell of his sweat invaded your nose, your mouth, soaked your pores, surrounded you and the air around you, so that by the time you stepped apart you smelled like him.

Then he made you wait two weeks, but when he called, right away you said yes, you said you were delighted—you used all the phrases your mother had told you.

You were in the front seat of his father's car—hand-washed and waxed that very Saturday morning in honor of this first date, Mark told you—and he was driving with one hand on the wheel, the other draped over the seat back, not touching you, not quite. The night was damp and sticky, but with the air blowing through the window onto your face and his arm that close, you didn't notice much about the weather, even though you used it as a topic of conversation when there was too much silence (advice your mother had passed on, that it was always safe to talk about the weather, that everyone all across the world always had an opinion about weather). You'd been to the movies, ducking in late, hurrying up the aisle right as the final credits rolled; you'd been for ice cream afterwards, sitting side by side on the splintery picnic tabletop, watching the moths spin around and around the streetlight over the parking lot—what had you talked about all that time? the movie? the moths? ice cream? But now, now that you knew where he was taking you and why, there was nothing to talk about except the hot, sticky night, the air like a wet sock, the feeling that what you were breathing had been trapped in someone's basement.

So, just before the turn-off to the upper level of City Park, you asked, "What's your favorite food?" (It's what your mother had told you, to be good at asking questions. "Boys want to talk about themselves," she'd said.)

"Chocolate fudge." He didn't pause to think, he didn't explain why, and he didn't ask what your favorite food was. By that time you were driving slow over the speed bumps on the road that wound near where they used to have the cement bear cages before animal cruelty was something to think about and then you were passing the duck pond that froze over for ice skating in the winter and then you were pulling into a parking space near the merry-go-round and then he turned the car off and then his arm drifted down and touched your shoulder.

You took a deep breath of that heavy, heavy air, let it out. A moment later you said, "Lots of crickets." Their chirps droned through the rolled-down windows. In fact, it seemed that somehow weather and crickets were related, that there was a way to tell if it was going to rain by counting chirps and multiplying something and you were about to mention this, but then he leaned over and kissed you and even though your teeth clicked together he kissed you again, harder, and you kissed back and you forgot about crickets and weather.

Why did you always, always believe them when they said they loved you? And how did they always know you would?

"You know you want it," he whispered in your ear.

You knew there was something you wanted. You thought it could be this.

Afterwards, you pressed your head against his chest and listened to his heart beat until he turned on the car.

The next morning, as your mother watered down her orange juice with vodka, she asked why you were reading *The Joy of Cooking*. Before you could tell her, she peered over your shoulder and said, "Chocolate fudge?" You didn't say anything, but she went on because she was happy to fill silences—that's what she called it, not conversation but filling silences: "Fudge is nice. I like fudge. But I wonder if this humidity will be a problem. Or is it divinity that you can't make in humid weather? Maybe it's taffy. I can't remember. People used to make candy all the time. No more. It's sad. Everything's different now. Everything."

The front door opened and slammed, and you watched her pretend she wasn't looking at the clock as your father's footsteps banged the stairs down to the basement guest room where he slept now. As if it weren't Sunday morning, she said, "Working late, I guess." She laughed. She sipped her juice once, twice. "Boys want a girl who knows her way around the kitchen," she said. "Don't forget." You'd heard her say that so many times you knew you wouldn't ever forget. She picked up her glass and you listened to her footsteps bang the stairs up to her bedroom, and then you listened to that door slam. Then there was too much silence and you concentrated on reading and rereading the recipe for chocolate fudge.

Because you were a girl who knew her way around the kitchen, it was easy to measure milk into a heavy pot, put it on the stove to boil.

You turned on the radio as loud as it would go, and that helped some. It was the DJ everyone liked that summer, Chrissy Z. She'd been as big as you can get in Chicago but then she almost O.D.'d and so she left the rat race and here she was. She played only the best songs, the sad ones when you were sad and the happy ones when you wanted to stop thinking and dance. She never talked about her unhappy life, but it was there behind every word she spoke; turning her voice up loud was like having a friend in the kitchen. Of course you had friends—you had lots and lots of friends—but they were the kind of friends who when they asked "*how are you?*" only wanted to hear "*fine*." They were the kind of friends who called you more often after that party where they saw how someone like Mark liked you.

Chrissy Z. was playing the sad songs. You watched the milk in the pot until it started to boil round, slurpy bubbles; then you took the milk off the heat and stirred in sugar and chocolate, stirring to dissolve them, feeling the sugar heavy against the spoon at the bottom of the pot, then melting away, disappearing as the streaks of chocolate blended. You put the dark liquid back on the burner and turned up the fire. The recipe said no more stirring, so you watched the red in the candy thermometer rise, waiting for 238 degrees.

The phone rang and you picked it up quick, imagining it could be Mark, but what you heard was that woman, and then your father's hurried whisper on another extension: "Not now," and you hung up as quietly as you could—not that it mattered, probably—and a door slammed upstairs and the red line seemed to have barely moved and you stared without blinking, willing it to rise, pushing it upwards with the hardness of your eyes.

Everyone liked Mark. You liked Mark. You liked the solid muscles in his arms, you liked how his smile tilted to the left. You liked his whisper hot and urgent in your ear, tickling itself into the places no one had been before. He made you forget the weather and the rules and everything else. One day he'd ask how you were and you wouldn't have to say fine.

You liked how fudge was his favorite food, how it could have been anything he liked best, but it was chocolate fudge, and you thought about how you would make fudge for him every day for the rest of his life if that's what he wanted. You could tell him to close his eyes and open his mouth and then you'd set tiny pieces of fudge onto his tongue and watch them melt and you'd put your fingers in his mouth so he could suck off the chocolate stickiness and you'd kiss his chocolatey lips and feel his chocolate-coated tongue slide hot and wet all over the inside of your mouth. You wouldn't be in his father's car then, you'd be together in your own house with your own kitchen and own car in the garage, and afterwards, you'd listen to his heart beat for hours.

The phone rang again, but you didn't look at it because you were watching the red line in the thermometer. And a moment later, your mother stalked back into the kitchen and snatched her bottle of vodka out of the cereal cupboard then left and you didn't look at her either because the red line had reached 238 degrees and you put the pot of fudge into a bowl of ice water to cool it back to 110 degrees and by staring hard at the disappearing bubbles, you could think about nothing, you could almost feel you weren't even really there and when all the bubbles were gone and the fudge was cool enough, you beat in butter, letting the clatter fill the kitchen. Then you beat in vanilla. Then you beat the fudge until it was no longer shiny and poured it into a buttered pan. You knew your way around a kitchen; you'd made fudge for a boy.

You cut the fudge into perfect squares and wrapped them in wax paper. In the pantry you found a tin with a picture of a family riding in a horse-drawn sleigh and claimed it for your fudge, arranging the pieces very carefully. You put a red peel-off sticky bow on the tin, and then you borrowed your mother's car, sneaking the keys out of her purse as she slept, and drove to Mark's house, after looking up the address in the phone book.

It was about three o'clock in the afternoon, another hot day. Going up his front walk, you felt the heat burning off the bricks and through your sandals, but you didn't change your pace. Mark's grass was very green, and you imagined someone remembering to run the sprinkler every other night, long conversations about fertilizer.

When he answered the door, he seemed surprised to see you and stepped right outside, shutting the door behind him, keeping one hand on the knob. You thought maybe he'd kiss you. Or hug you. Or ask how you were. Instead, he glanced up and down the street. He squinted when he looked back at you. "Not now," he said.

There was something you'd been planning to say, something cute and funny, but all of a sudden you couldn't think what that was. Nothing felt cute or funny. It was hard to breathe. But you smiled your pretty smile, the one you thought maybe he liked. "I made you chocolate fudge," you said. You flipped your hair.

He didn't speak, just squinted more so that his eyes became tiny and faraway, almost disappeared.

"Your favorite food."

He said, "My girlfriend is here."

There was a pause. Somewhere a lawn mower started up. You thought maybe you would cry, and you didn't want to, so you bit the inner part of your bottom lip. The tin of fudge was suddenly heavy in your hand.

Again he turned his head this way and that, looking up and down the street. He whispered, "What about tonight?," brushed one finger quickly along your cheek.

You listened to your own heart beat hard in your ears. Then you nodded.

You got home and sat alone in the kitchen while your parents did whatever it was they did behind your mother's closed bedroom door and Chrissy Z. or someone like Chrissy Z. played songs that were supposed to make you want to dance. You ate all the fudge yourself, letting it melt on your tongue bit by bit, sucking the chocolate stickiness off your fingers, watching the clock that was so slow to reach ten p.m., waiting, waiting.

The perfect
candy bar
would run its
fingers through
your hair while
you eat it.

The Chocolate Lady

Laurence Gonzales is the author of Deep Survival: Who Lives, Who Dies, and Why? *(W.W. Norton); for more, see www.deepsurvival.com.*

They spent Saturday looking for wedding rings in the Loop. To Hank's mind, jewelry stores were ugly. He and Terry had to ring a bell to enter through locked metal gates, as if they were trading in plutonium. They stood before the glass counters with light shooting around them like withering fire, ricocheting off crystals and chromium. Suddenly Hank felt a sickening dread at the prospect of marrying her, as if he were setting out on stormy seas in a boat full of holes.

Hank and Terry were engaged to be married in less than a month. How had he gotten himself into this? He didn't want rings. He didn't want cake or flowers. He hated it when one of her friends called and blurted out with strident cheer, "So are we all ready for the festivities?" He felt like saying, "No, I'm going to Alaska to become a bush pilot," and slamming the phone down.

But he didn't. He always chuckled and said, "Just about," or something noncommittal. Now he avoided answering the phone at all.

He was staring at a platinum ring with small diamonds set all around its circumference, thinking: It looks like a tiny model of the Space Station. All it needs are solar arrays. It looks like an IUD for a killer robot.

"What do you think, Hank?" she asked, turning her hand this way and that to catch the light. Her ring size had changed dramatically. Terry had gained fifty pounds during the seven years they'd been together.

"Great," he said between his teeth.

"I know it's more than we planned to spend—"

"A lot more," he interjected, but she plowed right over him.

"—but I'm going to be wearing it every day, all my life, and I think it's important to get something we like."

A revelation: I'm a coward, Hank thought. It's that simple. This is what cowardice is. Not failing to run in front of the machine gun. It's failing to run away from the machine gun. It's elective stupidity.

■

They were on the street again. The rings were theirs. They'd be ready in a few days. A train passed on the tracks overhead. The deafening roar and clatter shot off of coal-blackened stone buildings on Wabash Avenue and bounced around in crackling, rifle-shot echoes.

"Do you like your ring?" she was asking.

"What?"

"Your ring," she shouted. "Do you like the one you're going to wear?"

Hank suddenly realized that he hadn't even looked. He remembered that she had slipped a ring onto his finger at one point, but he couldn't remember what it looked like. Was it gold? Was it platinum? Did it have a stone? He didn't know. He needed a cigarette. He needed a drink.

But Terry didn't know that he smoked. He'd given it up years ago and only started up again recently. It was the stress. How could he tell her that he smoked? How could he tell her that it was because of the stress of knowing that he'd have to marry her?

She was prattling on about needing shoes to go with the dress. The dress! While she was at her first fitting, it had occurred to Hank that they could have bought an amazing amount of camping gear for the price of that dress. They could have outfitted an arctic expedition. They could have gone somewhere interesting. The seamstress came highly recommended. Hank guessed her weight at about three hundred pounds. She was very nice, he thought. But he couldn't help wondering if Terry had chosen her because by comparison Terry seemed positively slender.

Interestingly enough, Terry's weight had not bothered him. She was over six feet tall and carried it well. Hank's attraction to her had remained through everything. Just the week before, he had taken her to the Art Institute and had shown her sculptures of women in marble and brass, bodies just like hers. "See?" he had said. "You have a classic body. Your body is beautiful." He wasn't being disingenuous. He agreed with those sculptors. His struggle with Terry wasn't about sex, it was about power and control.

The noise of the L-train was drowning her out. Hank pulled her into a doorway. "Why don't you go over to Marshall Field's and look at those shoes and I'll meet you there in half an hour or so?"

She pouted. "You don't want to look at shoes with me?"

Lying effectively, Hank found, was a skill that required constant practice to develop good speed and timing. "I have to go and get a little surprise," he said coyly.

Terry smiled. "Gimme a kiss," she said and stuck her face out at him.

He pecked her on the cheek.

"On the lips," she said. "Do you love me?"

"Of course, I do," he said.

"On the lips, then."

He kissed her on the lips. She opened her mouth and tried to suck him in. People jostled past them. The train passed catastrophically overhead. Hank pulled away with a forced smile and patted her arm. "I'll meet you by the fountain at around four."

"I thought you said a half hour," she protested.

"I don't want to keep you waiting," he said.

"OK," she said and turned as if to leave. But she stopped herself and rushed back with an air of urgency.

"What?" he asked.

"We haven't talked about the cake," she said.

Hank didn't know what to say, and so he simply gaped at her.

"Well, Hank, don't you care?" She looked as if she might be on the point of tears.

"Of course, of course, I do," he said. "I was just thinking. I mean, don't you just... order a wedding cake?"

"Just order a wedding cake!" she said. Clearly he had betrayed her. He didn't quite know how. He had never thought about it before, but wasn't a wedding cake just some kind of tiered confection of white cake with white icing on it?

"Well... I don't know," Hank said, taking her hand. "What were you thinking we should do?" For he knew by now that far more important than any actual decisions they made was that he give the appearance of being involved in the decisions, the illusion of concern, as long as the decision in the end was Terry's to make. It was even better if Hank could find out by some subtle exchange what exactly Terry wanted and then give the illusion that he had made the decisions, had come to the very conclusion that she was after, so that she could then agree and say, "See? You're always saying that I make all the decisions, but I let you make decisions, too."

At which point Hank could say, "You're right, honey."

So it was now that Hank took a chance, a leap of faith, based on years of knowing her, and said, "How about chocolate?"

"Chocolate," she said breathlessly. "Yes, of course. That's it, isn't it? We'll have a chocolate wedding cake. Oh, my God, we have to start calling bakers right away."

Hank was grasping the idea now. She wanted the wedding to be completely traditional in every way but to have the illusion of being nontraditional. The pieces of the puzzle were beginning to fall together in his mind.

"What about the shape?" she asked.

Hank waited while a train thundered overhead. When it had gone, he said, "Well, I suppose either a sheet cake or one of those, what do you call it?"

"Stair step," she said.

"Yes. Not the traditional wedding cake shape, though, not if it's chocolate, right?"

"Right!" She hugged him. "Oh, Hank. You see? I do let you make decisions."

"Yes," he said. He looked at his watch. "We'll start calling the bakers on Monday and see what they can come up with."

"I love you, Honey."

"I love you, too."

He watched her walk away into the Saturday crowd. He breathed a sigh of relief. When he felt that she was at a safe distance, he lit a cigarette and inhaled deeply. People flowed around him. The trains clattered overhead. But he felt as if he were in a cocoon of quiet and safety.

■

He wandered for half an hour. He liked the coal-smudged, looming shadow-world of those old buildings. He could walk through the Loop all day and be content. He passed south of Carson's, past the cigar shop, the eateries, and an antiquarian bookseller. He came to a shop with a glass front that had been whitewashed from the inside. There was a single word painted on the window: Cake. He wondered what a cake store was doing in this seedy part of the Loop. But perhaps he could find out something about chocolate wedding cakes here.

He pushed open the door with the tinkling of bells. A fit, middle-aged man stood behind a glass case that might have held cakes but was empty. It was Saturday. Perhaps they had delivered all the cakes already. Chocolate stains looked like blood on the man's white apron. Hank explained that he was getting married and would like to have a chocolate wedding cake very soon, very urgently. After pushing out his lower lip in a thoughtful pout, the man answered with a French accent. "Well, we have had requests like this before. There is a woman just a few blocks from here in the south Loop who I believe might be able to do as you wish. I understand from her clients that she has made these, um, as you say, cakes like this before. This is of great urgency?"

"Yes," Hank said. "Yes it is." It would be the surprise he had promised Terry if he could come up with just the right chocolate cake now, before she even finished her shopping.

"Well, then, I suppose that I could call her for you and see if she is free."

"Yes, that would be great," Hank said, growing excited at the prospect. If only he could contribute something, perhaps make this feel more like his own instead of something that was dragging him along.

While the man dialed the phone, he looked up with raised eyebrows and warned, "She's a little bit strange. But then I think that is perhaps what you want…"

Hank was tempted to say, Oh, Terry and I are the king and queen of strange. But he only smiled knowingly. The man spoke rapidly in French, then hung up and handed Hank a business card. It said, The Chocolate Lady. There was an address and phone number beneath.

Hank hurried off toward Van Buren Street. He still had most of the hour before he had to meet Terry. He shuddered at the thought of what she might spend with an hour and a charge card in Marshall Field's. He should have given her less time. On the other hand, this might make it worthwhile.

The row of ancient buildings at the south end of the Loop had shops at street level and neon signs in some of the windows above. He passed a dark tavern, a disordered pawn shop, a pizza place, and an old tailor's that seemed to have gone out of business. He checked the addresses. The one on the card matched the number on the tavern door.

Hank went in and found the place thick with cigarette smoke. A few afternoon drinkers stood at the rail. A television was broadcasting the game, and someone in a dark corner thrust his hips urgently at a pinball machine in an ugly mockery of mounting passion.

Hank went to the bar, and the bartender placed a cardboard coaster in front of him and waited for his order.

Hank showed him the card. "I'm looking for this place," he said.

"You have an appointment?"

"Yes."

"Right though that door," the man said. "Upstairs on the left."

"Thank you."

Hank pushed through waves of smoke to the louvered swinging doors and entered a dingy hallway littered with trash. A metal staircase stood at the far end, lit from above by a dirty skylight.

Hank's footfalls rang hollowly on the stairs. At the second floor was another hallway with doors on either side. There was almost no light, and he walked right past the one with the fading gold lettering that said The Chocolate Lady. On his way back, he saw it and knocked.

There was no answer. He tried the door and found it open. He went in and was hit by a powerful odor of chocolate and sugar. "Hello," he called. He closed the door behind him. He could hear a machine working in the back.

The room was someone's living room. The furniture was Edwardian. The drapes were maroon, and cobwebs hung from them. At one end they had come unhooked from the rod and were collapsing. The Persian carpet was threadbare. A cat came out and looked at him and then disappeared into a far room.

Hank moved into the darkness, passed through a doorway, and found himself in an old kitchen. The Chocolate Lady stood at a stove stirring a pot. Light brown hair fell down her back. She wore jeans and a blue work shirt and a stained apron, and when he entered she was singing something from Edith Piaf and didn't hear him. She shook her hair away from her face with a toss of her head. She had a slim and shapely figure. Hank called hello again, and she turned with a smile.

She was beautiful in a lost and dissipated sort of way. She was in her thirties. She put down her spoon, wiped her hands on her apron, and crossed to Hank. She took both of his hands in hers. Hank felt their skin stick together. "Marcel told me you were coming," she said. "For my chocolate cake."

"Yes," Hank said.

"That's marvelous," she said. "Can you put down a deposit?"

"Certainly," Hank said, taking out his wallet. "How much would you like?"

"A hundred dollars," she said.

"That's an expensive cake," he said.

"If you are not satisfied, I won't charge you a cent. It's my policy."

Hank put five twenties on the table. She ignored them and pulled Hank toward a couch. He noticed that there was a bed and a piano in the kitchen as well. She sat close beside him on the couch and stared at his eyes. "Tell me about your wedding," she said. "Tell me about your fiancée."

Hank was filled with fear and confusion. He did not believe in love at first sight and in recent years had had to admit to himself that he might not believe in love at all, in the same way that he'd had to face the fact that he didn't believe in God. Yet here, undeniably, something had happened in his heart or in that place we call the heart, which is no heart at all. He didn't even know her name, but she sat holding his hands with her own sticky hands, gazing intently into his eyes, her knee touching his thigh. What was the source of her interest in him? Her smile was more than style, and her closeness was more than a French sense of personal space.

"It's my worst nightmare," Hank blurted out. He could hardly remember the last time he'd told the truth about anything personal. He saw her face fall.

"Oh, no," she said softly. "You don't want to get married?"

"No," Hank said. "I'm trapped. She's a witch."

"Oh, no," she said again. "Ah. So I see why you want my chocolate cake, then. It is—how do you say?—a last-ditch effort."

"Yes," he said.

"You want to do something, and you don't know what to do, and so you come to me to make things better."

"Yes," he said, thinking: How does she know? She's a genius, a fortune-teller. "Yes, yes, yes," he said. "It's horrible. We just came from shopping for wedding rings. I thought I was going to scream. I thought I was going to die."

"You've thought about throwing yourself under a train, haven't you?" she asked.

"Yes," he said, bowing his head in shame.

"Oh, no," she said again in that way she had. Like a little girl with a broken doll. "We must do something."

"Yes. But what?"

"Listen to me," she said, squeezing his hands tighter. "You have only one life. And it's over so quickly. How long have you been together?"

"Seven years," Hank said. He could feel his throat tightening. Tears welled up in his eyes.

"Oh, no. That is a long time, no?"

Hank couldn't speak. He simply nodded dumbly.

"And you feel now that you can't possibly back out. You've invested too much. The wedding is approaching. You are desperate, I can see that clearly in your eyes. Does she not see this when you look at her?"

"She sees what she wants to see," Hank said.

"And you don't look at her that much, either, I suppose."

Hank shook his head again. It was true. He hardly ever met her eyes anymore. How could he? He was too ashamed.

The Chocolate Lady hugged herself and said, "Oh. Oh-oh-oh," as if she were waiting for a pain to pass. "Think, think, think," she told herself. Hank watched her go through this, marveling at the way he felt in her presence. Marveling at feelings he hadn't known in years.

"Did you know that Century Downing said that every kitchen should have a bed?

"No, I didn't know that," Hank said.

"Yes. Food and cooking are so sensual, you know, when food is done right it is like love or it's an expression of love or an extension of love."

"What about the piano?" Hank asked.

"Oh, I play while I'm cooking. I cook so much, I have to have the things I need in the kitchen. I don't get to spend any time in the other rooms." She shook her head again and said, "What to do."

"It's not your problem," Hank said.

"Well, yes and no. If you came across a bridge and saw me in the water drowning, wouldn't it be your problem?"

"Yes, of course," he said.

"And you'd try to save me, would you not?"

"Yes," he said.

"So." She gripped his hands again and pulled him close. "What you are doing is even more dangerous. It is no joking matter. If you marry a woman you don't love, you will die. I have seen it happen."

"Oh, but I love her," Hank blurted out. But even as the words left his lips, he realized the Chocolate Lady knew him better than he knew himself.

She stared at him. She didn't have to say anything.

"No," Hank said. "You're right. I don't love her."

She nodded up and down in confirmation. She stood, lifting his hands. "Come," she said.

Hank stood, puzzled, enthralled. "What?"

"Come," she insisted.

She led him to the bed. It was a narrow bed, little more than a cot pushed against one wall. Chocolate was simmering gently in a double boiler on the ancient porcelain stove. "What? What?" Hank asked urgently.

The Chocolate Lady stood by the bed and undid the buttons on her work shirt with fingers that were stained permanently brown as if from tobacco. Hank watched her do this, his heart going like mad, his real heart. She dropped the cotton shirt to the floor. She had perfect breasts, small and soft, in elegant French curves. The nipples were natural jewels set in moons of chocolate.

"What are you doing?" Hank whispered.

"Shh," she said, undoing the button on her jeans. "Take off your clothes. Don't be afraid. I'm going to save you."

"I can't—" he began. But he knew he could. He knew he must. Suddenly he realized how right she was. He was a drowning man, and his clothes were an anvil carrying him to the bottom. His fingers had never been so nimble as they flew over buttons and zippers.

Hank had forgotten that he had a body.

The Chocolate Lady was naked before him, taking his hands gently in hers. She had chocolate on her neck, where she'd pushed her hair back and smeared herself. She smelled like chocolate and smoke.

"She has made you forget how beautiful you are," she said. "She never tells you that you have a beautiful body, because she herself does not. She has gained a lot of weight and feels that if she recognizes how beautiful your body is, then she must also realize how she has lost her own beauty. And so she makes you pay for her sins. She makes you pay and pay but you never get anything back. In this way, she slowly sucks the life out of you, and if you marry her, you are going to die. Maybe not today, maybe not tomorrow, but slowly, over the years." She pulled him down to the bed. Hank sat beside the Chocolate Lady. They were both naked. He could feel her heat where their hips touched. "When you came in, the light in your eyes had almost gone out, but now I can see it rekindling. Can you feel it?"

Hank nodded. His eyes were wide. He could feel the reanimation of his corpse, an energy that rose from his feet and up his legs to his groin and stomach and chest, until it reached his face like a warm wave. She had her hands on his face. Hank let her push him back until he was lying down.

"If you pulled me from the river, you would give me artificial respiration, would you not?" she asked.

"Of course," he whispered.

She put her mouth over his and blew air into his lungs. Hank relaxed and let her fill his lungs. She put her tongue in his mouth, and Hank held it there, and then put his tongue in hers, and back and forth they went.

"Breathe," she said.

Hank put his mouth to hers and filled her lungs. She sucked the air in eagerly. "Here, more," she said. She drew herself up until one of her breasts was in his mouth. She made soft noises as he sucked on the nipple, moving his tongue back and forth.

"Can you feel it?" she asked. "Can you feel the life you've been missing?"

"Yes," Hank said.

"This is not about sex," she said. "Don't you see how desperate the situation is? Desperate situations call for desperate measures. You see that, don't you?"

"Yes."

She slid off of him to one side. She lay on her back. Hank rose above her. She cocked her knees up toward her chest. The white soles of her feet faced Hank like two hands making peace with the air. Her long thighs angled back, and her face was framed by the gentle curve of her calves. She reached around her own legs and took Hank's head and pulled his face down into her.

Hank could smell the chocolate, mingling with her own aroma. Then she cried out and pulled his face up along her belly and chest until his mouth met hers again, and they breathed in and out of each other's lungs as Hank moved gently inside her. She said, "Let me turn over."

Hank moved off her and she rolled onto her stomach. He hesitated, hovering over her. She turned her head to face him. "Don't you want my chocolate cake?" she asked.

"What?" he asked, puzzled.

"My chocolate cake, darling," she said. "Don't you want it?" She smiled. Hank noticed for the first time that her teeth were perfect and straight and white as stones in a river.

Hank felt a rush of emotion. "Yes," he said. "Yes, I do. I do. Is that what you like? You really want that?"

She reached for a small tube from the table beside the bed and handed it to him. "Of course I do," she said.

Hank looked at the tube in his hand. The label said Astrolube. His heart was going like mad. His fingers trembled as he flipped open the top. He held it above her bottom, and for a moment it remained there like a censor in a sacred rite. A drop of crystalline liquid formed on the end of the small plastic nipple. It grew and hung, shaping itself in its minute scaphoid elegance, and then gravity released it into the air. Much later, as Hank went over and over it in his mind, he would imagine that he witnessed in that fractured second its plunge toward her perfect skin. The drop changed shape from tear to sphere like a new planet forming in mid-air. Then the slick fluid hit her cheeks and slowly drew a shining trail down into the smooth muscular canyon of her maximum world.

She arched up toward him. Hank fell upon her.

A voice said, "Oh, my God, oh, my God…" Hank wasn't sure anymore whose voice it was.

■

Hank stood beside the fountain in the Marshall Field's department store. He was an hour late and wondered if Terry had waited and had then gone home. She would be furious. Terry's fury had always been the most frightening thing in Hank's life, but suddenly he didn't care.

He sat on the edge of the fountain and opened the small brown paper bag. He selected another chocolate from the selection the Chocolate Lady had given him. There had been five altogether, and he'd eaten three on the walk over. Now he ate another. They were light and airy confections, each one flavored differently. This one seemed to have a kind of cognac in it, and it made him light in the head. Or perhaps he was feeling the thrill of freedom. His ears had been ringing since he'd left the south Loop.

Then he saw Terry coming through the Coach store. Her arms were loaded with packages. She had spent a lot of money. Hank didn't care. He stood up, swallowing the last of the chocolate. She hurried along, speaking before she reached him. "Oh, Hank, I'm sorry I'm late. Have you been waiting long?"

So she was the one who was an hour late. She thought nothing of letting him wait, but if he'd been late, he never would have heard the end of it. It only gave him more strength. How little she looked out for him. How little she cared. As she reached him, she saw the look in his eyes and stopped dead. Not even she, the queen of denial, could deny what she saw. Hank watched her face fall.

"What is it? Hank? What is it?"

"I don't love you and I'm not going to marry you," he said flatly. "I'm in love with another woman."

She dropped all her packages and burst into tears. There was no ceiling where they stood by the fountain. The airy atrium went up in tiers of balconies, floor after floor, straight to the roof of the building. Terry's wails echoed off the tiles, and people rushing past stopped to gape at the couple. She was howling uncontrollably like a dog that had been run over. Hank didn't know what to do.

"How could you do this?" she screamed. "What am I going to tell my parents? What am I going to tell my friends?" And she commenced to wail again.

Hank watched as long as he could. He picked up the packages and stacked them beside the fountain. Terry collapsed and sat heavily on the edge of the fountain. She put her head in her hands and wailed pathetically, the tears falling between her feet on the tiles. Ordinarily, this would have melted Hank's heart, he would have taken her in his arms and said he didn't mean it, he took it all back, he was just under a lot of stress—he would say whatever he had to say, and she would rearrange herself and they'd both deny that it had ever happened. That's how it was every other time they'd broken up over the years. That's how she managed to keep him prisoner.

But not now. Hank said, "I'm sorry." And he walked away through the crowd, leaving her sitting on the fountain. When she realized that he was leaving her there, she leaped up and screamed, "You son of a bitch! You never loved me!"

Hank heard the words echo around the big store, but they didn't touch him. They didn't touch his heart. And he kept on walking, right out onto Wabash Avenue, where he turned and headed back toward the south end of the Loop.

He lit a cigarette as he walked. He felt a great weight had been lifted from him. He floated through the Saturday crowds. The trains chattered overhead.

When he reached the block where the tailor shop and the pawn shop and the tavern were, it looked somehow different to him, but he couldn't say how. He entered the tavern and went straight to the back. As he pushed his way through the louvered swinging doors, he heard the bartender call out, "Hey, fella! Where do you think you're going?"

Hank stopped and turned back. The bartender was scowling from behind the bar. "That's private back there," he said. It wasn't the same man who had been there earlier. This one had an Irish accent.

"I know," Hank said. "I'm going up to see the Chocolate Lady."

"The Chocolate Lady?" the bartender asked. "I don't think so, pal."

Hank crossed to the bar to show the man the business card. He stood under the bartender's suspicious glare, searching his pockets, but he could not find the card. "Damn, I must've dropped it," he said.

"Dropped what?"

"The card, I had her business card." Hank realized that the card must have fallen out of his pocket while he was undressing. "Listen, I think I left it upstairs," he explained. "I was just up there." Hank moved again toward the louvered door. The bartender called after him, but Hank rushed through and hustled down the hall to the metal staircase, a kind of desperate fluttering fear forming in his chest.

As he vaulted up the stairs, he could hear the Irish accent calling out behind him, "Listen, Mister, if you've escaped from ISPI, I can call you a ride. The police will be happy to take you back there!" He could hear the footfalls behind him.

As Hank reached the second floor, he raced down the hall, looking at the doors. He found the one with the gold lettering and pushed his way through just as the Irish bartender reached the landing.

Hank stood in the semi-darkness a moment, letting his eyes adjust. He could hear the bartender running toward him. He lunged through the room, barking his shins on the edge of a couch, and burst into the kitchen. A blue flame flickered from the stove beneath a double boiler. The Chocolate Lady was on her back in the bed, and a man with a beard was on top of her. She screamed when Hank burst in, and the man rose, huge and naked, his eyes burning like filaments. He said, "What the hell..." Hank felt the bartender grab him from behind. He heard the Chocolate Lady shout, "Goddamnit, Sean, will you get him out of here, can't you see I am balling this customer?"

"I'm sorry, doll," the bartender said, "he just ran right past me."

"Wait, wait," Hank could hear himself saying. "I was just here. What are you doing? I told her like you said. I told her the wedding was off."

"That's very nice," the woman said. "Now will you please get the hell out? You are not my only customer, you know. Sean will take your money. You can come back later."

Hank felt the words gagging him. He couldn't speak. The bartender was dragging him out through the living room. Hank was coughing. He felt as if he might throw up. The world was spinning.

The bartender was surprisingly nice to him about the whole thing. He pulled him gently down the stairs and guided him along the hallway back to the tavern. Hank stood like a mummy, and the bartender helped him to a stool at the bar and then went behind it and put a cardboard coaster in front of him.

"Hey, I thought you were a cop, all right?" the bartender said. "Have one on me." He poured Jameson and Hank drank it, and he poured another. "She gets guys all mixed up, you know, when she could just be doing her business. I don't get it, you know. She and Marcel came here from Belgium a few years ago. They've got a weird thing going, you know, with this chocolate and all. But she does a good business, so we don't complain. Here have another. Cheer up. You can go up when that other's guy's through. So what's your story, pal?"

ANN ANDROLA

Cherry Cordials

Ann Androla lives in Erie, Pennsylvania, with her husband, the poet Ron Androla. She is currently working on two unfinished novels, "A Real Witch" and "Uncross."

She rolled over and squinted at the clock beside the bed. Almost seven-thirty. He must have turned off the alarm to let her sleep, since it was Friday and she didn't have to go to work. She stretched, hands touching the wall behind the bed and feet nudging the cat sleeping under the covers. Eyes open, she lay on her back for a few minutes and thought about last night, and all the nights before that, when she'd avoided having sex with her husband.

Thursday night was usually his window of opportunity, the only night her excuses didn't cover. She didn't have to get up early for her four-day-a week job, and she wasn't yet too tired from slaving over her novel all weekend. Last night she'd come right out and told him she didn't want to. She never really wanted to, but he already knew that.

She sighed and sat up. Married sex was like writing, she thought. She didn't really enjoy the process all that much, but she did savor the feeling of getting it over with for another week. In a novel, as in a marriage, there was only one way to get from the beginning to the end, and that was to keep plugging away at the middle.

She picked up her heavy white socks from the floor and pulled them on. The forecast for today was rainy and cool, just the way she liked it. A perfect day to get a lot done. She heard a muffled thud as the cat jumped down to follow her. Flicking on the bathroom light, she bunched her long nightgown around her waist and sat down. The cat rubbed his head against her shins and she stroked his glossy brown back. She scratched just at the base of his tail, and he quivered with pleasure.

The cat was called Bean, though his real name was Cocoa, and he had been her husband's cat before they met. When they were dating, she considered his preoccupation with dark chocolate charming, even romantic. Now she found it self-indulgent and annoying. He talked about chocolate the way other people talked about wine—bitterness, aroma, undertones and overtones and other qualities she had no appreciation for. Chocolate, for her, was like sex; a little went a long way.

As she brushed her teeth, she examined her puffy eyes and limp, unwashed hair. Oh well, she thought, it wasn't as if she was going to see anyone. The cat waited for her to finish, lifting one foot, then the other, in a quiet dance of impatience. Side by side, they padded down the carpeted stairs. She noticed the front door was still latched, which meant he hadn't brought the newspaper in yet. She frowned. Maybe he was making breakfast, even though Sunday was his customary day.

Soft gray light bathed the living room in a pearly glow as she came around the corner. She could barely make out the top of his head above the sofa back. Taking another silent step in his direction, she suddenly realized what he was doing.

He was slumped on the sofa, his legs spread as far apart as the pajama bottoms around his ankles would allow. The long fingers of his right hand encircled his erect penis, and his left hand traveled slowly, languidly, up from the candy box nestled beside him. The box of expensive hand-dipped cherry cordials had been cradled in his arms last night when he arrived home from work, a weekly gift not for her, as a stranger might assume, but for himself. Holding a chocolate-covered cherry above his open mouth for a moment, he dropped it in and made a slurping sound. From where she stood a few feet behind him, she could hear him chew and swallow. His right hand began to move faster. She tried to turn and leave without his knowing she'd been there, but Bean gave her away, meowing for breakfast.

She was seized with a powerful mixture of contempt and envy: contempt of her husband's constant desire for sex and envy of his ability to abandon himself so completely to sensation. His head turned toward her. She began unbuttoning her nightgown. Letting it fall around her, she knelt before him and placed her hand above his. He released his grasp and tried to move his hand away, but she gently replaced it, keeping his fingers covered with her own, showing him through her gestures that she meant no harm.

She watched the steady motion of their hands, unable to look at his face, as his cock stiffened again. Shuffling forward on her knees, she cupped her pillowy white breasts and surrounded him with flesh, provocatively lifting her ass higher as she leaned over. Continuing to squeeze and rub the shaft with her breasts, she inclined her head and flicked the tip with her tongue each time it rose from between the soft mounds. Her hair fell forward, and he lifted it away from her face. She let go of her breasts and took him fully into her mouth. In a short time she could feel him jerk and throb, on the verge of orgasm.

She pulled her lips away as he exploded, milky semen pumping onto his belly. Still on her knees, she delicately lifted a piece of candy from its tiny fluted paper cup, bit into the dark chocolate shell and sucked out the cherry and the sugary white syrup around it. For the first time that morning, she looked into his eyes. He seemed bewildered.

As she held his gaze, she used two fingers to scoop up some semen just before it ran into the shallow pool of his navel. She transferred it carefully to the empty chocolate shell, scraping it from her forefinger on the melting rim. After sucking sweet brown goo from her fingertip as suggestively as possible, she lifted the refilled cherry cordial as if offering a toast and plopped it into her mouth.

That ought to hold him, she thought, licking her lips.

NICK CARBO

Foreskin Crackling

Nick Carbo is the author of El Grupo McDonald's *(1995) and the editor of two anthologies of Filipino writing,* Returning a Borrowed Tongue *(1996) and* The Other Half of the Sky *(2000). Among his many awards are fellowships in literature from the National Endowment for the Arts and the New York Foundation for the Arts. He lives and writes in New York.*

She had this wild thought to dip my penis in a pot of Swiss chocolate. Must have been that stand in the mall, selling all kinds of fruit dipped in brown goo. The grapes were a good idea. She preferred the peach slices, I had the figs. She had that Catherine the Great look in her eye—ready to strap me on some harness so she could lower or raise me like a Lippizaner horse. Lindt and Suchard wrappers decorated the cherry-red linoleum floor, and the sweet scent of melting chocolate permeated the kitchen. This sure was not from the pages of that seventies' sex book, *The Sensuous Woman.* Maybe more from Xaviera Hollander's *The Happy Hooker.* Or was it straight from Anaïs Nin's *Delta of Venus?* The white apron and nothing else underneath convinced me this might just work. She led me to the warm pot like some big animal, spanking my bare bottom along the way with her wooden spatula.

Chocolate syrup on a lover's nether regions is proof positive of the existence of God.

JOANNE HARRIS

from Chocolat

Joanne Harris's novels include Gentlemen & Players *(Morrow, 2006),*
Sleep, Pale Sister, Coastliners, *and* Chocolat. *Half-French, she teaches
French at Leeds Grammar School and lives in Barnsley with her husband
and small daughter.*

FRIDAY, MARCH 28
GOOD FRIDAY

At some point quite early on I forgot what the party was all about
and began to enjoy myself. While Anouk played in Les Marauds,
I orchestrated preparations for the largest and most lavish meal
I had ever cooked, and became lost in succulent detail. I had
three kitchens: my own large ovens at La Praline where I baked
the cakes, the Café des Marauds up the road for the shellfish, and
Armande's tiny kitchen for the soup, vegetables, sauces and gar-
nishes. Joséphine offered to lend Armande the extra cutlery and
plates she might need, but Armande shook her head, smiling.

'That's all dealt with,' she replied. And so it was; early on
Thursday morning a van arrived bearing the name of a large firm
in Limoges and delivered two boxes of glass and silverware and
one of fine china, all wrapped in shredded paper. The delivery
man smiled as Armande signed the goods receipt.

'One of your granddaughters getting married, *hein*?' he asked
cheerily.

Armande gave a bright chuckle. 'Could be,' she replied.
'Could be.'

She spent Friday in high spirits, supposedly overseeing things but mostly getting underfoot. Like a mischievous child she had her fingers in sauces, peeped under dish covers and the lids of hot pans until finally I begged Guillaume to take her to the hairdresser in Agen for a couple of hours, if only to get her out of the way. When she returned she was transformed: hair smartly cropped and set under a rakish new hat, new gloves, new shoes. Shoes, gloves and hat were all the same shade of cherry-red, Armande's favourite colour.

'I'm working upwards,' she informed me with satisfaction as she settled into her rocker to watch the proceedings. 'By the end of the week I might have the courage to buy a whole red dress. Imagine me walking into church with it on. *Wheee!*'

'Get some rest,' I told her sternly. 'You've a party to go to tonight. I don't want you falling asleep in the middle of dessert.'

'I won't,' she said, but accepted to doze for an hour in the late sun while I dressed the table and the others went home to rest and change for the evening. The dinner-table is large, absurdly so for Armande's little room, and with a little care would seat us all. A heavy piece of black oak, it took four people to manoeuvre it out into Narcisse's newly built arbour where it stood beneath a canopy of foliage and flowers. The tablecloth is damask, with a fine lace border, and smells of the lavender in which she laid it after her marriage—a gift, never yet used, from her own grandmother. The plates from Limoges are white with a tiny border of yellow flowers running around the rim; glasses—three different kinds—are crystal, nests of sunlight flicking rainbow flecks across the white cloth. A centrepiece of spring flowers from Narcisse, napkins folded neatly beside each plate. On each napkin, inscribed cards with the name of the guest: *Armande Voizin, Vianne Rocher, Anouk Rocher, Carline Clairmont, Georges Clairmont, Luc Clairmont, Guillaume Duplessis, Joséphine Bonnet, Julien Narcisse, Michel Roux, Blanche Dumand, Cerisette Plançon.*

For a moment I did not recognize the last two names, then I remembered Blanche and Zézette, still moored upriver and waiting. I realized that until now I had not known Roux's name, had assumed it to be a nickname, perhaps, for his red hair. The guests began to arrive at eight. I left my kitchen at seven for a quick change and a shower, and when I returned the boat was already moored under the house, and the river people were arriving. Blanche in her red dirndl and a lace shirt, Zézette in an old black evening dress with her arms tattooed in henna and a ruby in her eyebrow, Roux in clean jeans and a white T-shirt, all of them bringing presents with them, wrapped in scraps of gift paper or wallpaper or pieces of cloth. Then came Narcisse in his Sunday suit, then Guillaume, a yellow flower in his buttonhole, then the Clairmonts, resolutely cheery, Caro watching the river people with a wary eye but nevertheless prepared to enjoy herself if such a sacrifice was demanded. Over apéritifs, salted pinenuts and tiny biscuits we watched as Armande opened her presents: from Anouk a picture of a cat in a red envelope, from Blanche a jar of honey, Zézette sachets of lavender embroidered with the letter B—'I didn't have time to do one with your initial,' she explained with cheery unconcern, 'but I promise I will next year'—from Roux a carved oak leaf, delicate as the real thing, with a cluster of acorns clinging to the stem, from Narcisse a big basket of fruit and flowers. More lavish gifts came from the Clairmonts; a scarf from Caro—*not* Hermès, I noticed, but silk nevertheless—and a silver flower vase, from Luc something shiny and red in an envelope of crinkly paper, which he hides from his mother as best he can beneath a pile of discarded wrapping-papers. Armande smirks and mouths at me—*Wheee!*—behind her cupped hand. Joséphine brings a small gold locket, smiles apologetically. 'It's not new,' she says.

Armande puts it around her neck, hugs Joséphine roughly, pours St Raphaël with a reckless hand. I can hear the conversation from the kitchen; preparing so much food is a tricky business and much of my attention is given to it, but I catch some of what is going on. Caro is gracious, ready to be pleased; Joséphine silent; Roux and Narcisse have found a common interest in exotic fruit trees. Zézette sings part of a folk song in her piping voice, her baby crooked casually into her arm. I notice that even the baby has been ceremonially daubed with henna, so that it looks like a plump little *gris nantais* melon with its mottled golden skin and grey-green eyes.

They move to the table. Armande, in high spirits, supplies much of the conversation. I hear Luc's low, pleasant accents, talking about some book he has read. Caro's voice sharpens a little—I suspect Armande has poured herself another glass of St Raphaël.

'*Maman*, you know you shouldn't—' I hear her say, but Armande simply laughs.

'It's my party,' she declares merrily. 'I won't have anyone being miserable at my party. Least of all me.'

'For the time being, nothing more is said on the subject. I hear Zézette flirting with Georges. Roux and Narcisse are discussing plums.

'*Belle du Languedoc*,' declares the latter earnestly. 'That's the best for me. Sweet and small, with a bloom on her like a butterfly's wing.'

But Roux is adamant. '*Mirabelle*,' he says firmly. 'The only yellow plum worth growing. *Mirabelle*.'

I turn back to my stove and for a while I hear nothing more. It is a self-taught skill, born of obsession. No-one taught me how to cook. My mother brewed spells and philtres, I sublimated the whole into a sweeter alchemy. We were never much alike, she and I. She dreamed of floating, of astral encounters and secret essences: I pored over recipes and menus filched from restaurants where we never could afford to dine. Gently she jeered at my fleshly preoccupations.

'It's a good thing we don't have the money,' she would say to me. 'Otherwise you'd get fat as a pig.' Poor Mother. When cancer had eaten away the best of her she was still vain enough to rejoice at the lost weight. And while she read her cards and muttered to herself, I would leaf through my collection of cookery cards, incanting the names of never-tasted dishes like mantras, like the secret formulae of eternal life. *Boeuf en Daube. Champignons farcis à la grèque. Esacalopes à la Reine. Crème Caramel. Schokoladentorte. Tiramisu.* In the secret kitchen of my imagination I made them all, tested, tasted them, added to my collection of recipes wherever we went, pasted them into my scrapbook like photographs of old friends. They gave weight to my wanderings, the glossy clippings shining out from between the smeary pages like signposts along our erratic path.

I bring them out now like long-lost friends. *Soupe de tomates à la gasconne*, served with fresh basil and a slice of *tartelette méridonale*, made on biscuit-thin *pâte brisée* and lush with the flavours of olive oil and anchovy and the rich local tomatoes, garnished with olives and roasted slowly to produce a concentration of flavours which seems almost impossible. I pour the '85 Chablis into tall glasses. Anouk drinks lemonade from hers with an air of exaggerated sophistication. Narcisse expresses interest in the tartlet's ingredients, praises the virtues of the misshapen *Roussette* tomato as opposed to the tasteless uniformity of the European *Moneyspinner*. Roux lights the braziers at either side of the table and sprinkles them with citronella to keep away the insects. I catch Caro watching Armande with a look of disapproval. I eat little. Steeped in the scents of the cooking food for most of the day I feel light-headed this evening, keyed-up and unusually sensitive, so that when Joséphine's hand brushes against my leg during the meal I start and almost cry out. The Chablis is cool and tart, and I drink more of it than I should. Colours begin to seem brighter, sounds take on a cut-glass crispness. I hear Armande praising the cooking. I bring a herb salad to clear the palate, then foie gras on warm toast. I notice that Guillaume has brought his dog with him, surreptitiously feeding him with titbits

under the crisp tablecloth. We pass from the political situation,
to the Basque separatists, to ladies' fashions via the best way to
grow rocket and the superiority of wild over cultivated lettuce.
The Chablis runs smooth throughout. Then the *vol-au-vents*, light
as a puff of summer air, then elder-flower sorbet followed by
plateau de fruits de mer with grilled *langoustines*, grey shrimps,
prawns, oysters, *berniques*, spider-crabs and the bigger *tourteaux*
which can nip off a man's fingers as easily as I could nip a stem
of rosemary, winkles, *palourdes* and atop it all a giant black lob-
ster, regal on its bed of seaweed. The huge platter gleams with
reds and pinks and sea-greens and pearly-whites and purples,
a mermaid's cache of delicacies which gives off a nostalgic salt
smell, like childhood days at the seaside. We distribute crackers
for the crab claws, tiny forks for the shellfish, dishes of lemon
wedges and mayonnaise. Impossible to remain aloof with such a
dish; it demands attention, informality. The glasses and silverware
glitter in the light of the lanterns hanging from the trellis above
our heads. The night smells of flowers and the river. Armande's
fingers are nimble as lacemakers'; the plate of discarded shells in
front of her grows almost effortlessly. I bring more of the Chablis;
eyes brighten, faces made rosy with the effort of extracting the
shellfish's elusive flesh. This is food which must be worked at,
food which demands time. Joséphine begins to relax a little, even
to talk to Caro, struggling with a crab claw. Caro's hand slips, a jet
of salt water from the crab hits her in the eye. Joséphine laughs.
After a moment Caro joins in. I find myself talking too. The wine
is pale and deceptive, its intoxication hidden beneath its smoothness. Caro is already slightly drunk, her face flushed, her hair
coming down in tendrils. Georges squeezes my leg beneath the
tablecloth, winks salaciously. Blanche talks of travelling; we have
places in common, she and I. Nice, Vienna, Turin. Zézette's baby
begins to wail; she dips a finger in Chablis for it to suck. Armande
discusses de Musset with Luc, who stammers less the more he
drinks. At last I removed the dismantled *plateau*, now reduced to

pearly rubble on a dozen plates. Bowls of lemon-water and mint salad for the fingers and palate. I clear the glasses, replace them with the *coupes à champagne*. Caro is looking alarmed again. As I move into the kitchen once more I hear her talking to Armande in a low, urgent voice.

Armande shushes her. 'Talk to me about it alter. Tonight I want to *celebrate*.'

She greets the champagne with a squawk of satisfaction.

The dessert is a chocolate fondue. Make it on a clear day—cloudy weather dims the gloss on the melted chocolate—with 70 per cent dark chocolate, butter, a little almond oil, double cream added at the very last minute and heated gently over a burner. Skewer pieces of cake or fruit and dip into the chocolate mixture. I have all their favourites here tonight, though only the *gâteau de savoie* is meant for dipping. Caro claims she cannot eat another thing, but takes two slices of the dark-and-white chocolate *roulade bicolore*. Armande samples everything, flushed now and growing more expansive by the minute. Joséphine is explaining to Blanche why she left her husband. Georges smiles lecherously at me from behind chocolate-smeared fingers. Luc teases Anouk who is half-asleep in her chair. The dog bites playfully at the tableleg. Zézette, quite unselfconsciously, begins to breastfeed her baby. Caro appears to be on the verge of comment, but shrugs and says nothing. I open another bottle of champagne.

'You're sure you're OK?' says Luc quietly to Armande. 'I mean, you don't feel ill or anything? You've been taking your medicine?'

Armande laughs. 'You worry too much for a boy of your age,' she tells him. 'You should be raising hell, making your mother anxious. Not teaching your grandmother how to suck eggs.' She is still good-humoured, but looks a little tired now. We have been at table almost four hours. It is ten to midnight.

'I know,' he says with a smile. 'But I'm in no hurry to i-inherit just yet.'

She pats his hand and pours him another glass. Her hand is not quite steady, and a little wine spills on the tablecloth. 'Not to worry,' she says brightly. 'Plenty more left.'

We round off the meal with my own chocolate ice-cream, truffles and coffee in tiny demi-tasses, with a calvados chaser, drunk from the hot cup like an explosion of flowers. Anouk demands her *canard*, a sugar-lump moistened with a few drops of the liqueur, then wants another for Pantoufle. Cups are drained, plates cleared. The braziers are burning lower. I watch Armande, still talking and laughing, but less animated than before, her eyes half-closed, holding Luc's hand under the table.

'What time is it?' she asks, some time later.

'Almost one,' says Guillaume.

She sighs. 'Time for me to go to bed,' she declares. 'Not as young as I was, you know.'

She fumbles to her feet, picking up an armful of presents from under her chair as she does so. I can see Guillaume watching her attentively. He knows. She throws him a simile of peculiar, quizzical sweetness.

'Don't think I'm going to make a speech,' she says with comical brusqueness. 'Can't bear speeches. Just wanted to thank you all—*all* of you—and to say what a good time I had. Can't remember a better. Don't think there's ever *been* a better. People always think the fun has to stop when you get old. Well it doesn't.' Cheers from Roux, Georges and Zézette. Armande nods wisely. 'Don't call on me too early tomorrow, though,' she advises with a little grimace. 'I don't think I've drunk so much since I was twenty, and I need my sleep.' She gives me a quick glance, almost of warning. 'Need my sleep,' she repeats vaguely, beginning to make her way from the table.

Caro stood up to steady her, but she waved her away with a peremptory gesture. 'Don't fuss, girl,' she said. 'That was always your way. Always fussing.' She gave me one of her bright looks.

'Vianne can help me,' she declared. 'The rest can wait till the morning.'

I took her to her room while the guests left slowly, still laughing and talking. Caro was holding on to Georges's arm; Luc supported her from the other side. Her hair had come entirely undone now, making her look young and softer-featured. As I opened the door of Armande's room I heard her say: '...virtually *promised* she'd go to Les Mimosas—what a weight off my mind...' Armande heard it too and gave a sleepy chuckle. 'Can't be easy, having a delinquent mother,' she said. 'Put me to bed, Vianne. Before I drop.' I helped her undress. There was a linen nightdress laid out in readiness by the pillow. I folded her clothes while she pulled it over her head.

'Presents,' said Armande. 'Put them there, where I can see them.' A vague gesture in the direction of the dresser. 'Hmm. That's good.'

I carried out her instructions in a kind of daze. Perhaps I, too, had drunk more than I intended, for I felt quite calm. I knew from the number of insulin ampoules in the fridge that she had stopped taking it a couple of days ago. I wanted to ask her if she was sure, if she really knew what she was doing. Instead I draped Luc's present—a silk slip of lavish, brazen, indisputable redness—on the chair-back for her to see. She chuckled again, stretched out her hand to touch the fabric.

'You can go now, Vianne.' Her voice was gentle but firm. 'It was lovely.'

I hesitated. For a second I caught a glimpse of us both in the dressing-table mirror. With her newly cut hair she looked like the old man of my vision, but her hands were a splash of crimson and she was smiling. She had closed her eyes.

'Leave the light on, Vianne.' It was a final dismissal. 'Good-night.'

I kissed her gently on the cheek. She smelt of lavender and chocolate. I went into the kitchen to finish the washing-up.

Roux had stayed behind to help me. The other guests had gone. Anouk was asleep on the sofa, a thumb corked into her mouth. We washed up in silence and I put the new plates and glasses into Armande's cupboards. Once or twice Roux tried to begin a conversation, but I could not talk to him; only the small percussive sounds of china and glass punctuated our silence.

'Are you all right?' he said at last. His hand was gentle on my shoulder. His hair was marigolds.

I said the first thing which came into my head. 'I was thinking about my mother.' Strangely enough I realized it was true. 'She would have loved this. She loved—fireworks.'

He looked at me. His strange skyline eyes had darkened almost to purple in the dim yellow kitchen lighting. I wished I could tell him about Armande.

'I didn't know you were called Michel,' I said at last.

He shrugged. 'Names don't matter.'

'You're losing your accent,' I realized in surprise. 'You used to have such a strong Marseille accent, but now…'

He gave his rare, sweet smile. 'Accents don't matter, either.'

His hands cupped my face. Soft, for a labourer's, pale and soft as a woman's. I wondered if anything he had told me was true. For the time, it didn't seem to matter. I kissed him. He smelt of paint and soap and chocolate. I tasted chocolate in his mouth and thought of Armande. I'd always thought he cared for Joséphine. Even as I kissed him I knew it, but this was the only magic we had between us to combat the night. The simplest magic, the wildfire we bring down the mountainside at Beltane, this year a little early. Small comforts in defiance of the dark. His hands sought my breasts under my jumper.

For a second I hesitated. There have already been too many men along the road, men like this one, good men about whom I cared but did not love. If I was right, and he and Joséphine belonged together, what might this do to them? To me? His mouth was light, his touch simple. From the flowers outside I caught a wafting of lilac, brought in by the warm air from the braziers.

'Outside,' I told him softly. 'In the garden.'

He glanced at Anouk, still sleeping on the sofa, and nodded. Together we padded outside under the starry purple sky.

The garden was still warm in the glow of the braziers. The seringas and lilacs of Narcisse's trellis blanketed us beneath their scent. We lay on the grass like children. We made no promises, spoke no words of love though he was gentle, almost passionless, moving instead with a slow sweetness along my body, lapping my skin with fluttering movements of the tongue. Above his head the sky was purple-black like his eyes, and I could see the broad band of the Milky Way like a road around the world. I knew that this could be the only time between us, and felt only a dim melancholy at the thought. Instead a growing sense of *presence*, of completion filled me, overriding my loneliness, even my sorrow for Armande. There would be time for grieving later. For the moment, simple wonder; at myself lying naked in the grass, at the silent man beside me, at the immensity above and the immensity within. We lay for a long time, Roux and I, until our sweat cooled, and little insects ran across our bodies, and we smelt lavender and thyme from the flowerbed at our feet as, holding hands, we watched the unbearable slow wheeling of the sky.

Under his breath I could Roux singing a little song:

> *V'là l'bon vent, v'là l'joli vent*
> *V'là l'bon vent, ma mie m'appelle…*

The wind was inside me now, tugging at me with its relentless imperative. At the very centre, a small still space, miraculously untroubled, and the almost familiar sense of something *new*. This too is a kind of magic, one that my mother never understood, and yet I am more certain of this—this new, miraculous, living warmth inside me—than of anything I have done before. At last I

understand why I drew the Lovers that night. Holding the knowledge close, I closed my eyes and tried to dream of her, as I did
in those months before Anouk was born, of a little stranger with
bright cheeks and snapping black eyes.

When I awoke, Roux was gone, and the wind had changed
again.

RIKKI DUCORNET

A Cup of Chocolate

(Letter to the Fan Maker from Sade)

Rikki Ducornet is the author of seven novels including the Fan Maker's Inquisition, *an L.A.* Times Book of the Year. *She was awarded the Lannan Prize for Fiction in 2004, and a Lannan Fellowship in 1993. She is currently working on a collection of short stories and a novel set in Algeria after the War for Independence.*

Little wolf, *my prize wench. The things you sent have at last arrived this morning, pawed over the by the contemptible Scrutinizer, a wretch who cannot keep his hands to himself; but nothing broken and it seems everything in place: the ink, candles, linens, sugar, chocolate—the chocolate! Untouched! And what chocolate! So that I may start the day just as the Maya kings with a foaming cup.*

Like a good fuck, a good cup of chocolate starts with a vigorous whipping and here I am, my little anis de Flavigny, *breathing the Yucatán as I write this letter. There are fops who swear by* amber gris *and would put that in their chocolate, but I'm particular to the classic cup—unadulterated—perhaps the one instance when I can say I prefer a thing* unadulterated!

A cup of chocolate, ma douce amie, *and my mood—and it couldn't have been worse—has lifted: why I am so buoyant that did God exist I'd be in paradise with my nose up his arse! But this is a godless universe—you know it as well as I—and therefore nothing in the world, or, for that matter, in any of the myriad other worlds, planets and moons, smells better than a good cup of hot chocolate!*

Or tastes better. Hold on for a moment, will you, as I take another sip... As I was saying: nothing! Not even those sanctified turds no bigger than the coriander seeds which falling from the sky into the wilderness fed the famished Jews. A pretty story... And here's another (although I warn you, it's not near as nice):

Yesterday as the clouds rolled into the city from the West obscuring the sky and just before it began to rain, I saw a young fellow, fuckable beyond one's wildest dreams, kneel before the guillotine. Now I know that all I imagine in my worst rages is only a mirror of the world. All day, over and over again, although the rain fell in torrents and the wind sent a bloody water surging into the crowd, Hell materialized beneath my window. At times it seemed a staged tableau, a diabolic theater as redundant as the bloodthirsty entertainments I have, poisoned by ennui, catalogued time and time again. To tell the truth, all day I wondered if thoughts are somehow contagious, if my own rage has not infected the world. I thought: Because I dared to dream unfettered dreams I have brought a plague upon the city.

The idea persisted. I could not let it be but worried it like a dog worries the corpse of a cat. Such redundancy is exemplary: a machine has been invented that lops off a head in a trice, and suddenly the world is not what it was. And I who have dreamed of fucking machines, of flogging machines—I am outdone! The plague I have unleashed is not only highly contagious, it is mutable: see how it gathers strength and cunning!

And now—a death machine, là! Là! Just beneath my window! Have I engendered it? It seems that I have. Even the clouds pissing rain, the air filled with mortal shrieks, with sobs, the laughter of sows—seems to pour out of me. I imagine that every orifice of my body oozes crime. A lover of empiricism (and this is a tendency that, on occasion, plunges me into a fit—for I would count the whiskers on the face of a rat and weigh the dust motes of air if I thought this would lead me somewhere...) it occurs to me that I might find a way to measure or track this seminal poison and direct it. For the gore that accumulates like the dead apples of autumn beneath my window sickens me, yes! It is one thing to dream of massacres; it is another to witness one.

Is this violence the bastard child of one man's rage? If so, all is irreparable, for I have imagined so much. Worse: I have put it to paper!

I recall the story of a notorious slut, Madame Poulaillon, who attempted to destroy the husband she despised by soaking all his shirts in arsenic. Arsenic she had in plenty as rats plagued her home. (But what marriage is not haunted by the midnight chatterings and scrabblings of vermin?) It is a venerable tradition: the poison garment. There is another story of a pagan queen, a Hindoo, a real piece, who made to marry the one who had taken her kingdom by force offered him a robe so deadly it caused his flesh to fall away.

My mind is like these: its poison is invisible but deadly. Far from the world, locked in ignoble towers, fed slop, forced to scribble away my precious days and years with a quill no bigger than a frog's prick—my venom soaks the city like a fog. What would things be like, I wonder, if I really put my mind to it? Could they be worse?

Ah! But another taste of chocolate, and all this dissolves. And I recall a fan you once made for the actress known as La Soubise: a fan of peacock feathers, a fan made of eyes! *When she used it, it seemed that an exotic moth, a moth from the Americas, had settled on her hand. You called the fan "Andrealphus" in honor of the demon who was said to transform men into birds. And thanks to your instruction in the languages of fans, when La Soubise glanced my way and taking her fan with her right hand and, holding it before her face, left the room, I knew she might as well have spoken the words:* follow me. *Crowing like a cock, I flew after her at once and spent a happy hour in her barnyard. (Now, there was a courageous soul who was not afraid of my reputation!)*

Remember when I asked for a flabellum? *How later, together, we laughed at the joke? A fan that represents chastity! That protects the host from Satan in the form of flies! Just* what *is supposed to*

happen, I would like to know, to a believer who swallows a con-
taminated wafer?

Wild Chocolate

for Rae Armantrout

Kevin Killian is a poet, novelist, critic, and playwright. His books include
Bedrooms Have Windows, Shy, Little Men, Arctic Summer, *and* Argento
Series. *With Lewis Ellingham he has written* Poet Be Like God: Jack Spicer
and the San Francisco Renaissance *(Wesleyan, 1998), the first biography
of the important U.S. poet. He lives in San Francisco.*

Mr. McAndrew offered Mark a glass of beer, which was notable.
Only time his father ever poured out any Rheingold was when he
wanted him to do some ball-breaking thing. "No? I suppose you
get enough of this on the sly, when I'm away."

Mark said nothing, just waited, his feet turned inward on the
polished oak floorboards. They were sitting in the living room of
a house tucked away on a side street in Smithtown, Long Island.
He looked at his shoes with their pinch tassels that seemed to be
faintly twirling. Or anyway moving, perhaps from the draft of air
that also moved the fringes of the hooked carpet...tousling them
helter-skelter so that they looked like colored fingers beckoning
and waving...

"Listen, Mark, I was talking to a friend at work today—nice
guy—Charles Carpenter. And um, he was telling me about this
little business his wife and her friend have, right here in town."

"Really?" his son replied. "What kind of business is it?"

"Catering concern," said Mr. McAndrew, in an expansive
mood. Ruthlessly, he brought his beer to his face and chugged

it down. Then he rose from his armchair with his empty glass, as though he didn't know what to do with it. If we were in England, Mark thought, he'd dash it into the fireplace. "Nice for the wife—keeps her out of trouble. I've met the wife and she's a piece of ass. How'd you like to work for her?"

Mark hated it when his father tried to talk man to-man with him. *You are probably great at banking or whatever you do at Chase*, he thought, *but you are no pal of mine*. He squinted down at his shoes and yes, the tassels were moving across their faces.

"She needs a few boys to help her out this Saturday, so I figured you and Kevin Killian could give her a hand. It's for some shindig at the club. Nice pay," he said reflectively, his hand on the doorjamb. "And she is some piece," he said.

At twilight the grounds of the Smithtown Country Club looked blue, and the evening was warm, spring-like. A white man in blue jeans stirred a giant net on a stick through the placid waters of the swimming pool. Mustangs rolled up the wide pebbled drive, pulling up to the front porch and depositing weathered barmen, maitre d's, coat-check girls. Mark and I walked around the low-slung Colonial-style buildings to the tennis court, where a huge statue of a tooth had been erected, spotlit by green and yellow headlamps. I gathered that this catered affair was some kind of benefit to help our town fight tooth decay. Beneath the statue a little ledge had been erected, around which a fence was strung with near-invisible ropes of dental floss; a tuxedoed man stood on the ledge gingerly, fiddling with an outdoor microphone, and casting his eyes around an imaginary crowd. Behind him the golf courses began, and beyond those shadowed dales a line of poplars separated the club grounds from the strip of beach on Long Island Sound, its shallow choppy tide.

"I suck at this menial shit," Mark said to me. "What I hate most about my dad is the emphasis he puts on meniality. Like I'm supposed to learn how to be a man by first being a waiter."

"It won't be so bad," I said, determined to put a bright face on the matter and to lend my friend some cheer. "Aren't you looking forward to seeing this famous piece of ass friend of your dad's?"

"Hmm," grunted Mark. "Well, there's the door, Pollyanna, give it a knock."

This was the beginning of March 1967. A week or so before, in the UK, police had arrested Mick Jagger, Keith Richards, and Robert Fraser after raiding Richards's rented country mansion Redlands, on a tip from a reporter from *News of the World.* The two great rock gods were in jail, charged with possession of heroin tablets and four amphetamine pills, later thought to be the property of Jagger's girlfriend, the pop singer Marianne Faithfull. Mark and I had read the story of the midnight raid and thrilled to the police testimony that Faithfull had been surprised in her bath and had come into the sitting room wearing nothing but a white fur rug. We didn't want to work, we just wanted to rehash the Redlands affair. Something in the air—some spirit of rebellion—whispered to us that we were too young, too special, and too good-looking to have to work, even if Mark's father had put his foot down, actually driving our asses to the country club himself in his big black Fleetwood sedan that looked like a pimp drove it. "You have to read between the lines in these news reports," Mark confided. "She was naked, brother Kevin. Nude as the day you were born."

I didn't want to admit that Marianne Faithfull had ever been naked. *Not her!* For she was a creature from a Fragonard, dressed always in exquisite laces, her blonde hair in these natural waves from the 1840s, shaded by a pink parasol. She had had a hit song the year before called "As Tears Go By," which I thought the most beautiful thing ever written. I didn't like Mark taunting me about her reported dishabille, it seemed sacrilegious, and if he wasn't my best friend I would have—well, I wouldn't have socked him one but I wouldn't, sure as shit, be here tonight on the grounds of the country club getting ready to be a busboy on his father's whim. The issue of Faithfull's nudity was a bone of contention between us that had rather spoiled the amity we felt toward each other—and the guilty crush I had on him—a feeling I didn't know what to do with, a bleak blast of suburban anomie. When I thought about her, and her blonde air of monied *tristesse,* I thought about him—Mark McAndrew—these two worlds of sensuality colliding and crashing together like dental plates: clack. Hurt my head.

One afternoon as we met after school, he told me what "friends in England" had told him had been omitted from the newspaper accounts. The police had raided Redlands for drugs, and had surprised Mick and Marianne having oral sex on a white fur rug on the living room floor, and Mick had been eating chocolate out of Marianne's—out of her— I couldn't even comprehend what my friend was telling me, it sounded too vicious.

Backstage, in the big kitchen, Mrs. Carpenter was directing her staff, standing in the middle of the wet tile floor, examining a list of hors d'oeuvres, when her partner tapped her on the shoulder and said, "Kiki, can I disturb you for a minute?" He stood six-and-a-half-feet tall, handsome, about twenty-eight years old, and he wore a frilly apron about his waist. Tiny scraps of dough still clung to his fingertips, and his fingers were arrayed like a king's—rings of many descriptions, some plain and masculine, but others studded with elaborate jewels.

"No, go ahead, William," she said absently. He lifted a hand and pinched her upper arm.

"Where are my boys? I asked you specifically for two young helpers. Are they here or are they somewhere else?"

"They're coming, William," Kiki Carpenter replied with ease. She moved to the pastry chef and sampled his rich, crusty pound cake. "Very good, Sam. Yes, William, I arranged with a friend to get you two young helpers."

"What size?" he said.

"Darling," she said. "I do hope—"

William looked furious. He towered above Mrs. Carpenter and his fists were knotted with red lines—veins, I guess.

Kiki gave him a cool look over her clipboard. "Back to work, dream boy," she said dryly.

Right outside the kitchen door, in the busy sunset, Mark and I stood downing a can of beer apiece. "What are heroin *tablets,* anyhow?" I said, suppressing a belch. Remember those old-fashioned cans of beer that you opened with a silver opener? Pop tops had just recently made their appearance and purists like ourselves disdained them. "Heroin 'tablets,' like St. Joseph Aspirin for Children? Do they come like pills, all buffered and shit?"

"Heroin is legal in England," Mark said.

"Oh, yeah, right, and that's why Mick and Keith are in prison."

"Heroin's legal there," he said, with utter certainty, for Mark was even more convinced than I that England was a magical land, one far more worthy of our attention than our benighted USA.

"Maybe it's just illegal to put it in tablets," I said brightly.

"What they're in fucking prison for," Mark said, tipping the empty can to the flagstone pavement, "is *eating Hershey chocolate out of Marianne's snatch*. It's not because of heroin tablets or anything else, just pussy eating."

"You knock," I said coldly, to defray further slurs against Marianne Faithfull's chastity.

"No, you knock," said Mark. "Pretend you're the inspector from Scotland Yard investigating *snatch abuse at Redlands*."

"It's your party," I told him, so he knocked, saying, "Here comes meniality."

Just then the door opened, hot air blowing out against us and the evening. A man stood in the steamy threshold, and his eyes lit up with surprise and quiet appraisal. "Hello my little fledglings," he said, trim and tall and very mod even in his frilly apron. He pointed a ringed finger at us. "You're late, but don't fret. My name is William, and you must be—?"

"Kevin Killian," I said, extending my hand.

The kitchens, which I saw over and around him, were steamy with white clouds and the insinuating smells of prime rib au jus, roasting in industrial-size ovens. A wheeled rack held tray upon tray of what looked like—deviled eggs? A thousand eyes.

The tall man stooped over to kiss my hand. His mouth felt like someone had just cooked a pancake on my wrist.

"Mark McAndrew," my friend said, but did not offer his hand. William looked at him reproachfully, told him not to be coy.

"Is Mrs. Carpenter here?" he said hesitantly. "My father told us to ask for her."

"She's busy right now, but I am William, William Lemoire, and *you are here to help me! I am the one who needs your help and I have uniforms for you to put on.*"

He shoved us toward an alcove hung with coats, hats, greasy-looking smocks. Above the coat rack, a small diamond-shaped window let in the light of the fading sun.

"You shall be busboys tonight," he said, handing us each a thatched bundle of clothing, red and brown and black. He perched himself on a little wooden stool with an expectant manner, his eyes gleaming as bright as the jewels on his hands.

Slowly I reached up and pulled my shirt over my head.

"Yes, ah, splendid," said William finally, when I stood before him in my underwear, and he handed me a starched white shirt that had both buttons and studs to do up the front. First I stepped into the long, absurdly baggy pair of dress trousers he held out. Then I felt William's deft hands, his fingers clutching pins, running up and down my legs, pinning up the inseam, and when I raised my eyes to the diamond of sunset, it almost felt like he was trying to arouse me, tickling the inside of my legs from the ankles, then, lightly—like a silken spider—touching my inner thighs and pressing the fabric against the tip of my prick. "That's good," he said. "Now let's move these over here and really give them a show."

"Say mister," Mark said, "did you hear about Marianne Faith-full?"

William flashed him a glance, his mouth full of pins.

"Did you hear about the cops in England came into the big house and Mick Jagger was eating her out on a white fur rug?"

With some effort, and now a sudden hard-on, I finished buttoning the difficult shirt with its silver studs. I turned away to the corner and slipped on the very baggy red jacket.

"In fact he was eating a Hershey bar out of her cunt," Mark said, stepping out of his jeans.

"I heard that, yes," William said. "But it was Cadbury, not Hershey."

I was feeling more out of the loop from minute to minute. Did everyone believe this baseless calumny about Marianne? Did everyone have "friends in England" with nothing better to do but get on the transatlantic phone and *lie* about a *great beauty and a great virgin*?

"Some people will believe anything," I said. I lifted my hair from under the blazer's collar and said, "Thank you, William."

"All I can say is," said he, moving on to my friend, "you can put chocolate on something doesn't make it taste any better."

"Say, William," Mark said. "Can I ask you a question, about all the rings you wear on your fingers?"

"Everyone says I remind them of Ringo," William replied, his hands stitching and sewing right under Mark's balls.

"No, that wasn't the question," Mark said. "My question is, do you get another ring for every cock you put in your mouth?"

"Oh, I wouldn't ask that question if I were you," William said. I looked around at the kitchens, laden with heavy, hot plates, steaming. There were little white clams with pink insides, they looked sexual to me, they made me think, is a pussy like that? There was molasses, dripping on hot slices of chicken, all golden and brown. A huge crystal bowl, filled with cold lemon punch, and a man wearing a tooth costume pouring a bottle of bourbon in it. He winked at me. I felt stupid having a hard-on tight in my tight black pants. Another chef was carving up a dressed turkey, chestnut stuffing spilling from its throat or whatever. Big plates of bonbons. Oysters soaked in port wine.

The winking tooth man capped the empty bottle and tossed it in a metal trash can, where it rang and clanged hollowly. He touched the lapel of my baggy red blazer. "The redcoats are coming," he said, his accent thick with some Caribbean patois. "But don't you go far without your hat, they make the boys wear hats like Jackie Kennedy."

Mark and William emerged from the alcove presently, and on Mark's head was perched a little black pillbox-style cap, tilted jauntily to one side. His face was red. William held out another hat for me. It came with an elastic band to fit under my chin: God, did I look dumb, all I had to do was look at Mark McAndrew to see how dumb I must have looked. He after all was the cute one, and I was the homely serious sidekick, like Horace in the Judy Bolton books for girls. And if he looked bad I must look like such an asshole.

Apparently the chocolate bar story was only a rumor. Marianne Faithfull's memoir recounts it as the kind of tale only dirty-minded people would invent or believe. "I laughed it off," she writes (in *Faithfull,* Marianne Faithfull and David Dalton [Little Brown, 1994], p. 113), "but my amusement began to wane when the damn story established itself as a set piece of British folklore." I don't know how these two, Mark McAndrew and William LeMoire, knew about it already: they were neither of them British. "By some mysterious means," writes the pop historian Philip Norman (in *Sympathy for the Devil* [Penguin, 1993], p. 199), "a rumour was travelling the length and breadth of England that, when the police entered Keith Richards's sitting room, they had interrupted an orgy of cunnilingus in which Jagger had been licking a Mars bar pushed into Marianne's vagina. The Mars bar was a detail of such sheer madness as to make the story believed, then and for ever after. No one needed any explanation of the line that appeared gnomically on *Private Eye* magazine's next front cover: 'A Mars Bar fills that gap.'"

Until I read Philip Norman's book I never heard that *a Mars Bar* anchored the rumor. Nor had I ever heard that 'A Mars Bar fills that gap' was a current UK advertising slogan and thus must have been hysterically, cynically funny to the in-the-know readers of *Private Eye*. I guess a certain level of salaciousness is to be expected from a pair of young boys. We were suburban sophisticates, after all. Am I wrong? My memory's bad: perhaps I knew it was a Mars Bar but, disliking Mars Bars personally—their bulky gloss, their chewy mass—unconsciously substituted my favorite, the slim, pure, milk chocolate Hershey bar. In the years to come, Mark and I quarreled about this too, as he reminded me over and over that it was a Cadbury bar, per William's correction. He ridiculed my attempts to place an American Hershey bar inside the English country house, indeed inside Marianne Faithfull's most secret place. "Cadbury is English chocolate," he said. "Obviously you think monkeys grow on trees."

William waved us up toward the head of the food line, his fingers twitchy and febrile in a way I found extraordinarily expressive, rings flashing like evening fireflies, as I made my way through the steam with Mark McAndrew, the two of us dressed more like bellhops in a Fred Astaire picture than busboys, each of us fourteen or fifteen and almost drunk. The cooks and chefs and food suppliers didn't so much as blink twice. As we stumbled by, they continued applying whipped cream to gingerbread, pineapple slices to ham cutlets. "Say, Kevin," Mark said.

"Yeah, did William give you a blowjob?"

"Brother Kev…"

"What," I growled.

"Did you hear about Marianne Faithfull and her pussy?" Mark asked. Under his jaunty pillbox hat. "Pussy smeared with chocolate, mmm, good, and Mick Jagger eating her out on that white fur rug?"

"Fuck you," I said, disgusted. I kept thinking of those little clams and how, maybe, a vagina might be very like one of those little cherrystone clams; experimentally I tried to imagine licking one, trying to decide well, it won't be so bad; and indeed I found myself getting aroused, thinking, well, then, it is only a little thing, a tiny, winking dime-size slot rather like the asshole of a boy which—

when smeared with chocolate—

which—and then suddenly a tall woman in a blue denim coverall and a severely bleached hairdo came up to us in the steam. An apparition. "Hello," she said in a cracked voice. She carried a clipboard.

"Ye gods," said Mark under his breath. The woman's face was lined, she must have been forty at least, and her dim blue eyes were lined with swatches of melted mascara. She looked hard and cold.

"Hello," I said nervously. "Can you tell us where we can find Mrs. Carpenter?"

"You must be Mark," she said, her manner imperious. "I am Kiki Carpenter. I know your dad."

"Oh, this is Mark," I said, with great amusement. I clapped my buddy on the back. "I'm just his friend along for the ride."

Today, whenever I see either Mick Jagger or Marianne Faithfull, both of whom have remarkably managed to stay on in the public consciousness, I always think of them having sex at Redlands, at the moment of the police break-in. The white bearskin rug upon which Marianne lay, her long skirt hiked over her hips. To describe the warmth and sensuality of that rug correctly I'd have to be Carole Maso, I suppose. Jagger's wide slash of a mouth, and that tongue, which even I *knew* was long, the tongue the Stones later used as the logo for their short-lived label—as though determined to keep the Mars Bar rumor floating in my head. They were tripping on acid and the heat of the fire excited their senses.

It excited mine, for it was an English fire I created for them, exquisitely detailed, all the requisite implements standing in a rack by the side of the hearth, and the mantel laid with cunning knickknacks of the Colonial era and Staffordshire china. And for thirty years I've followed the dictates of this dream, ruled by it, even asking my lovers to include chocolate bars—or chocolate syrup, ice cream, *mole,* Hershey's kisses—in our sex lives. At no time has it worked out well, though I wouldn't have believed it when I was a teen, constricted, a prisoner of my own thoughts and imagination, and I lived on Long Island with my mom and dad in a suburban house of bores, fleeing always to the basement with my records, drugs, etc., and importing various pop magazines to find out about the outside world... Thus it was that one day I opened the paper to find out about the arrest on LSD charges, in far-off England, of the pop stars Mick Jagger and Marianne Faithfull... Wild chocolate...

"Piece of ass," Mark muttered rebelliously. This was after the banquet when, worn off our feet, we sat propped up on a chrome counter in the kitchen. The dishwashers had gone home, Kiki Carpenter had gone home, all the helpers and guests had gone home. Piles of tooth costumes were folded into cardboard boxes for morning pickup. At the dinner we'd recognized many of our neighbors and people we'd seen in the paper. Local politicos, their wives, doctors, lawyers, a writer or two, a host of spinsters, Smithtown dignitaries and shop owners, the Chinese Nobel Prize winner from the local university at Stony Brook. Bankers, dentists, suburban housewives and their harried husbands. We took their plates as soon as they were done eating and some local Italian singer with big black hair mounted the stage. Then they ate more and we had to run around and do it again. Six hundred people, Mrs. Carpenter said, her springy hair escaping from its Aqua Net. Her glasses fogged up. "Go, go, go!"

"She was not my idea of a dream girl," I said to Mark. We had found part of a bottle of Johnny Walker Black on the table, and he and I were switching it back and forth, our chairs drawn close together, our hands touching. I loved him so much, but I was tongue-tied and he was the suave one.

"That's my old man for you." Mark belched. We were covered with grease and sweat. "He's fucking her," Mark added.

I was shocked.

"But what about your mother?"

Glug, glug, glug. "What about her, brother Kev? Y'know, I didn't really put two and two together until just now, but I bet anything he's fucking her. She is just his type and that's what he considers a piece of ass."

"You mean your father cheats on your mom?"

"Yeah," Mark said. "With pigs especially. Soon as I saw her I had one of those epiphanies like in James Joyce's *Dubliners*. He's putting it to her but good."

We each had a twenty-dollar bill in our wallets now. Fabulous pay for 1967. I looked down the clear neck of the bottle, saw this delicious brown whiskey, at least another inch of it. I was too upset to look Mark in the face. I felt so bad for him. I wasn't very mature, I guess. Had lots to learn. When he passed us the twenties, I had given William my phone number, scrawled on the back of a matchbook from the country club, and I'd told him to call me "if more work comes up." He took out a pen and asked Mark for *his* number; Mark said, "No thanks, brother William." So brother William kind of crumpled up the matchbook and thrust it in his breast pocket, his rings winking like fury. On and on Mark and I sat sharing the bottle and smoking these leftover Kent cigarettes that looked stained with chicken guts. They kind of tasted like chicken noodle soup.

About a month later, Mark mentioned that he'd heard from William and gone to see a boat show with him. *What?!?*

"He's OK, in my opinion," Mark said. "We've got a lot in common even if he is a fag of the worst description."

"Yeah, and he gives a great blowjob," I said, coldly.

"Um, he gave me some heroin tablets," Mark said. Again I believed him, though as I think back on it now, perhaps he was lying to impress or deflate me, though he didn't need to. I wonder if he and William actually ever met, but who's to say? And one evening, shortly afterward, when we were walking down by the river, Mark produced a plastic bag with three heroin tablets in it from the pocket of his jeans. "Want to split one?"

"OK," I said. He opened his palm and showed me this blue pill, under the shadow of the blue alders. Sunlight flickering through the leaves. It looked more like a diet pill than anything I would call a tablet. A capsule, like the ones that decorated the cover of *Valley of the Dolls.* Carefully he pried it apart and I licked the heroin off his palm, while he swallowed the other half, including the gelatin casing or whatever it was. I don't remember how it made me feel—romantic I guess. Now, thirty years later, I'm reading Philip Norman's book and I find Mick Jagger knew very well what Hershey chocolate is like. "They had been back on tour only a day or two when Phil Spector, in New York, picked up his office telephone to hear Mick Jagger's voice, speaking from a hotel room in Hershey, Pennsylvania. 'Everything here,' Jagger moaned, 'is fuckin' *brown!'* The Stones that night were performing in a town named, and largely decorated, in honour of its principal product, the Hershey chocolate bar. 'The phones are brown,' Jagger wailed, 'the rooms are brown, even the fuckin' *streets* are brown.'"

And a week or so later I called again on Mark McAndrew. His mother let me into the house, a modern split-level house on a street that made a complete circle—which, Mark boasted, was the way streets were laid out in the UK. "You can go right to his room," his mom said, gesturing with a Kent. I studied her with

the same worried, doleful smile I wear today when I go to the
hospital visiting pals with AIDS, how stupid of me. I felt deeply
for Mrs. McAndrew; her Chase Manhattan husband was cheating
on her with a blonde caterer. And she didn't seem to know it, as
she sat there at her kitchen table working a crossword puzzle.
Or maybe she knew and she didn't care. Or she had worked out
an accommodation in some "adult" way that repelled me. In any
case I ran up the steps, three at a time, to Mark's room, barging
in as best friends do. *Aftermath* was spinning on the turntable.
His hair was wet, he had just come out of the shower. He wore
a ribbed sleeveless cotton T-shirt and a towel round his waist.
He sat down on the bed and the towel fell off. Just for a minute.
Slightly erect, then his cock shrunk. I don't know, when that happens with a man I always feel a sympathetic reaction, a mutual
loss. Blushing, Mark put the towel back on and repaired to his
closet. When he next appeared, he had thrown on a pair of khaki
green shorts, wrinkled like seersucker. His blonde fair hair, when
it was long, looked like Lord Byron's: wet, pressed to his skin. He
looked cuter than I could understand. He threw me a beer and a
can opener and winked at me.

We bullshitted about this and that and presently I jumped
across on the bed with him. He was wearing a pair of khaki green
shorts and his legs were shorter than mine. "I value your friend-
ship," I said haltingly.

"Yeah, well…"

"Let's always be friends," I said—pleaded.

He turned his head away, then turned to me. His hazel eyes,
almost green, his ash-blonde hair. "OK," he said, then smiled.
"Yeah, me too." He leaped up, rolled on his side, stuck his head
under the box spring. "Here's a treat for you, Kev." I was watching
the waistband of his shorts peel down across his hips until he
straightened up, pink in the face, and showed me a Hershey bar.
Part of it was eaten, the "E" and the "Y" at the end of the word
"Hershey," and his teeth had made bite marks which somehow

had oxidized the chocolate, turned it a lighter color the way chocolate does. Mark unwrapped its brown face, its silver wrapper,
all the way, and he stuck the eaten part into his mouth. His thin
red lips. His eyes widened as if to show me what to do, drawing
me in. I put my mouth to the other end—the "H," the "E," at the
beginning of the engraved word—and we started biting in unison,
giggling. When our lips met we broke away, giggling louder. I was
perfectly happy and my heart was pounding away in my chest
like a thousand guitars.

I still haven't gotten the response I want from the question, "What would you do for a Klondike bar?"

NANI POWER

Cadbury Fruit & Nut

Nani Power went to Bennington College and the Corcoran Art School, and attended École Des Beaux-Arts Americaines in Fontainebleau, France, on a painting fellowship. Her three novels are Crawling at Night, The Good Remains, *and* The Sea of Tears. *She has been a finalist for the LA Times Book Award and long-listed for the Orange Prize, and her books have been listed as New York Times Notable Books of the Year.*

LILLIAN

One of the hardest things to get used to is their smell. Not that it is bad. Just different.

Sweat has its own language. It tells you things on different levels, sometimes you understand and other times, you understand but not up in your heart, but in your guts.

There's nerved up sweat, for example. It's oniony, sharp, and almost lemony, but not in a fresh way.

There's a lot of other sweat smells, too. Anger is hot, meaty. And love smells the best, they say, but I don't understand that one yet. Or maybe it hasn't hit my head yet.

But his smell confused me, lingering in the air after he came over, melting and mixing with the sweetness of the half-melted Cadbury Fruit & Nut bar he pressed in my hand, quickly, like saying "Here, take it, TAKE it!" while his other hand already scooted up my blouse, hot and hungry.

He was fast, nerved up, intense, and oh so sweet. He called me "baby girl" a lot. Which made me laugh. Because then, I had just turned thirteen.

∎

His wife used to cook crab at the High Point Grill with my mother. I used to watch them as they chopped conch on Saturdays. My mother loved conch salad, loved the way it burned her mouth all day long and tasted tough like rubber. It's good for the teeth, she said. I remember lots of things about her. She had one gold tooth in front that caught the sun sometimes and looked like the center of a flame. I'm getting her shape, they say. Miriam could shake like no one else, says my Grandma Carrie, and now, dumpling, you're getting the swing of things. And her hair was like mine but lighter. Gleaming red in the shadows, a dark red, like dried blood.

I used to watch the way that woman, his wife, fried crab in the hot sun and never sweat her blouse. She was cool and pretty, and they said he was lazy, that she worked all day long for him. Even then, I understand when I saw him walk up one day and lay his hand on her cheek, saw his pretty, pretty face, tan and light running around it like a river. His hair was blonde, but not light, the color of dust. Even as a little girl, I knew I wanted him.

I saw my mother look down real fast when he touched his wife. When I saw the corners of her eyes looking down that day, I couldn't read them. They glittered darkly like bird's eyes.

One day I was catching soldier crabs in the back garden with Mellie, to sell for soup, when I heard the screaming.

You can feel death creep in, you know, it's got a cold feeling and then you realize, yes, I've been waiting for this. I knew all along. All along, it was a dark shadow in the back of my mind, maybe from dreams or the unspoken words you can almost hear.

My mother got dead. I never knew how exactly, because Grandma Carrie wouldn't say, but years later I found out it was a knife that did it, and why was because of that man, Jimmy.

He must have felt guilty, Grandma said, under her breath.

He sent us things, like a big green sea turtle for soup, or bright pink coconut candy his uncle made.

One day, just a few months after I turned thirteen, he walks in the screen door, and stands there blocking the light. His hands are full of chocolate, Cadbury bars, and he shakes them at me.

"For you." His eyes are small and glint green. Half his dusty hair falls in his eye.

"No thanks." I try to cut an onion, to distract myself. I wished he'd go away. He comes up close, and I smell him, sharp. I disturb him.

His hands circle around my front, they're big hands, strong from surf fishing, and he lightly touches my breasts, soft as wind.

"Getting so grown every day. Where's Miss Carrie?" He looks around a bit. Voice is velvety soft, like the half-melted chocolate on the counter.

"She's out at Piggly Wiggly's. Shopping—"

And then he just kisses me, his tongue fills my mouth up and moves and wiggles in every direction and I follow him, follow him all the way he wants to go, and it doesn't last long, I sit on the counter and that's the first time he says "baby girl," the first time he pushes my knees apart, gets inside where he shouldn't be, but the thing is, I wanted it bad. I wanted it so bad I could taste it.

■

Afterwards, we sit back on the couch and eat the chocolate.

"Those crazy bitches at Piggly don't pay enough for. Look at this shit." He's peeled down the foil and the chocolate is whitened, grainy.

"That's ocean salt, Grandma says."

"Grandma says. Grandma says. I say they buying bad product."

He grabs the remote, and flicks on boxing.

"Oh, Willie boy go. Fetch me a Coke, darling."

He comes from Spanish Wells, across the water on the edge of Eleuthera, they say. Where the people look bleached out by the sun and talk like ducks. No brains in those folks, Carrie says.

When I come back with the drink, he looks at me for a long time.

"You love Jimmy?" he says sitting up and looking at me through his long lashes. Because he is a beautiful boy, this is the truth.

I nod and it starts again, the sweet weightiness falling through to the knees, the water, the tightness, the rocking waves, and the best part, his mouth crammed up against mine, sweet with chocolate, sounds coming from him like lost voices in a cave.

In the night, I keep a bit of the Cadbury under my pillow and sleep with my hands pressed against my crotch, all swollen and tingling. My mother comes to me in a dream with a rope around her neck and says to me:

"Be careful what eats and what you eat." But I don't understand her, and she smiles and goes on chopping the conch at the High Point Grill, smiling, humming a bit.

Only I can't tell her I see Jimmy coming up behind with a big knife, slowly like a snake. The words are stuck in my throat and then it's too late.

■

One day he comes by and says, meet me at the ocean by the Pink Sands at dark. He says through the screen, where I only see the outline of his body like a shadow, but his smell falls in the room, and the nervousness is there, and the need. I know he needs me.

"Sweets for the sweet." He says softly, reaching through the door just to push a tender square of Cadbury in my mouth. "These are from the Ruminette. Fresh."

He grabs my hand and presses it against the screen where his zipper lies and I feel the coiled heat there, and he sighs. "Hey, hey, baby girl," he whispers soft.

"Who's at the door, Lill?" Grandma Carrie yells from the kitchen, where she's stuffing crawfish.

He's gone and I tell her it's Jackie, asking I come for dinner and a party later.

Grandma doesn't say much. Stirs the stuffing full of pink chunks of crawfish smelling so good, I grab a chunk, and she slaps my hand so damn hard.

■

I walk fast down to the beach, barefoot, past the coconut trees that swish in the night, and heave out the smell of rotten coconuts, a soapy smell that excites me now remembering that night. I jump from side to side as I scoot down the narrow, sandy path to the beach, trying to avoid the tiny, hard prickerballs that lie hidden in the sand.

Finally, past the night-blooming lilacs my friends and I used to cram in jars with water to make perfume.

When I finally hit the beach, the waves are crashing and I smell salt.

He's sitting on the sand in the dark, just a rounded blob with a tiny orange ball that glows bright as he sucks his cigarette and then the ball darts down to where his hand rests on his knee. Rothmans, I remember, like all the boys from Spanish Wells because you can peel paper from the foil to make spliffs. I wonder if he does this.

I don't wonder too long, because he rolls one up and he gives it to me and I cough so hard my throat burns with fire and my eyes water and then I calm down finally, and then the waves sound so lovely, so loud, crashing and then I just laugh and fall back in the sand. He lifts my dress up, the one I chose after hours, the others in a pile of colors on the floor. And this time he's slow, and smells like rum and my mouth feels dry and every inch of my skin reaches up for the hot wetness of his mouth.

When he's inside me, it doesn't hurt anymore and he pushes, pushes toward something I don't have, can't give him. He's pressing on my head and surging, surging when I grip him and I feel looser and lighter until my eyes can't squeeze any tighter and I burst or blow up, like a comet in the sky. There is sand everywhere and he rolls back.

He takes me to a bar on the end of the island and feeds me chocolate with two fingers, and sometimes fishes it out with his tongue and we drink Yellow Birds, tall drinks for tourists with banana rum and little umbrellas. And we meet his friend, Sam, who captains the big boat in the harbor, the one there for days, as big as a city block, the fancy Arab boat, whose little pinlights up the sides say "come to me, children." He's with two women, all golden and sweet-smelling, shaking with chains and curls and they look at me like I'm a lost puppy.

"Look at Baby Spice." One says, and they giggle, and Sam grabs them both and kisses them on each cheek, and invites us to the big boat, and we all leave in a clot of laughter and zoom out there on a little white motorboat. I've always loved the little speedboats where the water spits up all around and as you hit the waves hard, it feels like you're crashing into rocks.

When we get on board, Sam shows us the swimming pool, where we all take our clothes off and swim and kiss and I feel hands grabbing and touching and it's all the strangest, oddest thing that I like it, I let Sam kiss me one time.

He shows us the big sitting room, with compartments that pop out like James Bond, and this huge bar of bottles of everything, and we drink some more. And by now I'm spinning like a top and Jimmy and I dance on top of the coffee table and the girls and Sam dance, too, and fall back on the big couches that eat you up when you fall back, soft as skin.

Jimmy's so happy he's singing, a song I'll never forget, the one that we loved that time about "Hannah, baby love." You know— *you're a sweet thing, Han-nah baby, sweet-est thing—my ba-by*. And then the drums go boom boom boom, and you're supposed to shake your butt, and we did, each of us with our hands on each other's hips and it felt so good, so much better than when I play the song to myself in my room while Grandma watches TV.

I can't get over the man he's so lovely.

When he realizes it's three o'clock, he grabs my hand and we take the boat back, but the engine conks and Sam has to bring us back paddling with a mop, and those girls and I laughed and laughed. At the dock they said, "'bye, Chickadee, 'bye Baby Spice" and I was sad to see them go, but the world was moving too fast then for me and when I reached the end of the dock, I fell down, he must've caught me and I threw up again and again and the world was a blur of lights and then I passed out.

GRANDMA CARRIE

To make a proper crawfish pie, you can't be using oleo. Marjorie Humphreys tried that one and the thing taste like diesel. You need butter, but not more than a quarter of a cup, and don't skimp. Don't get "lite" on me now. You pulverize that with the shells, see. In a blender, what else? It turns a pretty pink like a sunset. Coral or salmon, it's called.

She don't smell right.

Anyway, then you got your meat all separated, yes? In good chunks, don't be skimping, I said. Plenty of pepper, that's so you have bite. And strain that butter good, get the shell out.

And don't get skinny crawfish. Buy them fat and pink, go see Joe Petty down at the dock he'll get you good ones from his crew.

There's something, there's something *wrong* with her smell.

It's changed.

Some boil the crawfish in beer, and others in milk. I like to steam them in high heat with water and a chunk of butter. Some lemon. This way, they cook up sweet, sweeter than the other ways I can promise you because I've tried them all. And I do enjoy some good crawfish.

Put that meat in a good roux, I don't have to tell you that one I'm hoping. Add your season, Lawry's, dash of sherry, a good dash, mind you. Egg yolk. Mustard, a spoon or so. Add it to the shells. Spoon it high up, sprinkle with fresh bread crumbs and bake it until hot and bubbly. No cheese, lord. That'll spoil the flavor bad.

Add roe if you got it, the roe's the secret, and the younger, the better, more tender—

Her smell. Holy Goddamn Mother of—

Her smell.

LILLIAN

I'm lying with my face in the sand, I guess, and the next thing I know, Uncle Morton's there lifting me up and Carrie's there screaming, screaming at my face, and I say, "where's Jimmy" and she slaps my face and I got sick again.

She yells he's the devil. And I cry back No, no, no.

And I'm a mess, throw-up in my hair, in my nose. Uncle Morton's carrying me like a baby and Carrie is crying and I feel like a piece of shit, but worse, I just want Jimmy.

YOUR MOTHER BE DEAD FOR THAT MAN, she's shrieking. CRAZY, INSANE MAN, YOUR MOTHER LOSE HER HEAD AND NOT YOU, NO CHILD.

I don't know what I said, waah, waah, probably.

DON'T YOU KNOW.

DON'T YOU KNOW?

I must've answered or said nothing.

HIS CRAZY WIFE KILL HER ASS FOR OVER THAT MAN SHE'S A NUT THAT ONE SHE'S CRAZY AND I WON'T LET IT HAPPEN NO SIR NOT TWO NO HE WON'T DO IT. NO I WON'T IF I GOT A WILL IN THIS BODY.

IT'LL STOP RIGHT NOW OVER MY DEAD BODY I KNOW SOMETHING DON'T FEEL RIGHT. SOMETHING DON'T SMELL, FEEL RIGHT.

Oh lord. Come to me child.

And I did.

■

People say they're up in Spanish Wells now, say she opened a crab shop there. Grandma Carrie forbids me there until I'm eighteen, four years from now. But even then, I probably won't go.

In the Piggly Wiggly, most days I skip aisle 2, and get the bread just on the end, or ask Betty for it, she doesn't ask questions.

But once in a while my feet pull me there and I stand there, looking at the Fruit & Nut, the white wrapper, the gold foil poking out at the edges.

I pick it up and for one long glorious moment fill up with that sweet smell, and feel almost faintish as the blood rushes down between my legs.

Almonds can be painful.

SUSAN SMITH NASH

A Good Éclair Is Hard to Find

Susan Smith Nash is a poet and fiction writer who lives in Albany, New York. Her works include Lonelyhearts Pawn Shop, I Never Did Tell You, Did I? (Unsent Letters), To the Uzbekistani Soldier Who Would Not Save My Life, Doomsday Belly, *and* Channel-Surfing the Apocalypse.

She thinks she sees him in a red 1992 Honda Accord. He's in a Taco Bell drive-thru, and he's shouting his order.

She's sure he doesn't see her.

Their appetites have never had anything in common.

He's talking too fast and the sleep-deprived teenager is keying in the wrong items on the computer. He is going to get five cheesaritos and four beef 'n' bean burritos, but he probably won't care. By that time, he will have noticed Daphne walk quickly across the parking lot to a bakery, Le Chien du Chocolat, in the adjoining strip mall.

She feels his aversion to her. Knowing he hates her makes her want to bolt out of Le Chien du Chocolat bakery and, like a dog, run yelping after his rear wheels. She wants to crawl into the back seat of his pristinely clean Honda and soil it with drool and sweat.

What does he look like now? Has he metamorphosed into a gorgeous, stag-like creature with slender legs and thick, muscled haunches? Will his beauty trigger her obsessive nature, so that she will be forced to stalk him again, like she did for almost three years? He didn't like it. She couldn't help it.

The wind ruffles her hair. Its direction is indeterminate, suicidal.

Inside Le Chien du Chocolat, she checks her brash, blonde curls, her rhodochrosite lips. The bakery's clean plate-glass windows suggest that a quiet vista of pedestrian shrubs will improve digestion or at least encourage spending. Contentedness is a shade of green.

"May I help you, mademoiselle?" asks a man behind the counter. He is white haired, plump, and smiling. Très jolly, she thinks.

He looks down into the bakery case. His open hand invites her to enjoy the view of a dozen or so éclairs laid out in a row like good, dutiful sons, or spanking-new dildos.

"An éclair, please." Her soft voice counterposes her brazen eyes and her smile, directed squarely at his crotch. He is simultaneously offended and titillated. His shirt is dark blue with yellow dots in the shape of the constellation Orion. It is not the most phallic design he owns.

"Have you ever tried our *petits chiens*? Here we have two poodles and a darling little wiener dog—"

"Don't you mean dachshund?" she asks.

"Yes, it has a nice meat filling—goose pâté. The poodle has a nice crème in its tummy," he says without a tinge of double entendre.

He knows that if he refuses to be theatrical with his ironic wordplay, the ambiguity of linguistic intent will disturb her thoughts for hours, perhaps days.

"Yes, wonderful—both please." She is distracted by a red Honda Accord, which is pulling into a parking space in front of the bakery.

When a woman emerges from the driver's side, Daphne realizes that she has bitten her lip so hard that blood is welling up in the space between her lip and gum. Flesh wounds are just part of the hazards of stalking, she observes. It is then that she notices the differences. It's the wrong car.

She should have known. His car never would have sported a pair of fuzzy dice and a plush Bambi hanging from the rearview mirror.

A Taste of Gianni Mascarpone, Please

Jane Bradley, a writer of fiction, plays, and screenplays, teaches creative writing at the University of Toledo. She received an NEA Fellowship for her fiction and an Ohio Arts Council grant for her screenplay, "Blood Sisters," a script which was also a finalist for the Diane Thomas Screenwriting Award. Her story collection, Power Lines, *was listed as an Editor's Choice by the* New York Times Book Review. *Her novel* Living Doll *is often used as a text for interns and students working with emotionally disturbed adolescents. She is currently completing a new collection of stories titled "You Believers."*

Lizzy sat in the parking lot of the Spring Meadows mall and stared at the bright lights ahead beckoning with indoor fountains gushing into streams kept running by hidden pumps and copper tubes, plastic plants reaching toward skylights, and perpetual clearance sales. On dark winter nights the mall offered an oasis of warmth and light. And Gianni.

He ran the chocolate shop and was always happy to see her. When Lizzy saw his old handsome Italian face smiling, that gleam in his eye as if he knew her secrets and kept them wrapped in golden foil, she sighed with a relief that was quite simply barbitual. Gianni. She couldn't remember his last name, could only recall it was something like mascarpone, the essential ingredient for her favorite desert of layered cookies and chocolate and cream.

Lizzy leaned forward and checked her face in the mirror. In the dim overhead light, her face looked back asking, "Are you ready?"

"Never," she said as she opened the door, stepped on the pavement, and slipped a bit in her Italian boots too stylish for Ohio winters.

Above her the moon waxed full. Superstitious about such things, Lizzy knew she had one night to begin something because once the moon passed fullness, it was time to wrap things up, harvest those seeds of potential she usually let die. The last time Lizzy made love, it was a crescent moon waning. She remembered it precisely, the man rode her, hunched down and pumping like a jockey urging his thoroughbred to the finish line. His face shadowed in darkness, his hands gripped her shoulders for leverage as she sank deeper into the upholstery of his car. She squeezed her thighs against his hips, knowing the pressure would help make him come faster, and the exercise would help tone her legs. She looked up through the moon roof to the clear night sky and noticed the trees shuddering softly in the high autumn breeze. She watched the slivered bit of the moon. It was a season of completion, things coming to an end.

But now it was winter, and a dome of cold had descended on the city, sealing it in a black ice glaze that made sudden moves dangerous. Struggling to endure, she resorted to desperate measures, her methods for pleasure limited by her weakness for booze and men. A recovering drunk, a recovering Catholic, a recovering recovery, she was coming to believe that life was nothing but a process of trading addictions and you simply had to be careful with your choice.

Lizzy beeped the car locked, hurried across the parking lot, pushed through the revolving door, and entered into a warmth almost tropical. Surrounding the illuminated fountain, bronze sculpted fish eternally gurgled water from their grotesque open mouths. She didn't get it. Was it supposed to make shoppers feel exotic, as if they were in some foreign land? Was the gurgling from a fish mouth some kind of symbol to inspire them to spend as if money spurted perpetually from magical underground streams? Lizzy turned away and unwrapped herself from the scarf, the gloves, the hat, the coat—like armor to survive dangerous weather. She stamped the crusted ice from her boots, watched two teenaged lovers staring at the pulsing arc of spray as if it meant something. Old faithful maybe, that natural geyser that was losing its oomph in a world that was just getting too tired.

Lizzy liked to watch young lovers. The jet-black-haired girl stood tall in her stacked platform shoes, chin up, boobs out, ass a perfect mound—a genetically engineered sex machine, packed into a short thin black skirt and pink T-shirt emblazoned with "Hole." Back when Lizzy was the girl's age, going bra-less was enough to send preachers screeching on the moral decline of the country and politicians playing on the fear of a liberated nipple. Now girls strode the mall with lips painted the color of plumped-up vaginas. The boy, poor dolt, was clinging on the girl like a drowning man clutching a life raft. Lizzy walked past them as the boy cupped his hand around the girl's hip and stood close behind her in a gesture like affection. Lizzy wondered what such a babe was doing with a kid with his cap on backwards and his pasty face and khaki pants so baggy the crotch hung half to his knees. Lizzy smiled when she saw the girl staring off past the fountain, down the long glaring mall and looking nothing but bored.

Lizzy understood. Although she usually didn't go for small men like the last one, he had lured her with his sharp dark features that reminded her of Al Pacino. She had to admit she missed his long carpenter's fingers that could reach and wriggle inside her to pull orgasms out like dripping thick honeycomb from a buzzing hive. Problem was he could never make her come while they were screwing, and it pissed him off that he couldn't reach her G-spot. He'd insist, "I'm big enough to do it. Where the hell's your G-spot? Hiding up there behind your ribs?" Most guys didn't get it. A woman's G-spot was tucked safely and stubbornly in the dark shadows of her head.

Gianni would understand that. He was the old-style Italian who knew something about women and romance. He had told her long ago, while watching her bite into coconut truffle right there in his store. "It's a sure sign of love, Miss Lizzy, when a man feeds a woman. And I don't mean restaurants like these men these days putting fancy meals on expense accounts just to lure you ladies. No, a man must offer something made with his hands. My wife she taught me that." When Gianni talked of his long-dead wife, Lizzy couldn't tell if the tears brimming in his eyes were from sorrow or joy.

Gianni offered chocolates. He didn't make them, but he offered them in little gold foil bags or arranged on white doilies at the center of glossy pink plates. His store was called Sweet Temptations, but Lizzy thought of it as Sweet Substitutions since his fine chocolates could make her feel something like love, something like sex, keep her safely distracted in winter when usually her body became a heat-seeking missile that led her to new lovers whose forced fervor sparked her heart to glow, for a moment. Lizzy knew it was a biochemical response which in a short time only left her lonely and bored. Still she craved men, the smell of them, the sweet muscled heat of them, big men brought down to writhe with her touch.

When a man came in her mouth, she often thought of chocolate breaking between her teeth, the smooth hard surface spilling sweet spurts of cognacs, brandies, and thick, fruited liqueurs. Why was it everything she had always reminded her of something she didn't? Now she had to satisfy herself with chocolate, that pleasure of the firm silky surface between her teeth, the relief of the breaking on her tongue, the relenting thick cream.

But now her little weekly purchases of chocolates couldn't give her a high. She knew the taste, texture, smell before she unwrapped them, could replay the effect in her brain so well her body couldn't be bothered by the craving.

Again and again she returned to Gianni for new suggestions, but when she got them home they were too sweet, too gooey thick, sticking to her palate like some waxy foreign object that just didn't belong. That's how it was with addiction, no pleasure really, just the wanting to want to relive desire. Her chocolates were stacking up unused now, craved but unwanted. Little gold paper bags lined up on her kitchen shelf, untouched, like all those wineglasses she no longer used.

She wandered down the mall toward Gianni, and was already feeling warmer, softer, as if on vacation with the artificial trees reaching up toward skylights, white trellises wrapped in plastic vines. Lizzy half-expected wind-up parrots to come swooping down and eat caramel popcorn out of shoppers' hands. She walked thinking she should try a new chocolate, something totally different this time. She hoped Gianni could help her, hoped he had something secret on his shelves, some new confection that would satisfy something more than her body's needs.

The mall's clock read two minutes until closing. Was he waiting? Was he worried? Did he remember this was her night for his therapy of truffles and talk? Would he notice, or just stand there humming to himself, mopping up the floor, sealing the door shut to count up the day's cash and go? She hurried, moving as quickly as her high-heeled boots would allow. Surely he was missing her, watching the clock. Please. She ran.

Girls in black clothes wheeled the aromatherapy bar back into the Body Shop. "You're late," one called. Lizzy waved, moved on. Jesus, did everyone in the place know her habit? Was she as pathetic as that? Did they laugh? Inside, the girl bent at the entrance, pressed the button to lower the metal security door.

"Damn." Gianni was all the way down at the other end of the mall. She always parked far away to give herself a walk, to see the sales, enjoy the light, hoping maybe she'd see someone she knew.

She looked ahead and saw Gianni's shop, the red illuminated letters curling in the kind of script found on valentines. As the bells chimed the signal that the mall was closed, she saw him, her sweet kind Gianni, nodding to a tune in his head as he bent to press the button lowering the door.

"Gianni," she called, running now. He looked up just in time to see her slip on a puddle of some stranger's spilled hot chocolate. Her back wrenched for balance as her ankle collapsed, and she crumpled to the floor.

"Miss Lizzy!" he called. But she couldn't see him. Her eyes pinched shut as a flame surged up her ankle to her calf. She pulled herself up to sit, gripped her foot, and held it. She saw Gianni running toward her. "Miss Lizzy!" Her throat ached, and a knot like a fist was pummeling in her chest. She held tears back, took a breath, exhaled slowly, the way they'd taught her in recovery, to let the pain escape with her breath hissing between clenched teeth.

Gianni bent over her, touched her shoulder, "Let me help you," he whispered as he took her hand, held her waist, and lifted her up.

"Are you all right?" he kept muttering as he helped her to his shop.

She nodded, let him bear her weight, knowing if she spoke she would sob. She kept her body tight. Tight, she kept thinking, keep it tight. She pushed the hardness knotted in her chest up and out, making it envelop her like hard chocolate, the crust firmly containing an oozing center. She'd be all right if she didn't let the comfort of his touch sink past her skin. She pulled free of him. "Don't touch me." She saw the shock in his face. "Please," she added. "Just don't touch me now, please."

"I'm so sorry," he said, stepping away. "I didn't mean…" He busied himself with taking two up-ended chairs off the wooden table. "Sit," he said. "You can rest here." He turned and pressed the button. "You sit. I only come to help you," he said keeping his eyes on the lowering metal door.

"I'm sorry," she said. "It's just if you touch me, I'll cry."

He glanced back at her and moved toward his counter. "Can I bring you something? Water? An espresso? A hot cocoa. It will soothe you."

She balanced on the chair and lifted her aching foot to rest it on her knee. She could feel it throbbing, swelling already under the boot.

"You need ice. Get that silly boot off, and I bring you something." He headed toward the back room. "You shouldn't run. What in heaven is a grown woman doing running, shoes like that, running down a mall?"

"You were closing." Tears were squeaking up. "Oh god," she moaned.

He returned with a plastic bag filled with ice. "I would have opened for you, Miss Lizzy." He looked back toward his chocolate case, waved his hand. "I know you have need for your chocolate. I understand." He patted her shoulder. "You are my most loyal customer." He smiled. "And this old heart flutters like a dove when you walk in my store."

He put the bag of ice on the table and turned to go back behind his counter. "Get that silly boot off. I make something to soothe you."

She watched him work with the espresso machine. "Gianni, I've got to tell you something." He paused, looked back. She straightened. "You know all those little bags of chocolate I buy here. Every week I come, take your advice, select three perfect chocolates, carry them home. I haven't eaten them for a month. They sit lined up on my kitchen shelf. I can't drink, I can't date, and now I don't know why, but I can't even eat chocolate." She kept staring at her boot, her throbbing ankle, felt the heat swelling under the finely stitched seams. "I come here," she said. "I have to come here. But I don't want them. They're too sweet, too thick, too something." She glanced up at him, watching her with his arms across his chest and softly nodding.

"I just don't want them," Lizzy said. Oh god, she was whining.

"O Dio mio. This is worse than I thought," he said shoving napkins in her hands, pretty little designer napkins, borders printed with roses and unfurling green vines.

She stared at the roses. "It's so lonely. I sit in my dark little apartment, eating those damned chocolates by myself. I'm pathetic, Gianni." She kept her eyes on the roses, took her breath, tried to bring her voice back down to a normal range, but it kept slipping up again. "It was all I had, Gianni, my only pleasure, and now I don't want that. I don't want anything, Gianni. Nothing. How can you live when you don't want anything at all?"

"Elizabeth," he said, sitting beside her. "You want everything. I know this. This is the only reason you are so sad. Wanting everything can only lead to a broken heart."

She glanced up. He had never called her Elizabeth before. That was what her father had called her. "Elizabeth, a name fit for a queen," he had said. But her father was dead; her mother was dead. The mall was closed and the whole world was dead, except for Gianni who now looked at her with such kindness she was trembling. If he kept offering kindness, she'd soften, melt, and ooze like a caramel cream candy left too long in the sun.

Lizzy stared at the gleaming leather of her boot, knew she should take it off, but she'd never squeeze her foot back in that tight leather. She could see herself limping, like a bag lady in the darkness, toward her car.

"But your ankle is the only problem at the moment. And it's very simple. You want no pain in your ankle, and this we can fix." He pushed the bag of ice toward her. "Now take that boot off and let me see what you have done to yourself." She carefully began pulling down the zipper while he held the ice bag ready. "Easy," he whispered. He shook his head, "You silly young women wearing these designer boots in winter."

"They're good boots," she said. "Italian."

"I know they are Italian. You have the good sense to buy quality shoes, yes. But you young women." He watched her tenderly unzip the boot. "You try to look so sexy every day like sexy is some uniform. Sexy." He paused, leaned back, smiled. "My wife. She knew. Sexy is a thing to be saved. Like Christmas lights. No one would brighten at the sight of Christmas lights if we strung them all the year. *Capisc'?*" He stood and shook his head as she pulled off the boot exposing her stockinged foot pink and already going purple. "Look at those pitiful pinched toes." He placed the ice across her ankle and turned away. "When you are old you'll have bunions so big, you'll waddle like my old grandma in Italy." He crouched, squinched his face into a frown, and shuffled toward his counter. "You want to grow old like that?" He pointed to her foot. "You ruin those feet, the only feet you have this whole life. When you grow old, very sad, every step will hurt, you keep living like this."

She pressed the ice against her throbbing ankle, tried to see herself as old. "Gianni," she whispered without looking up, "you really think I'll be old one day? You really think I'll live long?"

He turned away. "I can't promise you that." She saw him pause, take a breath as he bent at the machine. "But you don't need to be old to grow a full life. My wife, we grew more love in fifteen years than most do in a lifetime." He flipped a switch, and a cloud of steam erupted with a hard hiss. She watched his back, his strong broad back, his body solid, thick with appetite. His wife, she must have loved this man. He turned to Lizzy with a cup, gently stirring. "What you need is some of my fresh cocoa. Ghiradelli. The best. My cocoa it takes tenderness, stirring, patience." He nodded to her. "You sit, be patient." He added more steamed milk to her cup and stirred. "You Americans. So in a hurry. So living in the future, you see only where you want to be instead of where you are." He turned, shook his finger, and smiled. "That is how you fall down, Miss Lizzy. Now wait, my chocolate will soothe you."

She eased back in her chair, closed her eyes, and listened to the spoon clinking against the cup. She heard him humming something, something foreign she figured. How could a man be so happy, his wife gone, grown children gone, living some West Coast high-tech life outside LA. She opened her eyes and watched the glowing light of the candy case, studied the chocolates arranged on doilies on the glass shelves lined with pink paper. There wasn't much in there she hadn't tried.

Gianni came toward her with a white china cup and saucer, placed it gently on the table, and sat. "My chocolate, I make the best, homemade, old style, real cocoa, fresh milk. You Americans have no business ruining a fine thing with these little powdered packets, dried milk, chemicals, and water just zapped in some microwave." He sat back and sighed. "It is no way to live I tell you."

Lizzy stared at the ridiculous mound of whipped cream.

"That's pure fat!"

"See, Gianni has you smiling now. Life isn't so sad. And you need a little fat on those bird bones." He lightly circled her wrist with his fingers and placed her hand gently back on the table. "A miracle you don't break like glass when you fall."

Balanced on the edge of her saucer was a thin wafer of dark chocolate. He pointed. "This one you haven't tried. Very nice. Delicate. In Italy, we serve these with espresso, cappuccino, cocoa. Such good warm things deserve a little extra on the side. We all deserve a little extra. The dolce vita," he smiled. "The sweet life. The good life. You Americans work so hard at living. Even for pleasure you have to take some class at some school. Go pay good money, study happiness someplace. As if God didn't give you the gift. No you have to go buy it in some mall, take lessons somewhere." He sighed and shook his head. "This, Miss Lizzy, is a sad thing. I feel for this country."

Lizzy nodded, not speaking of the yoga lessons, tai chi, facial treatments, massage, vibrators, the prices paid for someone, something to help her feel her own body's potential for pleasure in being alive. She sipped the silky warm milk, the whipped cream kissing her upper lip with coolness. She licked her lips. "Heavenly, Gianni," she said dipping her head to inhale the sweet warmth. "All this time I've come to you, and never tried this."

"My wife," he smiled. "She said she married me for my cooking. And all the time I told her, 'Not for my good looks?'" He laughed, shook his head, and she saw tears glistening his dark eyes.

Lizzy patted his hand. "Your wife knows you miss her. I'm sure she knows."

Gianni nodded. "Of course, but I have her still here. She's here." He tapped the center of his chest. Lizzy wanted to lay her head there, listen to that strong heart. "She tells me," Gianni said, "she whispers, 'Be happy Gianni, life is sweet. It is there for you to go on and enjoy.'" He straightened, smiled. "And I believe her." He reached and squeezed her shoulder. "There is a saying you can learn, Miss Lizzy. Sorrow looks back, worry looks around, but faith looks up." He pointed up and said, "Look up, Lizzy." She did and saw only the rose-colored ceiling, a thin crack in the plaster growing across the center of the room.

He pushed her cup closer. "You haven't tried your chocolate. Never overlook the free little extras. Most days they sit right in front of you, and you go on looking someplace in the future, missing what is right there."

"I told you, Gianni. That's my problem. I don't even want chocolate anymore." She stared at the wafer balanced on her saucer. "Maybe I should switch to pretzels. They're no-fat."

"*Macche*," Gianni shook his head. "Nonsense. A woman needs chocolate. I've seen books on this thing. A woman, her body, it needs chocolate." He smiled. "Go on."

She looked at the wafer, wondered why she'd never tried one before.

"Trust me," he said. "It isn't too sweet, not bitter, just good." He held the chocolate up toward her face.

She opened her mouth and let him place the wafer on her tongue. She closed her lips and let the chocolate break, melt, instantly merging with the wet warmth of her mouth. It wasn't like eating, but a soft coalescing, an instant sensation of pleasure felt, tasted, gone.

He smiled and squeezed her hand. "Tastes like *amore*, no?"

She smiled. "It's like communion," she said. "That's what the holy host should be, Gianni. More people would stay with the church."

He grinned, stood, moving toward the back of the store. "Think I should write the pope?"

She laughed, looked out at the darkened mall. An old Sting song was still playing on the mall's sound system, the one about everything a girl does being magic. "You're better than a therapist," she called. "You are a magician."

Gianni returned with a white towel, took the ice bag off her ankle, and wrapped the towel around her foot.

She leaned back and closed her eyes. "You are the kindest man I've ever known."

"Maybe you've known the wrong ones. You young women these days. Everyone fussing. Women saying men are so bad. Men saying women are crazy. When did men and women go to war? They argue; they fight; they write books; they say we come from other planets. This is silly talk." He sat back and looked around his store. "We are human, Miss Lizzy. All humans just looking for some bit of love before we die." He paused, hands gripping the table. "Most men, Elizabeth, we love women. Really."

Lizzy looked at his handsome puzzled face and laughed as tears came rising, tears for all those men who had plunged inside her, in and out and in and out and gone. It seemed she'd never really spoken to a one of them. Here in the soft rose light of Gianni's shop she felt she'd spent her life living like a reptile, driven by appetite, slinking up from moist heat, to a thrusting of silent muscle, then slinking back away to a slick dark river, moving silently, secretly along. "Oh Gianni," she said, "why can't I meet a man like you?"

"But you have," he said, stroking her hair.

She sank her head into his touch and closed her eyes. She leaned into him, feeling him like a lover, a father, a mother, someone nameless, timeless, a soothing steady touch of love.

He was kissing the top of her head. In the dark mall, the music suddenly shut off. Silence, just the dim glow of the chocolate case, a comforting steady hum. She lifted her face up, let him kiss her, a full kiss, a warm kiss, a kissing that wasn't demanding hunger, but rather just was another way of talking, a sweet silent syntax of pressure, easing back, searching out again.

They pulled back and looked straight at each other smiling. "Gianni," Lizzy said. "Are you superstitious?"

He shrugged. "I believe in magic. Even miracles sometimes." He took her hand, kissed it.

She sighed and looked up to the ceiling. "The moon is full tonight, Gianni. This means something. A completion of things begun." She paused, touched his face. "This began a long time ago."

He shook his head and kissed her palm.

"Gianni, listen. I'm serious," she said. "The moon is full. I know it. Above this ceiling, this roof of steel, above the parking lot lights, way above that cold dark freezing night out there, the moon is full. This is a completion, a good thing."

He pulled back, looked at her, and laughed. "The moon is always full, Miss Elizabeth. It never changes. This full moon, half moon, crescent moon, you young ones talk about in all your new age books. It's silliness. Think about it. You say the moon changes shape, but what you see is only a reflection of light." He took her hand, pulled her closer, "The sun, the moon are always there in fullness." He kissed her forehead. "Even in the dark," he whispered. "Nothing really goes away." He pulled her closer until she leaned into his chest, sank into his heat, his heartbeat, his breath.

She looked up into his warm and happy face and thought, It all goes away, Gianni. But she wouldn't say it, not to him. He believed in things like love. He believed hurts were healed with care and hungers could be satisfied. "Please kiss me," she said. And he did. He kissed her softly, deeply then. And she fed on his taste of chocolate and cream, wanting to be in his life, wanting to know his heart, to breathe his breath, hoping if she could visit his world long enough, she could find a way to stay.

Chocolate Factory

Cynthia Hendershot is the author of the book of stories and poems City of Mazes and Other Tales of Obsession *(Asylum Arts, 1993) and a book of criticism,* The Animal Within: Masculinity and the Gothic *(University of Michigan Press, 1998).*

When I told Mother about the job at the chocolate factory she squeezed me tight, took out her bottle of gin, and poured us both a drink. She talked excitedly about the things she would buy for the house, the sumptuous meals she would make, but she was most thrilled by the free chocolate bars we would get. I smiled, kissed her on the cheek, went into the bedroom, lay down on the pink bedspread.

If only I could reach out and touch his hand, slowly move my fingers up his arm, knead the muscles in his shoulder. I stared at his photograph and let the tears come. He died screaming on a Korean battlefield, now I will make chocolate bars and live in the cold shadow of his memory. My hands will wrap the bars in neat packages, hands that used to pull his face close. The faint taste of chocolate mousse on his tongue after one of Mother's dinners.

I turned out the light, tried to imagine him next to me, but the coldness cut me to the quick and I hid under the covers.

■

I took off my apron, hung it in my locker, looked at the tired face in the small mirror I kept next to his photograph. Fatigue overcame me and I sat on the bench until Sally, another factory widow, sat down beside me. She told me about the mysterious illnesses the kids in town had been suffering from. Tim, a boy who lived down the street from me, was hospitalized with nausea, hair loss, and fatigue. No one knew what was wrong. I smiled sadly at her. At home a neighbor was waiting for me at the door. Mother had been taken to the hospital with the same symptoms the children had.

Waiting outside her room I tried to conjure up his face, but all I could remember was the closeness of his body when he bent over to kiss me. That was real, not the face that stared out at me from dead photographs. The taste of hot chocolate on his mouth in winter. Working at the factory reminded me of him. The smell of chocolate like his body lurking just around the corner.

∎

When Mother died I was given two days off from work. She had been the only one who had died from the illness. I stared at the chocolate bars on the table, the ones I had brought back for her. I took a hammer and smashed them to pieces. I was alone and drained. In dreams he reached his hand out to me. I always missed it, grabbed air.

∎

The stranger was waiting for me at the locker room door. He introduced himself as Stevens, FBI, took off his hat, smiled at me. I eyed him suspiciously. He said he was doing routine security checks, then flashed a smile at me again.

After work I lingered outside the building, smoking, dreading the empty house. He came around the corner like a phantom. I cried out. His blue eyes were sparkling. I felt dizzy and sat on the bench. "What do you want?" my voice was flat and faraway, like someone outside my body speaking. "I just wanted to say hello again." He sat down beside me. "Hello," I said and walked away.

∎

He watched us from above, a god looking down on the factory. I rolled my eyes at Sally, continued wrapping. I could feel his eyes on me. My face was flushing. Damn him. Never another body but his. One day before we were married, we took a picnic basket into the woods. I dropped cake into his mouth, teased it, smearing the chocolate frosting across his pale face. As he devoured my mouth, our faces stuck together. I laughed as he entered me, our bodies merging in the hazy September afternoon.

The bar snapped. I picked up the pieces, walked away from the conveyer belt, asked the supervisor for a break.

He was waiting by the water cooler. He offered me a cup of water. I took it, sat down, put my head in my hands. When his hand touched my shoulder I jumped, stood up. "What do you want?" He backed away. "What's an FBI agent doing here anyway?" My body began to tremble.

Then I was in his arms and he was stroking my hair. "You smell so good, like chocolate," he kept saying over and over. He pulled me into the closet and his hands were caressing my breasts. He slowly unbuttoned my blouse. I sought his mouth with a ferocious hunger, probing it with my tongue, tasting the trace of chocolate there. He pulled up my skirt, ripped off my panties. He was warm and hard inside me. I cried out until he smothered my mouth with his.

■

The next night we met by the vats of chocolate, warm bodies, a small red blanket, cold concrete. No words. We sought out each other's taste and smell. While he was sleeping I opened a bar of chocolate, dangled it above his mouth, teasing his lips until he opened his mouth and bit. He woke up, a startled look on his face. I ran behind a vat. He caught me, carried me back to the blanket. I noticed that he spit out the chocolate. I looked up at him quizzically. He took a bar out of his briefcase, broke it in two, gave me half.

■

Lying in bed the next night, I thought of the FBI man and a fever seized me. I dressed and went to the factory, stood lurking outside the locked building. The door opened. I walked in and he was there, his arms open, his cock hard. "How did you..." He pulled me into the room with the vats.

As we made love, I imagined he was my husband. In the dark, cold room I could conjure him up, love a phantom on the floor, abandon myself to this stranger who tasted of his memory.

He put his coat over my shoulders, lit a cigarette, handed it to me. I still did not want to speak to him, didn't want to know him. He understood and we were silent. He inhaled my hair as I rested my head on his lap.

■

At work I avoided him. He stopped watching the workers and spent his time with the manager. One evening I saw him leave the manager's office, his hard face haggard, his hair disheveled. Fire surged through my body. I caught his eye and saw a spark there as he nodded.

He made love to me sadly and slowly that night and I held him tight, asking nothing, just wanting the warmth of his body. As the sun rose we parted outside. "We should meet in a hotel," he said. "It is not safe here." I nodded. He put a matchbook in my hand, kissed my cheek, and was gone.

Emptiness filling me up inside, I looked at the matchbook. It advertised the Desert Lodge, a well-known adultery motel in town. I sighed, sat on the steps, watched the smoke rising in the orange dawn.

■

We made love frantically in the sagging bed, but the joy was gone. He clung to me as if to life itself. Afterwards he took out a bottle of whiskey, poured each of us a drink, began speaking, breaking the silence that had bound us. "You've got to leave the factory. It's dangerous." I sipped my drink, watched him pacing up and down the room. "I can't tell you why, but you've got to leave." "And go where?" I sounded lost. "I will take care of you. You don't have to worry. I don't want to see you…" "What?" I asked, rising. "I don't want to see you dead," he spit out.

We embraced, fell back on the bed together. Hands blue in the moonlight seeping through the tattered curtains. My heart pounding, losing *him* now that the FBI man was no longer a phantom.

■

We met one last time in the room with the vats for old time's sake. A ticket to Washington in my purse, his house key on my key ring. I smiled widely at him when he walked in naked, carrying his clothes. He sat down beside me. "Let me taste your mouth," I said, pulling his face close to mine. The hint of chocolate. His face breaking into a smile as I ran my hand down his chest.

Dressed, we stood still in the center of the room. I looked into his blue eyes, alive and dancing now and as blue as the light emanating from the silver vat.

I think my whole problem with sex and chocolate is that putting the two together would show up any man. The appeal of chocolate is that it never fails. Men sometimes do.

IVY GOODMAN

Her Affair

Ivy Goodman is the author of two collections of short stories, A Chapter from Her Upbringing *(Carnegie Mellon University Press, 2001) and* Heart Failure *(University of Iowa Press, 1983). Her work has appeared in many literary magazines and anthologies, including* Grace and Gravity *(Paycock Press, 2004). She lives in Ellicott City, Maryland.*

In a long tweed coat and stylish high-sided brown leather pumps, briefcase in hand, she hurried across the station's marble floor, one hundred feet below the arched coffered ceiling. She was late. Her seven-year-old son and his after-school baby-sitter expected her at home right now. To her shock, a male colleague had way-laid her at the office to declare his love. She could not remember when—in what year—she had last had intercourse. She needed a chocolate bar.

Her heart was seized with anxiety, and she was already craving cures: chocolate bars; chocolate eggs; chocolate pinwheels; chocolate crisps; warm chocolate syrup on a bowl of mocha almond fudge ice cream; a serving of a cake known as chocolate sponge, its baked-on chocolate topping blackly glossy and of pudding consistency; a hunk of chocolate fudge so big that she had to eat it in bites, leaving teeth marks almost imperceptibly uneven, maybe by a millimeter.

She'd been divorced four years; he was just divorced himself. He had brown eyes, huge with earnestness and sorrow. He said, "You may not believe this, but after all the time we've known each other, I think I'm in love with you. Or maybe I should say 'enamored.'

I've checked, and there's no office policy against it." He smiled at this, but she was certain that he had indeed paged through the office manual or inquired at personnel. He was sincere and yet capable of reticence. Even then, as she stood in the corridor not knowing what to say, she felt him observing her and performing little secret tests of character.

"I'm not good enough for you, Dan."

"Don't." He frowned. "Please don't think of me that way. I'm not judgmental."

"I'm sorry."

But she had struck, perhaps, on the crucial flaw, the accusation that he denied in his home but heard confirmed in the marriage counselor's suite, where the twin armchairs convened with a third wiser, bigger chair. And her own flaw, what was hers? Surely he knew her reputation as an egocentric bitch?

He took her hand, and she clasped it too hard, as was her habit even when meeting other women professionally.

Would he be rakish enough to know what to do for her? She imagined him approaching her in the way most familiar to her, these past solitary years: she would have her first orgasm up against his palm, his fingers inside her instead of her own, his tongue in her mouth, the light pincer grip of his other hand turning and tuning at her nipples. And what was his fantasy of her? Did she kneel before his open fly front as he ran his fingers through her hair?

She said, incongruously, "Oh, it's so late. You know I have a son?"

He nodded yes; he seemed to know everything, or his eyes knew. He had two sons, one slightly younger, one slightly older, than her own.

■

She hurried on, through the opulence of the station's grand hall and then north, toward the suburban trains, down one of the side galleries where fancy shops were devoted to single precious items, luxuries devised for the hard-working, high-earning, commuting class: men's couture ties, lacy lingerie, leather goods, body unguents, chocolate solitaires displayed on pedestals, like jewels, in a black-walled space so rarefied that it smelled simply of the cold.

She had grown up in the era of the long-vanished, redolent local candy shop, where her mother had bought candy by the half-pound or pound, and a smiling woman, dressed all in white, like a nurse, had fulfilled her mother's wishes as her mother pointed at the glass and spoke candy names: turtle, bark, buttercup, trio, nougat, cluster, heavenly hash, caramel nut. The candies, in their brown pleated cups, were placed in a box and buffered from the lid with a sheet of cottony batting quilted to cellophane. At home, in the dimness of the dining room, she would bend down before the middle drawer of the buffet. She took only a piece at a time, but often she returned for more, leaving a dishabille of fluttery wrappers and the quilted batting sticking out crookedly beneath the lid.

Susan, have you been in the candy?

In the dim light of the dining room, after biting into a piece she didn't like, she would have to spit the figgy, fermented mess into her hand.

∎

She joined the single-file walkers on the left, who launched themselves double time down the moving escalator. Below, through its glass side wall, she saw the news agent's stand, and she already felt the heaviness of musty, basement air. Though she had no time to stop today, she could afford the news agent's treats and actually preferred them to those of the luxurious chocolatier upstairs. Reaching past the brightly colored pyramid of familiar wrappers and trademarked names, her left hand would offer money to the clerk while her right held up her choice of chocolate bar, its red wrapper pinched and fused shut at the ends. Sometimes, on her way to the platform, she would tear it open with her teeth. People lined up separately for lottery tickets, and one could also request toiletries in miniature sizes: vials of aspirin, tampons in boxes of eight, assorted condoms out of reach on a wire rack. But holding up her choice of chocolate bar to the news agent's clerk was the closest she had come, in a very long time, to revealing her most intimate desires.

Her train's lights flashed, and just before the doors shut, she ran aboard and came to a halt flush against the backs of other passengers in their winter coats. She found a handhold on the nearest pole. She stood for the entire trip, but like all habitual commuters within the crowd, she felt transparently self-enclosed. She daydreamed of the spreading dark denseness of a square of bittersweet melting on her tongue, and then she allowed the sensation of melting coursing through her whole body as she imagined her colleague in her bed. She felt arousal as a kind of active languor, focused on what he might do to her. She was excited in part because she'd never thought of him that way before, though once when they'd sat in adjacent chairs at the end of the oval conference table, during one of his more fervent speeches in a meeting that had gone on and on, she had stared at him for so long, in such proximity, that she'd had to stop herself from acting on the crazy impulse of leaning over and kissing him.

He was highly accomplished, even brilliant, though sanctimonious at times. He seemed to think that his honest, ruthless criticism of his colleagues' output—never hers, thank God, as far as she could tell—was morally necessary, a measure of being true to himself. But these last months, as his divorce proceeded, he had become more fragile in his conference room entreaties, so that his voice cracked at the ends of sentences, reminiscent of the way that nervous, novice women finish statements in questioning tones.

Why had he said he loved her, poor fellow? So they could skip the prerequisite nonsense and go straight to bed? Why else? There she was, and so was he, near to hand and suddenly discovered, like a candy laid aside at work and forgotten beneath the papers in one's drawer.

■

It was dark; she was cold. Always, these were the worst moments of her day. On the walk from the station, she tried to keep pace with those more distant shadowy figures, like the winning pieces in a game who entered boxes of light and reached "home" ahead of her.

He, and her fantasies of him, were no more help to her now than the empty sleeve of her ex-husband's overcoat with which she had once linked arms, or the stiff, suede, top-stitched fingers of her dead father's winter glove.

As a child, she had scoffed at her father when he had told her to eat chocolate bars against the cold.

"Ricky! Questa!"

Questa, Ricky's baby-sitter, stood in the living room, arms crossed beneath her bosom, wristwatch as near as an instantaneous downward glance. Ricky, who did not look up, was kneeling at the coffee table, sorting a pile of loose wrapped candy.

"Ricky, hi sweetheart! Questa, I'm so sorry I'm late." She wanted to run to her son and ruffle that deep mass of bangs that fell forward from the crown of his head and kiss those chapped spots that came out on his cheeks in winter, like rouge on a doll's face. But first she had to excuse herself to Questa. "I got called in by a senior colleague," she said. It was a lie, yes, but also an honest appeal to Questa's understanding of how relations between employer and employee, or boss and underling, range so easily from tenderness to exploitation.

Questa considered this. Her pretty bow mouth and high cheekbones she skillfully enhanced with makeup hues of rose, plum, and concord grape, the reds and purples on a color wheel in dark shades. She wore a bright pink sweater with starched and ironed blue jeans that were always uniformly deep blue, never worn pale in circles at the knees. Her professionalism was like the high barrier of a bureaucratic front desk. Even meeting her for the first time, one felt an instinctive need to court her a little bit. "You couldn't telephone?" Questa asked.

"But it's just six-thirty now. I'm within our time frame, aren't I? Granted, at the far end of it, but still…"

"You see, the problem is, I'm expecting Curt tonight."

"Oh, I'm so sorry, Questa!" She was the same age as Questa, they were both single mothers of precious only sons, but her Ricky was seven and Questa's Curt was twenty-two.

"Well you're home now, and we'll just forget about it, won't we? Ricky's had his supper. I heated up the mac and cheese."

"Thank you… and I am sorry, Questa."

"It's all right, all right… Ricky, baby, Questa loves you. Bye bye now." And then, more formally, "Goodbye, Sue."

"Enjoy Curt! See you tomorrow!"

The front door shut, and she threw off her coat, got down on the floor, and put her arms around her son, who was still entranced by cataloguing candy. "Sweetheart, where'd you get so much? Was there a party at school?"

"No, Mom!"

This tone of contemptuous disbelief was new from him and comical to her now, though it presaged years of a multitude of more important things that she would also completely misunderstand. "Then where did it come from?"

"Questa gave it to me."

"Really. Is there a piece for me?"

He gave her a chocolate mint patty, which she knew he didn't like and which she unwrapped and ate whole. The force of her bite immediately cracked through the brittle thin chocolate and shot peppermint cream throughout her mouth. Dinner it was. Her divorce had made her gaunt, and she'd had to coax herself back to food, but she was almost eating normally now, with the exception of tonight. She had recovered thanks in part to those alternate weekends when Ricky was with his dad and she fixed herself hearty, balanced meals of which she partook as if she were a rodent chewing through the insulation in the walls.

"Did Questa give you vegetables and fruit? She said she heated up the macaroni?"

"Yes, Mom."

"With what vegetables?"

"Peas and carrots."

"Fruit?"

"Apple."

She couldn't bring herself to ask if he'd actually eaten those foods, or if they were only served.

His head bent, he continued examining his candy, touching, turning over pieces, smelling certain ones, contemplating and designing his future pleasure with the stern single-mindedness of a man browsing through pornography. "Can I eat some, Mom?"

"How much have you already had?"

"Oh…a couple."

"Just one more."

"No, two!"

"OK, two."

"No, three!"

"How about zero then?"

"Oh, Mom!"

His lighthearted silliness returned when he put the candy in his mouth and began galloping about the room.

"Careful, sweetie, please! Or you could choke on that!"

She wanted to be with her son and no one else. And yet their precious evening hours were bedeviled by her contrary wish to end the continual coaxing and negotiation and tuck him speedily in bed.

While he dawdled in the bathroom brushing his teeth and peeing one last time, she fell in exhaustion on his narrow bed, beside the smooth white wall. For his own good, she wouldn't let him sleep with her; it was a taboo in the therapeutic lore with which she agreed, though sometimes all she wanted was to lie down and hold his body against hers. On nights when he slept at his father's, maybe she would feel better if she slept alone in here.

At the bang of the toilet seat, she knew she should get up, but she did not. She believed in the taboo, but she was too tired not to manipulate those urges for her own ends tonight: to get him into bed as fast as possible. He was still the pajama-clad little boy whom she'd seen naked only minutes earlier when he'd changed: thin arms and legs, a sturdy, straight trunk, and a vestigial babyishness rounding out his abdomen. And yet, in his urgency and determination on seeing her in his bed—as if he were tricking her—she could see the future young man, in early adulthood or late adolescence, sprinting toward his mattress as a beginning, overeager lover.

"Don't move, Mom, don't move."

"But sweetie, I've got to."

"No, lift your legs. Get under the covers. See? Isn't it nice?"

"Oh, Ricky, sweetheart, you know I can't stay in here."

"Why not?"

"I'd keep you awake. We'd keep each other awake." With an ungainly bounce, she pushed herself up. "Besides, I can't go to bed for a while."

"Why?"

"I have a problem I brought home from work."

As she leaned over him and brought the blankets to his chin, he grabbed her fingers so tightly in his fist that, soon, in another dreaded moment, she would forcibly have to pull herself away.

■

Beneath the phone books in the kitchen pantry, she found the office list of birthdays, home addresses, spouses' and children's names. His divorce was so new that his ex-wife's name was still beside his in parentheses. Dan and Jody, Jody and Dan. And so they would remain linguistically coupled for a long while, in the minds of old, astonished friends.

She dialed the first three digits and then hung up the phone. It was too late to call, especially if his sons were there asleep. Or perhaps this listing was now solely his ex-wife's, the unhappy residence from which he'd fled.

Through the open pantry door, she stared at the box of baking chocolate on the top shelf. Maybe she should grate several ounces by hand—that would take fifteen minutes, longer if she nicked her knuckles and had to stop for first aid, longer still if she accidentally overturned the bowl. She would need to melt the chocolate in scalded heavy cream—if she had cream—and when the mixture reached body temperature she would mold gigantic truffles big enough to fill her mouth.

Because she didn't want to talk to him. She didn't want to regale him, nor did she want to hear him plaintively confide. But she was years ahead of him in that regard, already at the juncture when one is able to wring out a single sentence from a painfully amorphous past. In answer to inquiries about her marriage, she could simply say, I'm relieved it's over with. No, he was not for her; he was too recently hurt, too guarded, too perplexed. Besides, her daydreams were not of any man in her acquaintance, and even the woman involved, though she saw through her eyes and felt through her skin, did not entirely resemble herself.

But sooner or later they would meet and talk. To this end, in the next two weeks, they would rearrange and secretly coordinate their ex-spouses' weekend schedules with their children. Or she would do it secretly, and he with total honesty. She would dress as if for work. They would go out to dinner. Even before they got their wine, he would disclose intimate, unsavory details, and she would feel as men must feel hearing women's confidences about their menstrual periods.

"But you know all about this don't you, Susan?"

"Not really, no. Not in general. Just my own little case."

"It was such a shock, the night Jody broke the news. Oh, we had our problems, sure."

"Like everybody does?"

He nodded. "Well put. Absolutely right."

Yes, everybody did, but they belonged to the group of spouses who had failed.

"She told me, in retrospect, if you can believe it, that things might have been different if I'd come home now and then with flowers."

"She said that. Really. Amazing."

"And the irony is, every day, at this intersection near the house, I pass a vendor who sells bouquets."

"Oh, right, those guys are everywhere. They've got these dyed carnations in unearthly colors, like royal blue? Does he sell them from a can?"

"I don't know. That was exactly Jody's point, that I don't notice things." He would shut his eyes in annoyance, yearning painfully for Jody.

At last the waitress would bring their wine.

"Cheers, Dan. To better days ahead."

"Cheers." And then, wanting to be fair, in recognition of her exquisite feelings, he would ask, "What happened? With you and your ex-husband?"

She would swallow and hesitate, sloshing down another mouthful. "He lied." This suggested, falsely, an enormity of sins, not just adultery but felonies, awful things that were better not discussed, like theft or money laundering. Of course, she had also lied to him about her feelings.

"How long has it been?"

"Four years. I mind the weekends most, when Ricky's with his dad. I get out, the way a person should, you know, go to museums, go on long walks for exercise. And then, God help me, I stare at the families, those perfect worlds of four."

"We were four, the boys and Jody and I."

"Oh, yes, I know! Those fours are riddled through and through! But we were never even four, we were only three. So I stare, and the parents eyeball me and hold tight to their kids. As if I might try to steal them, maybe by offering some chocolate bars."

He would smile, but she would see that she had frightened him. He would invoke his therapist in passing, as if to recommend she get one of her own, and she might dare to raise her glass: "Damn therapy and all 'professional help.' I decided I would rather have a cleaning lady." If she was lucky, he would laugh.

They would make their way through the meal. But would they make their way to bed? Contemplating this, she would be embarrassed to watch him chew. Would he want to pay her share or split the bill? She could not afford fancy meals, even every other Friday. But just this once, when the dessert cart sidled up, she would choose a slice of Black Forest cake, the chocolate layers inky dark and every mouthful syrupy with kirsch.

If he was thinking chocolate and flowers in regard to her, she hoped he would please skip the flowers.

On that long day when he first made his feelings known, he came to her a final time. She floated in the hallucinatory state prefatory to sleep, in which the sleeper's body seems suspended, her mouth slips open, and she begins, perhaps, to drool. He offered a chocolate bar wrapped in plain white, the matte paper folded and tucked to the dimensions of a business envelope. He parted the wrapper down the back seam and broke off a corner for her. She was so relaxed that she was able to concentrate on one sensation at a time, first the exquisite melting and then their kiss, which tasted of the chocolate on their tongues, what else?

After all, she had forgotten how another person's mouth really tastes. Naked, his body hers to traverse, he was taller than she had realized, long from clavicle to hip. Her curiosity about his scent, in the thicket of his chest hair, beneath his arms, in the crevices between his groin and leg, was answered in her brain with overpowering whiffs of chocolate, not yet entirely refined, with an almost human smell.

RICHARD
GRAYSON

Those Old Dark Sweet Songs

Richard Grayson is the author of The Silicon Valley Diet, I Brake for
Delmore Schwartz, With Hitler in New York, I Survived Caracas Traffic, *and* Lincoln's Doctor's Dog. *Recent work has appeared online at*
McSweeney's, Yankee Pot Roast, Mississippi Review, Pindeldyboz,
Hobart, Monkeybicycle, *and* Fiction Warehouse. *He teaches English at
a Phoenix high school.*

THE CANDY MAN

Of all the lovers I ever had, Terence Rosenthal was probably the
only one who wouldn't care that each year more and more cocoa
farms around this overrated planet are failing, under siege from
fungal diseases, viral diseases, and insects.

"Think of *me*," I said to him that Monday morning last May
when I'd first heard the bad news on National Public Radio. "What
am I going to do when there's a shortage of chocolate?"

He just smiled in that lazy way of his. He was six-foot-two, 135
pounds, a fashion designer the color of Hershey's Kisses. Terence
took up two-thirds of my bed, pressing me up against the wall all
night. He didn't like to lie next to the wall.

"Hmm?" I said to him. "So tell me what I'm going to do?"

He stretched, making himself impossibly longer. "What do
you need chocolate for when you have me?"

"You're disgusting," I told him.

"*Disgusting*?" He blinked, scratched his chest—I liked the
stubble that resulted from his forgetting his last appointment to

get it waxed—and propped himself up on two pillows. Either he didn't understand or was pretending not to understand.

"What kind of weird racial remark is that?" I asked. "Equating yourself with chocolate?"

"I didn't mean it that way," said Terence, starting to get angry now. "If I were white, I would have said the same thing."

I turned toward the wall. "You think I like you just because I'm hung up on African American guys," I said softly. "That makes me feel like shit."

"You *are* the one who's race-conscious," he said.

"Not me," I said to the wall. "I'm chocolate-conscious."

He put his hand on my shoulder and turned me around. I'm only five-eight and I outweigh him by ten pounds, but he's a lot stronger than I am. Usually Terence didn't like to kiss in the morning, either because he thought he had bad breath—he didn't, despite the cigarettes—or he thought that I did. But that morning he kissed me repeatedly, and for the moment strategies for the sustainable farming of cocoa—partial reforestation for biodiversity, avoidance of large doses of pesticides or fertilizers, a shift away from large plantations to smaller farms where cacao trees can grow in the shade of larger trees—disappeared from my brain. I wasn't chocolate-conscious, I wasn't race-conscious—I was only Terence-conscious.

FEELINGS

"How would *you* feel if there was going to be a coffee shortage?" I asked him as he put on his black dress pants, one leg at a time. "Or a tobacco shortage?"

I didn't smoke or drink coffee. Terence and I had conducted our courtship in coffee bars, but I always sipped iced tea, hot chocolate, bottled water, or Odwalla fruit juice while he downed latte after latte.

Terence just put on his shirt and shrugged. "I plan to quit smoking on June first, you know that." This was the third date he'd set since I'd known him.

I didn't want to argue again about tobacco, so all I said was, "You know you're going straight to Starbucks when you leave here."

He bent down to kiss me and I gingerly touched his hair. He'd had it twisted recently, with smaller-size twists than he had before. Terence-consciousness overwhelmed me.

SEASONS IN THE SUN

After he'd gone back to his condo to take a bubble bath as usual, I sat at my kitchen table munching my Cocoa Puffs. That's when Terence-consciousness receded, and chocolate-consciousness took over. W.E.B. Du Bois wrote about "double consciousness."

I'd been writing a paper comparing Du Bois with Henry Adams for a graduate class in American ethnicities. Its thesis, of course, was that race is culturally significant but biologically meaningless. After the Oklahoma City bombing, in the rubble of the Alfred Murrah Federal Building, they found a severed leg which top forensic anthropologists identified as belonging to a white man. It turned out to be from a black woman.

Disgusted with the lack of progress in civil rights, Du Bois left the United States when he was in his nineties. He died the day of Martin Luther King, Jr.'s "I Have a Dream" speech at the Lincoln Memorial during the March on Washington. That was in 1963, the year before the civil rights bill passed.

Du Bois lived the last year of his life in Ghana. Did he think about double consciousness to the end? Did he think about chocolate?

Finishing my cereal, staring at the cartoon toucan on the box—what was his name?—I think about the Double Chocolate Fat-Free Frozen Yogurt I bought at Safeway. I eat two four-ounce servings of it (eighty calories each, no fat grams) every afternoon. I know, I know—I'm cuckoo.

Supposedly Du Bois went to Ghana to write an Encyclopedia Africana. But maybe he really went because Ghana produces so much cocoa. Ghana produced 324 thousand tons of it last year, down sharply from the year before.

AFTERNOON DELIGHT

Second-place Ghana's production was dwarfed by the leader, Ivory Coast, with well over a million tons last year, more than three times the amount of cocoa Ghana farmed. But a new species of black pod disease—a cousin of the potato blight that depopulated Ireland—has evolved and spread to the Ivory Coast border. This disease is now sitting on the frontier, where a million tons of cocoa a year is under threat.

When I tell Terence this, he doesn't know what I'm talking about. "Ivy Coast?" he says over the cell phone.

"*Ivory* Coast," I say distinctly. You know, like 'Ebony and Ivory.'"

I hear him talking to an empty-headed model in the background. So I say, "Sometimes the country is called Côte d'Ivoire."

I figured he'd prefer that, the way he preferred to call himself Terence Rosenthal instead of his birth name, Robert McKillop.

No response, so I tell him, "Your ancestors might have come from there. You really should know about it."

All he says is, "Paul McCartney's OK, but you know how I feel about Michael Jackson." And then: "I've got to get off."

TIE A YELLOW RIBBON

But later he calls back. As usual, he doesn't give his name or say hello. When I call him, he always knows it's me because he has caller ID. I think he forgets I don't have caller ID and I don't like to be taken for granted.

This is how he begins on the phone:

"Turn to page C-eighteen of the *Times*." No greeting, just a command. Because I am powerless, I get the newspaper and do as he orders, just the way I did everything he told me to do during our time together last night.

From the rustling, Terence knows we are on the same page. "See the Futures columns on the right," he tells me. "Look down to the Agricultural stuff under Financial. At the very right, under Hogs and Pork Bellies, you'll find Cocoa."

I study the columns of numbers. I once dated a commodities broker, as it happens, so I can figure it out. The price of cocoa futures on the New York Coffee, Sugar and Cocoa Exchange is going through the roof.

"My thing is, let's buy some March '99 delivery," Terence says. "It's at 1,750 now, but I bet it'll go over 2,000."

I am shocked. He expects us to still be together in March 1999.

"See, I *do* listen to what you're saying," Terence tells me. "I think about you all day, baby," he says in a silky-smooth voice. Even the cell phone can't conceal that.

KUNG FU FIGHTING

We fought all the time except when we were in bed.

Terence was a born-again Christian; I was a Jewish agnostic.

Terence was pro-life; I was pro-choice.

He thought people on welfare were lazy. I thought he was crazy and didn't know about poor people's problems. Like the way he talked about people in Baltimore's ghetto: "They're so stupid they've never been north of North Avenue." Easy to say if you grew up in suburban Owings Mills, with professional, upper-middle-class parents.

I grew up in Brooklyn, not in the greatest of neighborhoods. When I did something Terence thought vulgar, like cursing, he would say disdainfully: "That's *so* Brooklyn."

The first night we slept together, I made him an egg cream. Explaining it was like the Holy Roman Empire—neither holy nor Roman nor an empire—I told him he wouldn't get the taste of any eggs or cream, just chocolatey deliciousness.

At the time, I didn't realize that to Terence, chocolate was about as appealing as that gunk that's left over on a Biore nose strip when you pull it off to unplug your pores.

I spent so much time making that damn egg cream. You've got to put in the milk, the seltzer, and the traditional Fox's U-Bet Chocolate Flavor Syrup in just the right order or you end up with something resembling Yoo-Hoo with fizz, like the bottled Arizona Lite Chocolate Fudge Float Soda Pop I once tasted at an Internet cafe on Melrose.

I was so sure Terence would love that egg cream. But he took one small sip, wrinkled his brow, and said, "To be quite honest, it's a little too sweet for me."

It was four hours and three orgasms later (two his, one mine) before I cheered up.

MUSKRAT LOVE

My mother was seventeen and working as a waitress after school at a 5 & 10 cent store in Flatbush when my father and a few of his friends came in for egg creams. My father, like Terence, was very handsome, and my mother was very attracted to him. However, after drinking his egg cream and making very little conversation, Dad left with his friends, leaving Mom to think he was not interested in her.

The next night my father came in alone, ordered an egg cream, and asked to take my mother home after work. Because she knew his sister and that he came from a nice family, Mom agreed. Dad was a perfect gentleman. They dated for two years, during which they became engaged.

To this day, in their retirement home in Melbourne, on Florida's Space Coast—not far from Cocoa Beach—Mom teases Dad, telling him she never made anyone else an egg cream like the one she made for him.

That was the egg cream I tried to make for Terence.

Torn between Two Lovers

I didn't know then that Terence didn't like chocolate because he didn't like food, period. He'd been anorexic and bulimic when he was a teenager, until finally his grandmother—who'd been head nurse at Walter Reed Army Hospital—checked him into Sheppard Pratt's eating disorder clinic, where they watched him as he had to eat everything on his plate and then wouldn't let him go to the bathroom for ninety minutes after meals.

Supposedly he's cured now, but he often forgets to eat. We'll be climbing all over each other and then at two a.m. he'll realize that he hasn't eaten since early the previous afternoon. Naked, he'll wrap himself in one of my sheets and sit down at my kitchen table while I put one of my Weight Watchers frozen dinners in the microwave. He likes Spicy Szechuan Chicken with Kung Po Noodles the best. I know better than to try to give him anything for dessert. I guess I should be grateful he lets me feed him at all before we get back into bed for the night.

You Light up My Life

Working on my paper, I think about all the recent arguments Terence and I have had. We both love to argue. Early on in our relationship we had this incredible debate about the doctrine of transubstantiation. Although he was raised Catholic, Terence didn't believe me when I said the Eucharist was supposed to be the actual body and blood of Christ. It's a symbol, he told me. No, it's not a symbol, I screamed at him, don't you know *anything* about Catholicism? We kept arguing until the point where I got so mad—I should be ashamed to admit this—that I went over to the sofa where he was sitting and I sort of punched him. Not hard, but in the shoulder, and before I knew it, we were having a fist fight/wrestling match in my living room over the nature of communion.

At that point in our relationship I figured I could take him because even though he was taller, he was so skinny and effeminate, and I'd played sports like hockey and soccer back in high school in Brooklyn while he was sketching dress designs in his notebooks in the 'burbs. Not that I was going to beat him up, of course. I despise domestic violence. We were both half-fooling around, but because we'd spent the better part of an hour disputing Roman Catholic doctrine when we should have been getting off, I think we were a little crazed. Anyway, that's the night I discovered Terence was stronger than I was.

He got on top of me and held my arms above my head and wouldn't let them go. I kept trying to force my arms up, but I couldn't budge. He was on top of me, looking triumphant—which was sort of nice, since I'd been on top all the times we'd been together. That's how I discovered I like what Terence calls "light bondage."

The sex was unbelievable that night. So much so that later, when he was hogging the covers in bed as we were trying to sleep, Terence said, "I don't know what came over us back then."

"Me neither," I said, although I think I actually did.

You're Having My Baby

So I don't know why it is that Terence is the latest of my last three boyfriends who falls into the category of tall, skinny, dark—OK, black—and handsome.

In hopes of increasing cocoa production, some farmers in Malaysia have planted hundreds of acres of trees on cleared rainforest land. But the trees, bereft of shade from taller trees, appear to be far more vulnerable to pests and fungal diseases like one called witches'-broom.

Maybe I'm just like cacao and need the shade of taller trees to keep me healthy.

Both Terence and I are HIV-negative.

BILLY, DON'T BE A HERO

That night I tell Terence I don't like the idea of profiting from others' misery, especially not my own, and I won't speculate on cocoa futures with him.

"Suit yourself," he says. Is he getting bored with me?

We're so totally different. Sometimes I think: I'm with this guy whose whole life is the superficial world of fashion and beauty, who hangs out with rich people all day, whose only anger at the oppression in our society occurs when he's stopped by the police for driving his Lexus in his own very ritzy neighborhood because they can't imagine what a black man is doing there. Otherwise Terence is practically a Republican.

And then I think:

I'm actually with someone who tells me that he had sex with any rich older guy he could when he was a teenager, someone who was into every drug under the sun until one night, strung out on Special K—the animal tranquilizer, not the breakfast cereal—he heard a gospel song on an R&B station and was born again.

That was the night Terence called his grandmother, who made arrangements for him to check into Shepard Pratt immediately. First he was in the multiple addictions unit, and then, when he was off drugs, they put him in the eating disorder clinic.

This is a guy who now believes it's always wrong for teenagers to have sex. Even with each other. It's like with abortion always being wrong, even to save the life of the mother. Terence is such an absolutist sometimes. It drives me crazy because it's like he doesn't see shades of gray.

Terence looks at me across the table. He sighs. "Maybe you're right about the futures market," he says. "I mean, if scientists can send a robot to Mars, they can probably take care of this chocolate shortage."

I smile at him. "When you say Mars," I ask, "do you mean the planet or the candy company?"

THE NIGHT CHICAGO DIED

The following summer, we are staying over in what used to be Terence's bedroom in his parents' house in Owings Mills.

"I'd be freaking out if you weren't here," he tells me. He still takes up most of the bed, and it's smaller than my queen-sized bed back home.

This wasn't the bedroom he'd grown up in. That was a couple of miles away, in a house that was destroyed when a freak tornado hit Baltimore's northwestern suburbs in 1990. Terence came home from high school to find that his house was nothing but rubble.

They actually got into the new house rather quickly, probably because Governor Schaeffer was running for re-election and wanted to look good. Terence didn't live in the new house very long because he moved to New York to start Fashion Institute of Technology the following fall.

But three years ago Terence's grandfather, a lawyer, had died in that bedroom. He'd gotten AIDS, had been divorced for many years, and Terence's mother, his only daughter, took family leave from her job and cared for him till the end.

His grandfather's dying there was what made Terence ask me along on the visit, I'm almost certain. He didn't want to sleep in that bedroom alone, not in the bed where his grandfather died.

Given the nature of his grandfather's illness, and that Terence's mother and stepfather were in the next room, all we did was snuggle and cuddle that night.

In Terence's *old* old bedroom, the one in the house that had been destroyed, he'd slept with a teddy bear—even when he was practically, by his own admission, a teenage prostitute. Of all the possessions he lost after the tornado had struck, Terence missed Fluffy the most.

THE PIÑA COLADA SONG

So the next day, while Terence hung out with his parents, I drove up to Hershey, Pennsylvania, and made an apprehensive pilgrimage to the chocolate factory. I came away slightly reassured, my endorphins racing.

There is an emerging consensus that the future of cocoa beans lies with small farmers on more shaded, forested, intensively tended land. The big plantations that produce large yields of pods in the first few years can't sustain them because the cost of maintaining those endless fields soon becomes prohibitive. That's because if there's a disease, it runs rampant across a much larger acreage than in a small-farm situation, where one farmer may have a problem but it doesn't leap to the next farm.

In downtown Hershey, the streetlights are shaped like Kisses.

At a souvenir shop I buy Terence a Hershey teddy bear. It's not Fluffy, but it's fluffy, and mostly brown. The bear's stomach is white, like mine.

The Hershey Bears used to be a National Hockey League franchise.

The only time I've ever lost consciousness was playing hockey: after I checked him, this guy on the other team hit me over the head with his stick. I got a concussion and was dizzy and weak for months afterward.

There are relatively few black hockey players.

Driving over the Mason-Dixon line between Pennsylvania and Maryland, I let a tiny Mr. Goodbar—a free sample—melt in my mouth. I'll see Terence soon. The thought of him gets me hard.

Everyone has at least one incredibly passionate love for another person, but most people aren't as lucky as my parents.

Usually one of two things invariably kills passion: you break up, or you stay together. It'll be that way with me and Terence, I'm sure.

But chocolate is forever. It has to be.

MARY ANN CAIN

Wired on Chocolate in the Midget Bed

Mary Ann Cain's fiction and essays have appeared or are forthcoming in journals such as Many Mountains Moving, Under the Sun, Yfief, First Intensity, Porcupine, The Sun, 13th Moon, The Little Magazine, The Nebraska Review, Labyris, *and* Artful Dodge. *Her book,* Revisioning Writers' Talk: Gender and Culture in Acts of Composing, *has been published by the State University of New York Press (1995). She was awarded residency fellowships at the Mary Hambridge Center for the Arts in 1996 and 1997. Currently she is associate professor of English at Indiana University-Purdue University Fort Wayne.*

I stayed awake that night, as I am now, in the futon, Derrick snoring in gargled gusts, in what I have come to call, in my most deviant, furtive, and self-destructive thoughts, the Midget bed. There's not a single thing to complain about anymore, not even my toes, which the mice are still nibbling away, the way I used to nibble on the ears of those cute chocolate Easter bunnies my mother hid around the house, saying the Easter Bunny had left them. I used to love yet dread eating them because it seemed like a betrayal, like eating a pet. I must have known on some level even then that betrayal was my destiny. I was already an accomplice to my mother's lies, willing to believe her for the sake of my desires. I confess these aberrations to illustrate the depths to which my life has sunk since that night of Death by Chocolate.

The server at the Grand Hotel had called it Death by Chocolate, but who would have guessed it would jolt me awake at four in the morning? Even Derrick, who can sleep through an earthquake (and has, believe it or not), woke up to ask me what the matter was.

"Since when does chocolate keep me awake?" I practically shouted into the tight corners of our new bedroom. "How many times have I had chocolate right before bed and slept like a log? Can you believe this?" I stared at Derrick, shaking my head. Derrick knows how protective I am of my sleep time, after years of breaking out in a sweat every night at exactly 2:06.

"You sure it's the chocolate?" Derrick stretched his arms up and yawned. He always thought that my sweats were provoked by my Evil Boss, who relished keeping me in the dark about decisions. I, on the other hand, thought the sweats were purely hormonal, a signal from Mother Nature that my biological clock was slowly winding down. Derrick didn't believe me until I showed him the article that said hormone changes started as early as thirty. Even then, he thought the Evil Boss was what brought on the changes. I still don't know which came first, or if one has anything to do with the other.

"Damn!" I punched the futon, our recent replacement for the pillow-top mattress that I had suspected was giving me lower back pain. I had been reading the best-seller *Voluntary Austerity* and was looking to simplify our lives when it struck me that a futon would work much better in the tiny rooms of the new old house we'd just bought than the king-sized Sealy Posturepedic pillow-top mattress. We could use it as a sofa AND a bed, instead of buying two separate pieces.

"I've given up caffeine. I do my aerobics now in the morning instead of at night. We ate early tonight. What else could it be?" My fist left a small dent in the futon, unlike the pillow-top, which absorbed whatever blows I dealt it without a trace.

"Sex?" Derrick was growing a little beard like Brad Pitt, its tender fuzz scattered over his square chin. But the upturn in his voice only reminded me of the guilt I felt over breaking my resolution to get to sleep twenty minutes earlier each night for the next week, to ease myself into my new routine of walking the treadmill before breakfast.

"Oh, come on."

He always slept like death but would wake in a flash if sex was involved.

"No, really. Maybe you're still a little—overwrought."

We'd given each other two really good strong orgasms, cuddled and whispered and, on my part, bit the fleshy saddles behind his shins until my jaw ached. I could hardly believe, after all that exaltation and collapse, that I could be "overwrought." Then it hit me—the foreplay had been entirely chocolate inspired.

"Derrick." I leaned over, pushing my hair out of his eyes and mine, barely able to modulate the furry bubble rising up my throat. Derrick's forget-me-not-blue eyes clouded momentarily, as if perplexed by my excitement. "That wasn't ME—it was the chocolate!"

As I breathed those last words over Derrick's face, relief gushed through my limbs. I had been flopping around, the sheets twisting (no more fitted sheets, part of *Voluntary Austerity*'s advice to make better use of what one already possesses instead of endlessly consuming new goods) between my legs, hating myself for my utter lack of willpower. A litany of sins whirled through my brain: staying up later than I'd planned; eating more dinner than I was really hungry for; spending more than we'd budgeted on the new house; quitting my job and working freelance because the roof at the office was literally and figuratively caving in. But then, remembering the simple wisdom of *Voluntary Austerity* ("You can't control other people's disasters, but you can control your own") lead me to this sudden, blessed insight: It wasn't ME who'd kept me awake—it was the CHOCOLATE!

"Oh." Derrick's eyelids fluttered, his reply blurring into a snore.

"Isn't that great?"

A "Mmrph" signaled Derrick's quick departure into dream time. This only further reinforced my conclusion. Derrick hadn't ordered Death by Chocolate, so of course he could sleep. I could claim some relief and absolve some guilt knowing that I had had the willpower to put myself into bed at the appropriate time. It wasn't my fault I stayed awake when I got there. The only way I could get myself to bed as planned was if Derrick came, too. Otherwise, I'd hear him knocking around the house, which was too small to mask each other's movements, except in the basement, which smelled like rotting chrysanthemums. Of course, Derrick took my invitation as—an invitation. And maybe I—or rather the CHOCOLATE—meant it as such.

Derrick's towering obelisk of a body would have collapsed my gusher into sleepy contentment hours ago, had it not been for the chocolate. In fact, I had fallen asleep for a few hours, but then the chocolate bomb ticking inside me exploded, a terrorist plot against my personal sovereignty. Now, when I most needed his support, he had sunk back into sleep. Who could blame him, after I attributed our first passionate night in weeks not to his Brad Pitt goatee or his wide chest but to chocolate? Would he forgive me? Did he even care? If the end result was sex, maybe it didn't matter.

I didn't want to wake him after all that. But if I didn't wake him, I faced the even more horrific prospect of insomnia now that Derrick, as was his habit, had claimed over half of my half of the futon. We were, after all, both tall and if not large, certainly solid, people; futons, I realized too late, were designed for smaller, more compact bodies. Despite its size, the futon had, in fact, relieved my lower back pain, but probably because I was positioned upright more than prone in my struggle to adapt to its admittedly cramped space. One false move and sleeplessness came staring me in the face.

Of course I knew before I bought the thing that I would have to learn to do more with less. But because it looked so urban chic, so tidy and simple and economical, it appealed to my newly awakened austerity: *People adapt to their spaces.* Now I was beginning to suspect this author had never had the pleasure of adapting to a King-Sized-Ultra-Pillow-Top Sealy Posturepedic. *Clearing away clutter opens room for new creativity.* It's true that our old condo's bedroom had gotten so crowded that getting to the closet meant a belly flop across the mattress. But remember, it was our choice (I'm speaking to Derrick here), our CHOICE to buy the smaller house so that we could simplify with our one solid income and my precarious venture into self-employment.

I probably could have penetrated his subconscious with a gentle but firm nudge. It has worked before, even during his volcanic snores. But at that point, I had all but given up on the idea of sleep. What I really needed was rescue from this chocolate mania. My confidence levels were boosting to cosmic proportions yet at the same time something was quietly nibbling the toes off my feet. Or was that the sex talking?

I gave him one resigned elbow-in-the-armpit, while still flat on my back. It didn't take much skill, just a quick jerk over and up. No matter—nothing happened.

But then, after that night, everything happened. I lost ten pounds and gained tons of energy, enough to wake up at five-thirty every morning, sunrise or not, and hit the treadmill in the basement, which no longer smells like the back alley of a funeral parlor. After I did a little feng shui detecting in the basement, I discovered a pipe dripping over a collection of Rumanian peasant dolls in a Seagram's box under what used to be a bar sink. I replaced the pipe and recycled the sink into a mushroom farm to grow my own wood ears, propping up the peasant dolls to watch over the crops. Every morning I change out of my bathrobe into something I might wear to the mall, if not an office. I brush my hair and teeth, even use mouthwash, so the phone receiver won't stink when I breathe into it all day. When I sit down to write I have tons of ideas; I've taken to recording them onto 3" x 5" cards that I store in an alphabetized file box, so whenever I begin a new project, I browse there first. But I seldom need to since I'm always brim-full of ideas.

My voluntary austerity churns ideas out better than coffee or chocolate or, yes, even sex. I am so in control of my life that I want to scream. Because "voluntary austerity" means I can have anything I want, in time. If I want chocolate, I budget my intake of sweets. Time between Derrick and me are "dates" that I schedule into my calendar along with the dentist, hair appointments, pap smear, and grocery shopping. If I decide to take a break, walk down to CVS drug store for a Fruit & Nut Cadbury bar, I don't feel guilty anymore because I know when and how much I can indulge my chocolate passion. The same with sex, which we have more time for now than ever, because Derrick, too, has become austere and organized, and the open slots on our mutual date calendars are now so harmonious it seems like a cosmic intervention. And now that CVS is open twenty-four hours, we've discovered a whole new rhythm to our pursuit of pleasure.

The thing is, I like the tingly feeling, the lightness, the wobble my foreshortened toes lend to my stride. I like feeling a little unbalanced, not knowing from one moment to the next exactly what I will feel, or what the feeling even is. In the midst of all this outer control, I like knowing I can still be surprised.

Those little gray mice kept nibbling away tonight, efficient little dustballs, while Derrick and I tangoed on top of the futon. Now, as Derrick snores like a hangman, and I give a deep, chocolate-scented sigh, they raid the bedroom floor for crumbs. I hold my breath, clenching my digits, until I feel their needle teeth again, gnawing the epidermis at the edges of my piggies. They have finally begun to show signs of erosion, forcing me to reconsider my footwear, since my toes no longer can clutch the ground. It's a liberating feeling, sort of like a free fall from an airplane. Derrick doesn't know, a little secret I keep that's not written into any schedule. I've already checked to see if his extra longs have been affected, but, alas, his snoring seems to discourage the critters. I, on the other hand, am as quiet as—funny how such sayings take on a life of their own.

Now, as I lay awake once more, strung across the horns of a dilemma, I wonder: If I wake Derrick up, will he bring me the relief I need to go back to sleep?

I reach over Derrick for the rest of my thirty-two squares of Hershey's Special Dark from the pound we'd split earlier. The night stand, a Pottery Barn crate, both table and storage, wobbles a little when I lean into its edge. Alas, the gold foil is empty except for some chocolate crumbs that for some reason never seem to interest the mice. I forgot we'd finished our halves together, my craving so strong I almost believe that chocolate will be there just because I want it.

Derrick's breath is hot then cold on my breasts, which dangle over his open mouth. I crouch over him, clutching the bed crate, elbows akimbo like a lion before its prey, and lick the foil in long, luxurious strokes. As I lick, the crumbs meld with my taste buds in little chocolate explosions. Derrick's snoring settles into a purr. The mice abandon their nibbling and shuttle out from under the covers in search of other toes.

It's true, I do more now on less sleep, but my days of freedom are numbered, and soon the mice will have nibbled off my toes to the point where I am no longer able to move independent of support. This will no doubt come as a surprise to Derrick, who up until now has heard that my only desire to go unfulfilled is my inability to fall asleep as easily as he. Yet such desires have always been here, the sheddings and seepage of our nightly dance, the Death by Chocolate we suffer willingly, even gratefully, in this midget bed that cannot contain it. What tender cruelties; what exquisite lies. So marvelous that I can believe that when my toes are finally gone, I will learn to move without them. With or without my Derrick for support.

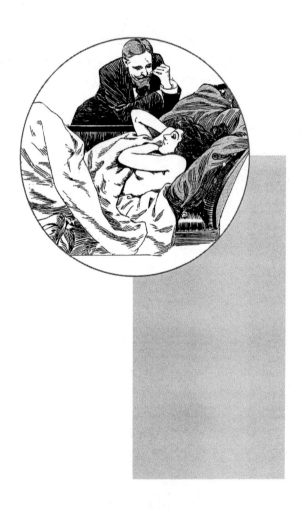

from # Bittersweet Journey

Enid Futterman is a lyricist, librettist, editor, and photographer. She lives in Claverack, New York. Her Bittersweet Journey: A Modestly Erotic Novel of Love, Longing, and Chocolate *was published by Viking in 1998.*

CHAPTER 8/PARIS

In a small hotel, in the Marais, a ravishing seventeenth-century room opens onto a balcony overlooking a courtyard. In the seventeenth century, women greeted men in this room with a question.

"*Voudrez-vous du chocolat?*"

But Charlotte and her lover would fall in love with Paris first, using it, as lovers had always done, as an aphrodisiac, arms wrapped tightly around each other—one person with two pairs of eyes and four legs. There was no rush to see anything, so they would see everything, without effort or judgment. They would see that all of Paris was beautiful and erotic. They would prolong the agony to heighten the ecstasy.

It was October, and the light was even more beautiful because it was becoming scarce. If it was possible to paint this light, she thought, it should be possible to photograph it. She had meant to photograph the light in Vienna, but she had gotten caught in the shadows. This was different; his desire surpassed hers, and her desire confounded her. When she glanced at him, quickly, from a distance, she saw a boy; at close range, he had no age and neither did she. He was like a shadow picture; after a while, the background becomes the foreground. The shadow becomes the light.

In bed, he was a man. He took the lead in the first, slow, catlike dance, pawing as she purred, licking as she stretched, biting as she scratched, until she felt as if she could be penetrated any-where. When he finally entered her, he said, "Don't move," and they stayed together, glued together, without speaking, for what could have been an hour, or a minute. He told her that he loved her and she was so moved she said it back.

Paris was the last stop. Mecca, Jerusalem, Oz. But not even the chocolates of Paris could compete with him, and for three days, she forgot to bring her list of chocolatiers along. For three days, they wandered the streets in a languid haze, never ventur-ing more than ten minutes from their bed.

On the fourth day, they stumbled into Angelina, a *salon du thé* in which well-dressed, well-mannered Parisiennes found themselves in the afternoons. When Charlotte led him to the center of the large, crowded room, she could feel them watching. When she was seated, she returned the glance of the woman at the next table, and when the woman, who had Patrizia's eyes, averted them, a bowl of whipped cream and a little Limoges pitcher streaked with something that looked darker and thicker than tea came into focus. It wasn't tea. It wasn't coffee either. It was chocolate.

She looked around. There were Limoges pitchers and bowls of freshly whipped cream on all the marble tables. All of the women were drinking chocolate, or pouring it, from little pitch-ers into large cups.

"Melted truffles," he said, taking his first gulp. Charlotte had thought so too, but her voice had gotten stuck in her throat, reveling in the warmth of the unctuous liquid—so thick it could be eaten, so smooth it was impossible not to drink.

"*Qu'est-ce que c'est?*" she asked the brusque, matronly woman who carried the silver trays but seemed oblivious to the powers of what they held.

"*Chocolat chaud.*"
"*Oui, mais qu'est-ce que c'est?*"
"*Le chocolat et le lait.*"
"*C'est tout?*"
"*Et la patience,*" she added, somewhat derisively. Charlotte thought she said "*la passion.*"

Here was the link that was missing in Vienna, to Charles V of Spain, and Cortés and Moctezuma. Here was the Spanish princess betrothed to the French king, arriving in Paris with a carved and gilded chocolate box and a maid, whose only task was to beat chocolate with a *molinet* for an hour before serving it to her mistress in bed, but was herself permitted only to smell it.

Charlotte closed her eyes and drank from the Limoges cup. She was permitted. She was the Queen of France.

"*Voudrez-vous du chocolat?*" she asked, before refilling his cup.

He drank it all, almost in one swallow. He was a young blood in a Covent Garden chocolate house at four-thirty in the afternoon, and the drink was an elixir, a potion, an initiation. As another, wiser Englishman once said, it was the end of the beginning. That day ended at four-thirty, and the night began.

"*L'addition, s'il vous plaît.*"
"*Oui, Madame.*"

At five, they were in their heavy, dark bed. "Take off your underpants," he said. She did what he said. "Turn onto your stomach."

He lifted her soft, short black skirt above her waist, and looked at her for a long time before he parted her legs, just enough for his fingers to intrude, and even then he didn't touch the insides of her thighs, but only the wet hairs between them.

"Open your legs."

He asked if she wanted more, and before she could form the word with her lips, he withdrew his hand, and she could feel all of the air in the room between her legs. She was exposed; it didn't occur to her to wonder whether it was the same as being open.

The next day, they went beyond their *quartier* and crossed the Seine. The streets of St. Germain no longer belonged to Picasso and Janet Flanner, but they were paved with the same beloved cobblestones, and the waiters were still arrogant at Deux Magots.

"What will become of us?" he asked.

When she smiled, and said, "We'll always have Paris," he didn't know she was quoting. He seemed not to have a past, not even a childhood. He talked about her instead of himself. He said she saw endings in place of beginnings. He knew the answers without knowing the questions, but she couldn't help correcting his English, not to mention his French. It would be easier if he were just a kid. What do women want, Dr. Freud? To want.

The darkest chocolate is not eighty, ninety, or ninety-nine percent cocoa. It is not the one that looks darkest, and tastes bitterest; it is the one that tastes bittersweetest. The darkest chocolate is not only dark; it is smooth, fine, complex, pedigreed, and French.

"I want chocolate."

"You shall have chocolate."

"I want Manjari."

In Paris, Manjari was no further than the nearest *pâtisserie*, and for Charlotte, it was still the perfect bittersweet balance. For him, the balance tipped at seventy percent cocoa, in Guanaja. It was the most aromatic, and perhaps the most exotic, but it was too bitter for her. That night, he took her to the other side of his sweetness. He made her wait too long.

The next day, they walked the streets as usual, but with an unusual sense of purpose. She had remembered to bring her list, and she couldn't forget it. Chaudun. Hevin. Constant. Maison. She could hear the names in her head like a song. The names of chocolatiers and the names of chocolate are all lyrical, because they are all French. *Couverture. Bonbon. Ganache.*

In France, chocolate has depth and chocolates are pure. In France, food is art and chocolate is food. But unlike wine or cheese, chocolate is not improved with age; *ganache* ought to vanish somewhere between the tongue and the palate. So why did Charlotte want to possess what could only be consumed?

Michel Chaudun's *truffes*. Jean-Paul Hevin's *pralines*. Christian Constant's exotic, erotic perfumes. Ylang-Ylang. Verbena. Vetiver. Charlotte never met any of these Frenchmen, but she knew them all, and they seemed to know her.

She consumed it all, and she wanted more. But her English boy had had more than enough.

"Let's go home."

"There's one more."

"No more."

"But it's…"

"On the list?"

"Yes."

"Am *I*?"

That night, he used the same slow, masterful touch, but with a harder edge. Something had shifted, from the heightening of her pleasure, to the heightening of his. It was apparent in his eyes; the more heat they reflected, the colder they became.

The next morning, she looked into those eyes and asked for more. "*One* more."

"Bloody hell."

"The best."

"Why wasn't it the first?"

"I was saving it."

On a street crowded with women who traveled with their jewelry, he stopped in his tracks as they approached the wooden doors with brass letters.

La Maison du Chocolat. Paris. New York.

She should have prepared him for that. Yes, she had been to the shop on Madison Avenue. No, it wasn't enough. This was a pilgrimage. If Paris was Jerusalem, La Maison du Chocolat was the temple wall, and no other house of worship would do.

If Paris was Oz, Robert Linxe was the wizard. His chocolates were subtle, layered marriages of chocolate and fruit, chocolate and spice, and chocolate and chocolate. His truffles left final, unexpected, whole notes. With six shops on two continents, he couldn't possibly make his chocolates himself, but he made every one, whether or not he ever touched them.

If Paris was Mecca, Charlotte was in heaven, and in control, shining, without jewelry. Her English boy, suddenly ragged, saw it; she let him see.

"Let's get out of here."

"We just got here."

"I'm stuffed."

"Four days ago, you were starving."

He swaggered past her and out the door like the rocker he was. But Charlotte was the addict.

"*L'addition, s'il vous plaît.*"

"*Oui, Madame.*"

Paris had swallowed him up by the time she retrieved her American Express card. When she opened the door to their empty room, she was almost relieved.

He was out on the balcony.

"I couldn't find you."

"Here I am."

"No, you're not. I can't even smell you."

"I'm not chocolate."

"I'm sorry."

"Don't apologize."

"I'm s…" She caught herself, and reached out to stroke his hair, but he flinched like a moody adolescent. When she put her arms around him, he let his arms hang at his sides, and eased back against the exterior stone wall, leaning on it, his mouth against her ear, her hands pinned against the wall.

"Can you smell me now?" he whispered. She closed her eyes and nodded, while he raised his hands to lift her skirt and lower her silk underpants to the tops of her thighs. It was late morning; they were in full view of the windows on the courtyard. Over and over, he asked her if she could smell him while he leaned back so she would have to lean forward. He held her skirt above her waist with one hand, and played with the widening space between her legs with the other. Over and over, she nodded, like one of those dolls in the back of a car. She was aware of being exposed, and not just to him, but she didn't care. She pressed herself against him, but he did not melt into her, and she tried not to kiss him, or cry.

"Please," she said, finally, in desperation.

As soon as the word had been uttered, he took his hand away, leaning forward against her until they were both vertical. Before she had a chance to steady herself, he left her there and went inside. She heard the door of the room open and close. Still breathless, she went cold. She pulled up her underpants, pulled down her skirt, and ran down the stairs after him to prowl the streets they had wandered.

Hours later, she returned to find a message from Nathan, and three boxes of chocolate from three men she had never met. Henri Le Roux. Joel Durand. And Michel Belin. She opened them as she made her way nervously up the stairs.

Le Roux sent *Truffes de truffe*. Truffles made with truffles. Real ones. Durand, who numbered his chocolates, sent numbers 1, 3, 13, 14, and 16. Belin sent a small, curious assortment, accompanied by hand drawings and five words—Cinnamon, Licorice, Ginger, Jasmine, and *Orgeat*.

All the boxes were from Bill, of course, still trying to give her what he thought she wanted. The Englishman would trump the English boy, by paying for other men's magic, because he had none of his own. The English boy was gone, of course, and so were his clothes.

On a beautiful day, the City of Light had grown darker than the City of Dreams. She had been away for so long, fighting a losing war, until she surrendered, but not to Paris. Charlotte never saw Paris, not even through a lens. She succumbed to the wizards—the men who knew magic, and used it in a conspiracy against her until she was spellbound and blind.

"*L'addition, s'il-vous-plaît.*"

"*Oui, Madame.*"

Antony Oldknow

Bluebells, Lilac, and Chocolate

A native of Peterborough, England, Antony Oldknow now lives in Portales, New Mexico, where he teaches writing and literature at Eastern New Mexico University. His stories, poems, and translations have appeared in many North American and British publications, including The American Poetry Review, Antaeus, Ghosts and Scholars, The Literary Review, The Nation, Poetry, *and* Wisconsin Review. *His books include* Ten Small Songs *(Paraiso Press, 1985) and* Consolation for Beggars *(Song Press, 1978).*

Spring. White sun. Sudden fresh breeze. Grass long and lush. Its wet leaves leaning back. I am wandering through them barefoot. They are springing back wetting my legs. Above, among clean new leaves, there are festoons. Lamps of lilac swung bouncing in the fresh breeze. In front as I turn—a sea of wet bluebells. Then... A girl. Long gold hair. The hair touches grass. One hand is on rock. She leans to touch a shoe. She is bent over removing the first. Then she bends the other way, hopping there. She ties the shoes to her waist, straightens up. She tosses back her gold hair, stretches up her arms.

As I am following with my eye the curves of her white shorts, her hands come together behind her. They explore, slide across and around each curve silkily, enter and withdraw from the two empty back pockets. Then I can see from the way her elbows are up and out she is searching her front. It's one of those fresh clear days when it's an intense joy just to be alive. With her, I feel I could stroke and linger, smell and lick and fondle. All at once, she thrusts up her hand, jumps, laughs—echoing notes. She has a chocolate bar in her hand. And stock still, silent, I watch. She is unwrapping it. Black chocolate.

Silver. Held up. Two hands together. Sun-dazzled, the silver opens. Delicate fingers draw the sheath. Slowly, the silver skin slides back. Slowly, the black column pushes upward out. Then those two hands descend, at first slowly. You feel from your distance that they are reluctant. Then abruptly those hands are hidden behind her gold hair. And you see a jolt—she is like a sword-swallower. Then it is raining, the wind sweeping great drops into my face. The grass and the bluebells are swirling around her. The sun shines intermittently into this rough sea. You hear branches crack, see lilac cages dither, shuddering, black wood bouncing as it falls. I gaze around me happily, surveying the savagery of a spring morning casting off its old clothes, flaunting the new flags of heaven. When I look down, she is gone.

Gone! I rush. Wade through shimmering. Wet crashes into me. Wind tangles up my eyes. And then, there she is—lying. Slid down in mud beside the stone. Chocolate smears all over and around her mouth. She has a crushed silver ball in one hand. The other is up in the grass under her head. Branch. Black branch. Heavy, snakelike, dead. Bluebells and grass crushed. Their wet leaves curled over. Curved and rippling over her face. Flinching up and away from the snake. Then springing back, nestling around it in wind. That black branch lies beside her like a lover. Her gold hair ripples gently like a bleached dry fern.

Since her skin is damp and cold like marble to touch, I touch it. I touch her forehead with my fingers lightly, then I use my lips. Thinking of stone taste, metallic blood taste, sick with laughter at this leaden prank of spring, I bow down to this stone.

Chocolate! Chocolate smell. Warm chocolate taste. Mud, powder, and chocolate. Also that almost obscene smell. The pungence of grass in rain. Rain pocking and slapping onto my back. Water sliding off my hair onto her face. Water beginning to make her smears of chocolate run. Her blue eyes suddenly open and stare up at me.

Alive! I gasp. She smiles then. And I smile back. And then I see blood. Blood from under her hair trickling. Diluted blood and rain from the branch. Thin liquid trickling down her turned raised face. Raised slightly toward mine, smiling now, blood meeting chocolate. And as her face comes up, I meet it. I clean her hurt softnesses with my slow delicate tongue.

I think she understands; I believe that I too understand. I am for all smells and tastes in the spring: chocolate and mud, blood and death and fish. And part of me swims like a fish in this glove of water and flesh. We lie on the bottom like warm slick cats among the swirling blades of weeds. Over and over we turn together, injured and gasping, and full of wounds in the grass, chocolate and crumpled bluebells in our mouths and hair.

If only everything we put in our mouths tasted as good as chocolate.

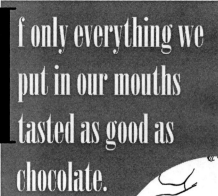

ANNA GEYER

Sleeps with Chocolate

Anna Geyer is a writer and an award-winning experimental filmmaker. Her written work has appeared in Gargoyle, The Underwood Review, Wasted Space, *and* Centipede. *She teaches at both Solano Community College and San Francisco City College. Her website is www.dr-yo.com/loquat.*

Arthur got a job working graveyard at a convenience store and became nocturnal. He hoped it would help his sculpting, for he preferred to work in natural light yet he had to have a job on the side to pay the bills. The night shift seemed the obvious answer, yet the transition was a bit difficult, for the time we spent together, or with friends, was gone.

To try and make it easier on me, he would stop on his way home and wake me up with breakfast and kisses. I would lie on my stomach with the plate hanging over the edge of the bed, carefully spreading jam on the flat, mini-pancake-like Tater Tots of the fast food joint. He sat next to me, or on my back, watching me eat, waiting, finishing my eggs for me on occasion. The first time I spread jam on the taters, he said, "Hey, what are you doing? There's plenty of catsup there for the potatoes."

"Look at them. They're not French fries. They're not even Tater Tots. It looks like they've been smashed. They're hammered tots. Besides, it's tastier this way. They're too salty with the catsup and too bland alone. Ya gotta try it." After that he always made sure he asked for extra jellies. I would work my way one at a time through all the Tater Tots, conserving enough jam for half the English muffin. Then I'd eat half a muffin sandwich-style with the eggs and finish off with more jam and the other half a muffin. It was all about the lingering. I would rip the muffin into chunks before adding the jam.

One morning as I started on the final muffin half, I heard a bag rustle on the floor next to the bed from somewhere around my hip. He said, "Try this," and he handed me a small square of dark chocolate. I added it to a jellied muffin bit. "What are you waiting for?"

"To see if it will melt."

"You know that muffin's stone cold."

"Yeah, I know. I was just hoping. This is good."

"I know," he said and kissed me.

Shortly thereafter he stopped ordering the eggs. Then, he switched to bringing muffins home and toasting them himself. Most mornings I heard him pull up; his car was built and sounded distinct enough to make its way into my not-quite-conscious morning anticipatory state. The first morning he used the toaster, I pretended I was asleep until I could hear him and smell the warm muffins in the room with me. I knew something was up when he didn't make his way immediately to the room—shedding clothes as he moved through the apartment—but clanged around in the kitchen for a while first. We never used the toaster and kept it behind a bunch of pots and pans in a cabinet and he was forced to locate it.

The chocolate melted better than ever before. Arthur knew that I hate butter; he always requested them to hold the butter. Yet, everything was still slapped on the grill to heat, leaving an unidentifiable residue I preferred not to think about. That's why the jelly was so important, and it was all right with me if he finished the muffin and then began to lick my fingers.

His muffins were far superior. They had no butter and, just out of the toaster, the chocolate melted into the jelly. One morning he switched to orange marmalade. I was in heaven. Propped up on one arm, my legs curled around his naked body, I stared at the marmalade and chocolate, "Ya know, this would be great with peanut butter." He was back from the kitchen, jar in hand, in no time. Marmalade and chocolate. Peanut butter and chocolate. Marmalade and peanut butter. Peanut butter and marmalade and chocolate. It was all good.

A candy store opened up in a strip mall between our apartment and his job. He would stop on his way to work and do his best not to eat all the goodies before he got home. If he was successful, he had bought enough to last through the night, the first thing he would do once he got home was turn off my alarm. He would then present the candy to me and I would be late to work. If he had eaten all the chocolates, or had no time to stop, he would crawl into bed next to me. We would both sleep through my alarm and I would be late once again.

"Oh shit," he was in the kitchen. He closed the refrigerator door, opened the freezer, and closed it as well. I had heard his car drive up and rolled over onto my stomach to wait. He had a bag with him, which he put down to take off his socks. He pulled off his T-shirt, pulled down the sheet, climbed on my butt, and placed the bag off the edge of the bed. He took a single piece of candy and placed it high between my shoulder blades where it was particularly difficult to reach even if he hadn't been sitting on me.

"What's this?" he whispered.

"Chocolate."

"No, come on, what kind?"

"Wait a minute…You asked….I answered. I win. What do I get," I said as I began to squirm.

"Please, just play a little." He made a semicircle of candy across my shoulders.

"OK, give me a kiss." I arched back and turned to look at him over my shoulder. I could not see the chocolates as they slid toward the small of my back. He pecked me on the cheek. "No, I mean a real kiss." He began to rearrange the chocolate on my back into its original position.

"This is a blind study. Besides I know what you're doing and it's not going to work."

"Oh, come on. I deserve a hint."

"Not today," He picked a piece of chocolate up and popped it in his mouth. "You better guess before it's too late."

"Now you sound like my old baby-sitter. She insisted we take naps and brought bubble gum with her as a 'reward.' If she heard us making any noise at all she would say things like, 'I know you're not in bed. I'm going to eat half your piece right now,' and she would. It was horrible."

"I know what you're doing. If you don't guess I'm going to eat another one." He began to draw little circles around them with his finger on my back. "Come on, it's not that hard. You better guess." I closed my eyes and began to enjoy his swirling nails. He kept his right hand long to play guitar yet never scratched hard enough hurt me.

"OK, dark chocolate medallions."

"See, I knew you could do it. Now for your reward." Arthur picked a piece up off my back and leaned forward on his knees. I tilted my head back. He kissed my forehead then held the chocolate out for me. I kissed his hand before I ate the chocolate, then rolled over under him. The remaining chocolate fell off my back and I grabbed one. "Hey, what are you doing?"

"Cheating of course." He kissed me again.

That was it. It was my turn to come up with something. I was alone after ten p.m. nightly. I began my research and although I had no specific goal, I knew I would find one. Thank God for the Internet.

The difficulties of remaining covert became obvious. I never bookmarked anything, deleted cookies endlessly, and cleared the history and the cache. Instead, I made copious, categorized lists with little stars for my favorite sites. Many categories would overlap and then I was left to decide whether to go with double entries or cross references. I encountered the dichotomy of chocolate. *Chocolate as love*, a love offering or a prelude to love, versus *chocolate as a substitute for love*.

There were innumerable chocolatiers whose sales pitch was buy chocolate for your sweetie. They would sell in the shapes of hearts, stars, pink dolphins. My favorites were slogans. "HE HAS RISEN" being the best of the bunch, although I would have preferred HAVE YOU RISEN? or I HAVE RISEN.

JUST SAY NO seemed the least appropriate of slogans. What were they thinking when they made that mold? Or were they playfully pandering to the anti-establishment crowd? For some reason you could buy the phrase "I LOVE YOU ERIC" in every shape imaginable. Eric must have worked hard for his prize. Perhaps Erics are eminently more lovable. I decided against that particular research project.

Chocolate as a substitute for love. Often these sites sold the same products, but the shapes of candies were more sentimental: lots of doggies and cuddly beasts, with little or no emphasis on slogans. "WHEN ALL ELSE FAILS HUG YOUR TEDDY" appeared as a popular phrase. Yet it somehow seemed to miss the point. What about a direct message to the lonely customer? WHEN ALL ELSE FAILS I AM HERE FOR YOU or WHEN ALL ELSE FAILS EAT ME.

Chocolate as an edible indulgence versus an indirect almost voyeuristic form of consumption. I found there are many different ways to have chocolate in your life. It seemed you could easily quench your desire without actually digesting anything. What blasphemy. What good was chocolate if you couldn't eat it? Instead you could buy exfoliating foot polish—go to the bakery without putting a foot in the door? Chocolate shampoo was at least thought provoking. It wasn't what I was looking for, but how would he react to a chocolate-scented coif?

I didn't want to buy chocolate or chocolate products. The candy store was right down the street. Among the articles on chocolate, one of my favorite quotes was, "In susceptible individuals, for instance, it can fuel an addiction like desire, especially among people who exercise excessively, such as dancers. Among ballerinas, chocolate is a food fetish. They crave it. Talk about it endlessly—dream about it." What is excessive exercise? Does my six to twelve hours a week count as excessive? I shut off the computer.

He came home without me hearing him. My face was toward the window. He kissed me on the shoulder. "Late night?"

"Research. Not really getting anywhere," I mumbled. He pushed my shoulder with his forehead.

"Roll over." I turned onto my stomach and he jumped on my back.

"Hey, could you massage my left shoulder?"

"OK, but only for a second." He rubbed it and I began to wake up. He then reached into the bag and pulled out a piece of chocolate. I had tried to peek as he reached for it, but he had gotten really good at hiding the bag just out of reach.

"What is it?"

"If you close your eyes, I'll give you a hint. You've got to promise not to cheat."

"OK I promise." I squeezed my eyes closed. He picked the candy off my back and held it in front of my face.

"Smell."

"Oh my God. It smells like one of those chocolate oranges that my sister brings over from Wales. You didn't unwrap anything before I woke up, did you?"

"No, but you're close."

"I give up, just let me have it." It was hard to linger over chocolate.

"Here, try it and then tell me what it is."

"It's so orangy and tart."

"Give up?"

"Yep, you win."

"Chocolate-covered orange peels." At that moment I knew I had to make my own chocolate: it wasn't only the taste; I had to have that smell filling the room.

I had noticed a general lack of imagination and humorlessness in the world of chocolate making. The one exception arose as I began my search for "chocolate tools," a term I expected to mean the tools necessary to produce chocolate. The dichotomy reappeared. Not only were there numerous pages selling utensils, but there were also several selling chocolate in the shape of tools. You could purchase a pipe wrench, a hacksaw, or—my personal favorite—vise grips. This site came with a disclaimer, as many did, "We do not sell the molds themselves." I noticed a distinct division between the people who sold molds and those who sold molded chocolate, and each side made it eminently clear which they fell on.

The vocabulary of chocolate in respect to production, and the tools of production, was more imaginative and sexier than any chocolate I could buy. I have always been a gearhead, and I must admit the equipment used to make chocolate is some of the sexiest-looking stuff I've seen—unbelievably beautiful, sleek lines. Obviously there was the old standard chocolate fondue pot; each manufacturer seemed to be trying to outdo its competition in sheer elegance.

Even the terminology for the equipment itself was provocative. A melangeur would grind and mix your chocolate for you. Although the fact that you were grinding your "nibs" seemed a bit frightening, the term still fit the picture.

You could purchase an eight-cavity mold and if you did so from the "adult mold" section you could end up with eight chocolate penis pops. Not that I wanted to make penis pops—I mean, how clever is that? And, if you didn't want to make your own penis pops, you could easily order them ready made from another site. Why aren't the chocolatiers inspired? Now if they all got together and had a contest on who could make the best penis pops, that would be hot. They could divide the tournament into all kinds of categories, best tasting, best rendering thereof, best interpretive piece. Whatever.

Even chocolate-as-fetish sites seemed lacking. I didn't want to purchase a white chocolate vagina complete with piercing. There were no chocolate whips, only gummy whips or chocolate handcuffs. I wanted something humorous. Or something that initiated sex, not imitated the necessary anatomy. Breast pops weren't it either.

All I could think of was the email I had received, probably an urban legend, of the man in Australia who bemoaned the fact Easter was so commercial and non-Christian. In an effort to return the holiday to Christ, he made his own jelly-filled candies which portrayed Jesus crucified. He called them Sweet Jesus. His act was decried by the Catholic Church as sacrilegious. He felt hurt.

Eventually chocolate-covered orange peels would be made. But Easter was coming up. At first I naïvely believed I could make my own molds. Through my research, I learned most are made of plastic today. And the antique metal ones didn't seem as if they would be very alterable, or at least not in a fashion to produce identical, repeatable results. I ordered a variety of bunny molds in various poses to practice, as well as several squeeze bottles to help properly fill the cavities and some dark chocolate.

The problem of not getting caught intensified. I so wanted a marble pastry board and stainless steel pastry scraper with which to temper my chocolate, but it would be impossible to justify my newfound interest in cooking. I settled for a stainless steel offset spatula. I had the tools delivered to work and hid them once they arrived. I printed out a multitude of how-to pages and recipes, then carefully applied the three-hole punch in order to keep them in an old binder of school notes. Even though I knew it was a truly risky proposition, I bought a couple of books, one on candy-making, the other on the history of chocolate. Arthur had a ton of cookbooks he read through regularly, so I didn't dare shelve my books with his. Besides searching for recipes, he liked looking at what he called the erotic food shots. "Look at this one. It's the real money shot, soft focus foreground, red background, white plate, slightly wet, glistening berries." And if he didn't find the books, I was afraid he would smell the night's endeavors before I could surprise him. I made a multitude of chocolate chip cookies as I advanced in my studies.

"What's with the chocolate chip cookies?" He asked after he found the third batch left on the kitchen counter. He had worked his way through the chocolate-covered figs and ginger, moved on to truffles from the candy store and, through his studies, become completely disinterested in what he called "low-end" product.

"I've been craving them lately."

"Chocolate chip cookies, but they're so pedestrian," he said with a tone of utter disappointment. It was clear he would never eat another candy bar again.

"Well, my brother's birthday is coming up and they're his favorite so I thought I'd send some to him."

"Oh." He had no idea I spent my nights learning how to temper chocolate, for in order to make chocolate candy, you had to temper it first. I was elated though surprised by the severity of his disdain. How could he not notice the plastic gloves in the trash, or the endlessly clean double boiler in the dish rack? I was glad Easter was approaching and he worked Saturday nights.

My competition from the candy store was unbeatable; therefore I focused on presentation. Because I couldn't alter the molds, I had to fix the bunnies themselves. I had the hardest time properly applying a prosthetic penis that wouldn't fall off. The bunnies weren't warm coming out of the molds. If by chance I got it to stick, there was always some kind of scar-like blemish in the groin area. If I built the penis directly on my bunny, gravity took hold—it dripped or became limp and misshapen. Someone else could probably produce my desired results, or maybe after years of experience, I would be able to find the perfect temperature. I was determined not to resort to the anatomically correct chocolate bunny molds I had finally found on the Internet. They were too exaggerated, and although they won points for silly, they just didn't go well with my girl bunnies.

Instead I discovered "chocolate plastique." I found the mixture of chocolate and corn syrup much more workable. I decided my boy bunnies would have a platform to which their penises attached. I added the plastic chocolate penises to the upside of medallion molds as the medallions themselves hardened, and then added the bunnies. I mapped out my diorama with a centerpiece of boy bunnies in a circle back to back. The girl bunnies wandered, as if trying to pick the perfect mate, around the periphery. There were pairs of bunnies, some playing hide and seek around chocolate eggs, others nuzzling noses. All on a bed of Easter grass encircled by jellybeans and smaller boy "guards" facing outward.

On Easter Sunday I stayed up assembling the display, adding the final touches. I had made a pedestal and placed it on the counter/bar/island which separated the kitchen from the front room. Bunny production had commenced several weeks early, although I decided to make one last batch of penis platforms and attached the male bunnies. I did not make any cookies, though the scent of chocolate permeated our apartment. I then changed all the lights in the kitchen, living room, and hallway to blue, green, and pink bulbs and placed a bunny mold in the dish drainer. I was exhausted but could not sleep.

Arthur's car pulled in. I had parked in the back space, leaving the front open for him; on the off chance I actually fell asleep, I knew his vehicle would wake me up. "Oh my God." He noticed my work immediately. Forever passed. Then, from the other room, he yelled, "Did you really make all this?" I did not answer. Finally, he stood in the doorway of our room. "I know you're awake." I didn't move. He crossed the room to straddle my back, pulled the covers down, kissed my ear, and tickled my left side. "Can we eat them?" I reached off the right side of the bed next to the wall where I had placed the bunny cache. He stood on his knees so I could turn over. He kissed me and then took a bite of the bunny.

"I wouldn't eat the boy bunnies, or maybe not the penises themselves. They have a lot of corn syrup in them."

"These are good. Can I have another bite?" I put the bunny in my mouth. The head and ears were sticking out. "Please," he said. I sat up and he bit the ears off and most the head, then undressed quickly. I rolled over to the far edge of the bed as he got in, grabbed another bunny, and rolled back over him. "Beg for this one," I said.

He too became obsessed with the idea of chocolate production. I told him about the penis pops, to which he responded, "Are there any life-size chocolate penises?"

"Not that I was interested in. They almost all look the same; even the three-D ones looked odd, like they're from the same mold. Some of them didn't have balls, others had white chocolate at the tip, but they were all basically the same. Most of them have a visible mold line."

"Oh, that's probably lazy casting."

"Well, whatever, I found nothing like the larger than life candles my mom's ex-boyfriend used to make. He sold them on Telegraph in the sixties. I saw one once and have been forever jaded. The best part was not only was it lifelike, like a sculpture, but it was red, white, and blue."

"I'm not into figurative sculpture, but I bet I could make a mint selling them on the Internet."

"I'm sure you could, but would you want to?"

"We've got to check it out. If there really aren't any good ones out there, you could help me make a website. I could hand sculpt each one. We'd be rich."

"Chocolate's not that easy, Arthur. And one thing you've got to worry about is ambient room temperature. I worked at night, so there wasn't a problem, but I don't think I could even do that around here during the summer. I'm not trying to shoot you down or anything... all I'm saying is you better do your research." I showed him my books, recipes, and websites. I even gave him what was left of the eleven-pound standard-size block of dark chocolate I had purchased. When I came home for dinner for weeks, he was on the Internet or reading. He surpassed my knowledge quickly. He joined discussion groups, talked to the guy at the candy store, and bought a ton of books. He called in sick for work and took a two-day local chocolate-making class, then actually flew back East to take a chocolate-sculpting class.

We ordered the marble pastry board as well as the stainless steel pastry scraper. Our days off were spent practicing tempering chocolate the hard way, looking at recipes, and comparing notes. For a moment, he too contemplated ordering beans to make his own chocolate, when he discovered terms like conche which included a machine with steel ribs and a series of blades that repetitively scrape against the lining of the drum in order to prepare the beans. We finally made chocolate-covered orange peels together and basked for hours in the aroma.

Soon he was setting up shop, and I was designing his website. Once he had devised a production method he was satisfied with and had a couple pieces made, we took pictures and posted them on the web. We added a couple gif files of the artist at work. He had wanted to call them Sweet Willy, but there was an English candy company selling Sweet Willies already. John Thomas Candy Co. was what he finally settled upon. Hours were spent thinking up promotional slogans. He sold Chocolate Packages. "Package for Mrs. Hershey?" and "How About a Hot Rod?" were his tag lines. I recorded audiofiles which played back automatically if you enlarged the corresponding picture. He asked me to include a line stating that the artist would make custom products upon request. Furthermore, he would personally deliver the product for an additional delivery fee and the price of airfare.

"Why would you want to do that?"

"Hey, haven't you noticed, it's all about the gimmick. It takes a gimmick to become an art star. You know, meet the artist and all that. I doubt anyone will ever take me up on it. It's there for the mystery, the intrigue, that certain 'I don't know what,'" he added in his sexiest French accent.

"But what if that certain-I-don't-know-what does call?"

"Janie's jealous...She thinks I'm gonna run off to Wisconsin and never come back."

"More like Brentwood or Paris."

"Don't worry, there's nothing better than watching you in your little red-and-white-striped apron, with your butt peeking out the back, working your pastry cutter, tempering your chocolate."

"Whatever."

His first order didn't come in for weeks. Arthur spent his spare time Googling his website and carving "fine wood penises," or "peni," as he liked to call them. He wanted to add a Morning Wood or a Hard Wood Package. He made five wood penises and began on his sixth, before he got his first Chocolate Package order. He was so elated, he produced and delivered his product in a week. Orders were slow but steady. He had an occasional special order. My favorite order—"I want the Hot Rod with dual piercings"—sent Arthur into a flurry of research. Most special orders were for a specific penis, in which case photos or video stills were necessary. He wasn't able to quit his job, but cut back to three days a week. Arthur was happy.

One day I got home, and there was a plate of chocolate-covered orange peels on the table with a note. Went to Florida for a delivery, be back tomorrow. He wouldn't talk about his trip when he got back.

I didn't act upon my first inclination to pile all his belongings in the driveway and set them on fire. Instead I asked him to move out.

Shortly thereafter, Arthur moved to Florida. I see his name on occasion. He hasn't become an art star yet, but he has had several shows. It seems he has quit sculpting, other than chocolate.

Imagine the French equivalent of the Hershey Kiss.

MOIRA EGAN

Lady Godiva

Moira Egan's first book of poems, Cleave *(Washington Writers' Publishing House, 2004) was nominated for the National Book Award and was a finalist for the ForeWord Book of the Year Award. Recent poems have appeared in* Gargoyle, Notre Dame Review, Passages North, Poems & Plays, Poetry, Smartish Pace, 32 Poems, *and* West Branch, *among many others. Her work is also featured in the anthologies,* Kindled Terraces: American Poets in Greece *and* Lofty Dogmas: Poets on Poetics. *Two of her Bar Napkin Sonnets won first prize in the Baltimore City Paper Poetry Contest, 2005.*

Once a month
I give in to my cravings, listen
to the howling of my appetites.
The wolves at the door of my self-
control are epicurean. I feed them
filet of hand-massaged beef,
single malt scotch, exotic desserts
from Africa or Chile. Only then
are they silenced. This month
it's bittersweet chocolate they demand.

So I go to Godiva.
Prancing across the foil the color
of sunset, she and her noble steed
are like a gender-bent centaur. Strange
story, a woman, naked on horseback.
Truth is, her ass and thighs,
pressed tightly to the hide,

would have itched and prickled.
Bruised bones. When she finally
dismounts, emerges from under
the umber waves of her hair,
she'll need relief
from all that heat.

Suddenly it's me
on the horse, a wild fall day.
He is skittish: dogs bark,
leaves rattle on dry dirt. He sees
a snake in every garden hose. I twist
my fingers through his
chestnut mane, the wind blows,
out of control. I try
to rein him in, but my lessons
have evaporated, sweat.

That was the day I learned to trust
my muscles, slow him down
with the pressure of my thighs.
My boyfriend meets me in the barn,
first lessons in heat, in hunger.
Even now the scent of hay
disturbs me, strokes my belly
like a cello sonata.

Or like good chocolate.
Its slow, voluptuous melt reminds me
of the vow I have taken,
solemn as a monk,
that I will seize each day
and distill its essence,
sweet as chartreuse,
potent as Benedictine.

But I never remember the moral
of the story, I fall in love with
priests and Geminis. How easy
it would be to grow used to this,
sunlight streaming in, warm
on his face, our breakfast of bread
and chocolate. How well I know that
each time he will leave
my psyche tangled as my hair,
and as fragrant.

If the man who persistently fills my thoughts were chocolate, I'd have put that box of bonbons in the alley, half-uneaten, weeks ago. But he is 6'1" and refuses to squeeze into the box.

A Period of Silence

Deirdra McAfee's stories have appeared in Willow Springs, Confrontation, The Baltimore Review, *and* The Rio Grande Review, *and online at* The Diagram, *among others. She won the 1998 Poets & Writers Writers Exchange Prize and the 2005 Seattle Review Fiction Prize.*

Bobby Renfrew said to his wife Jean, "The Fulbrights know all about siding now."

"Yes," she answered dryly, playing with him, "you're a teacher, too."

"I am," he said solemnly, playing right back. "Not as good as you, though. Mrs. Fulbright says you made their kids the stars of kindergarten." Jean laughed, and then Bobby told her he got the job. She laughed again and ruffled his hair. It was a big sale, a rambling house in a nice neighborhood Bobby wanted to get into. "We covered soffit, rakeboards, and wall vents," Bobby said, "and they decided to trim it out."

Jean poured Bobby a bourbon. Then she poured herself one, too, something she rarely did. Bobby watched Jean and thought of her teetotal Baptist grandmother toasting their wedding. Blue-black and bent-over, in a bright purple flag of a dress, Granny hoisted a beer mug with both skinny hands and said to Jean and Denise, "Y'all watch out, now! Las' drink I took was the night I brought you girls' mama in this world."

Bobby smiled at the memory, but something in Jean's face stopped him before he could mention it. Then she told about that afternoon, when the technician took extra pictures. "They said call tomorrow." Jean taught preschool three mornings a week, but not tomorrow. "Bobby? Could you stay back?" It was April 13, 1998, three months before their thirty-third anniversary. Bobby got up in the dark the next day and rearranged his schedule.

At nine, they sat at the kitchen table on their second round of coffee. After busy signals, beeps, and choices, Jean cut on the speaker: "You will experience a period of silence," the recording said. "Please continue to hold." Then Jean hung up.

"Now, honey. They said to hold."

"I know," she said, turning off the speaker to redial. "Let's talk to a person."

After twenty minutes, or nine periods of silence and three repeating messages, the nurse finally picked up. "Doctor isn't in. Emergency." Jean told Bobby this, muffling the phone by mistake against the breast under suspicion, the one she'd already started thinking of as the bad breast.

She wanted to explain to the nurse about Bobby missing work in his busiest season, wanted to ask why the doctor took that other emergency and ignored the emergency lurking in herself. Jean remembered her grandmother. And her mother. Her sister.

Granny was just the first. This was how it started. A bump egglike and calm beneath the soft unsunned skin. A space before it starts: that's your life. A space after. The bump breaks every-thing, but not right away.

"Ask when to try back," Bobby said; he worked phones every morning. "I'll continue to hold," he told Jean, smiling like it was an ordinary day. Jean herself showed him this, that seeming calm gives others strength. He freshened their coffee and put his hand over hers, a hand years of sun had darkened almost to the color of Jean's own.

Strength was not what you thought of when you looked at Bobby. You saw a guy weathered like a sunbleached boulder, his thinning hair scorched blonde, white lines around his eyes from squinting into the sun so hard the wrinkles can't tan up. Still broad-shouldered and narrow-hipped, Bobby was fifty-one now, and packing a little paunch. He seemed smaller than he really was, and quick instead of tough, but he was both.

Bobby made something of himself. Or Jean did. They've been together since high school, when Bobby's dad, who worked construction, moved Bobby and his mom down here to Georgia from Connecticut. Bobby came in as a senior, small and tetchy and talking funny, a Yankee who had to stand up for himself, a white kid who paid the price, in this fight or that, for who he was, even before crossing the color-line to date Jean.

Bobby finished fighting on a steamy spring night in 1965. Bobby and Jean couldn't park at the usual high-school places, so they were off in a field in Bobby's creaky old Ford. That was another April, unseasonably hot and damp, loud with early gnats and pulsing peep-frogs. When Bobby remembers those nights, he thinks about which liberties Jean allowed and disallowed. Unlike the ample Italian girls back in Bridgeport, all trying to prove they were Gina Lollobrigida, Jean never would let him undress her. He didn't know why and doesn't know now. She probably couldn't tell him.

Jean's delicious magnetic body was still the same, solid, determined, and warm, and her thoughts and feelings were still hidden and infinitely complicated. "You," she'd said on their second date the fall before, at the harvest dance in the darkened gymnasium. "It's you. We're in trouble, baby." That sticky night in the field, they decided that they'd marry after graduation and Bobby'd join the Air Force. "They'll make their peace," Jean said about their families. Then the heat between them ended talk.

Until shouts shattered their trance and blows shook the car. The Ford rocked sharply. Once. Again. Fierce pale faces pressed against the fogged windows. "C'mon out, nigger-lover!" a hoarse voice hollered, "or I'll bust yer damn windows."

"Bust 'em anyhow!" urged another voice. Inside, Bobby pulled Jean close, tucked her head into his chest, and folded around her. The next wallop webbed the windshield, making the shouts and catcalls sound louder. A face peered into the star-shaped hole, shouted, and spat. Slime crawled down Bobby's cheek. He wanted like hell to wipe it away, but something said not to move. He tightened his grip on Jean.

"Out! Out!" they yelled, and the Ford took another hit, the back windshield this time. Bobby felt Jean breathing. He straightened up to fight.

"Don't, Bobby," Jean whispered. He looked at her, and a flashlight glared through the hole. "Sit still, Bobby," she said calmly. "Make them come to you." The light picked out her face and shoulders, and she pushed her hands through her hair and stared out.

Whoever it was could see her as clearly as Bobby could. She had on a blue cotton shift Denise made; she'd pulled it up over herself when the yelling started. Now she moved out of Bobby's arms, reached back, and zipped it. To Bobby she looked like a queen, her polished face ablaze in the dangerous light, her posture straight, her expression intent, as if pondering a serious question. She gazed past the light, trying to see them.

Then they doused it and went back to banging on the car. She pulled Bobby's handkerchief out and cleared the passenger window. "Hank Shiflett over here," she said. "Probably his brothers in front, Ronnie and Shorty. Spud Conklin in back, tagging along as usual. Football team must've had a beer-bust."

"What now?" Bobby whispered. Jean didn't seem scared, but he had every symptom, including a pressing need to pee.

"Wait," she said. And, just like that, she swung the car door wide and stepped out. They got quiet. Jean stood behind the door, searching the darkness. "You Shifletts," she said into the silence. "What you want?" Her voice became more like theirs, slow and blurry, hard for Bobby to understand.

"That's between us and your nigger-lovin' boyfriend," Hank said. Hank played fullback, and nobody got through Hank. The light snapped back on, and Hank stepped way too close to the car door and faced Jean.

"You got somethin' to say?" Jean asked, still with that look.

"Yeah, we wanna know why he's bringin' them Yankee ways down here."

"You mean you have a question for my boyfriend?"

"Yeah," said Spud from the shadows.

"Bobby," Jean said, leaning down into the car and looking at him. "These gentlemen want to talk."

"Sure," Bobby said.

"Good," Jean said, smiling to show he'd given the right answer.

"What you carryin'?" Jean asked.

"Baseball bats," one said.

"Well, put 'em down," she said, and the bats thumped into the grass. "That's better," she said. "Now, you Shifletts listen, and you, too, Spud. I was the best little shortstop in two counties when we were kids, and y'all know I joined your team because you played fair and treated me right. We won every game, remember?"

"Yeah," they muttered.

"Now I'm down at the bottom of my daddy's field makin' plans with this man here—" they came to attention when she called Bobby a man, but she'd reached them now, made them see her— "and y'all come round actin' rude.

"You boys and I been friends since we could walk; y'all know I'm no nigger. Y'all shamin' yourselves to talk like that. Your mamas wouldn't like it, or my mama, either, that baked you cookies and brought you cool water when you came over our place to play.

"Now he and I got private business. Y'all shouldn't've come here and messed up his car and called names. Y'all can talk to him, but then you gotta leave us be."

That was it; she'd changed them from beasts to men. They stood around awhile in silence, and finally Hank Shiflett leaned down, picked up his bat, and walked off through the woods.

"'Night, Hank," Jean called, which Bobby thought was going too far. But then Hank called goodnight back, and the others echoed him and melted away. Hank's souped-up Chevy roared, then stalled, then caught in a storm of gravel. That was the end.

Though it never completely ended. Now it was a look or remark instead of baseball bats. Those, like Lester Maddox's axe-handles, went out of style in Georgia. Now, too, it's sometimes black people who feel about Bobby as the Shifletts felt about Jean. "Just skin," Granny'd said.

"They'll make their peace," Jean told Bobby, but their parents took longer than she thought. Jean's folks were teachers. Like their students, and their children, they'd left the tar-papered Colored School for the brick one where the books were sometimes brand-new and always had all the pages. So they knew Bobby, of course. In Jean's mother's chemistry class, he made a C. They didn't dislike him; he had good manners and treated Jean right.

He just wasn't what they had in mind. Bad enough Bobby was white, but he was no student. What kind of life could he give her, Jean the Honor Roll Queen, as Denise called her, Jean the Negro valedictorian with a much higher average than the white one, and a far better speech?

Only Jean's old granny, her vision failing even then, saw the truth. "Daggone it, Leona," she told Jean's mother, "they in love. You an' Willy best back off, 'cause they gone do what they will, yea or nay. It's jus' skin, Leona. That's all, jus' skin."

But nobody backed off. Jean's father thought daughters should obey their fathers; he thought wives should obey their husbands, too, though Jean's mother had too much Granny in her for that. Willy and Leona agreed about Jean, though, and sat her in the living room for a talking-to. Bobby's folks, meanwhile, got mad and yelled and stomped around. They made futile threats and predicted funny-looking half-breed children that neither side would claim.

The Saturday after graduation, Leona lay in the darkened bedroom with a sick headache. Willy sat on the back steps whittling branches into twigs while Jean and Denise helped each other into the chiffon dresses Denise had made. Meanwhile, Bobby's mother wouldn't speak to Bobby, or to Bobby's dad, who put away a few too many beers and pretended nothing was going on. Even though he lent Bobby a necktie.

Jean and Bobby rode up the coast to a minister they'd found; Denise and her boyfriend Charles, who married the next year, were supposed to meet them for the service. But the preacher had already started when Denise and Charles arrived, bringing along the reason they were late: Granny, toting a sack as big as she was. The old lady hobbled up the aisle, leaning on Denise and talking across the minister, loud in the empty church.

She'd never seen such a handsome groom, Granny declared, and the preacher was right pretty, too. She got up beside Jean and opened the sack, handing Jean an armful of bright zinnias, daisies, and yellow roses from her garden. Then Granny sat on the groom's side, across from Denise and Charles—"jus' evenin' things up, sugar," she whispered loudly to Jean—and the minister resumed.

In the café where they stopped for a wedding supper, Granny fed the table's jukebox and punched in Elvis and Sam Cooke. Granny was the only one old enough to drink. When she raised that schooner of beer, they clinked their Cokes, and she said, "Im'a pray ya make it, churren, 'cause this world is hard. Peoples is mean. Everybody mixed, but most don't want to know.

"Get up and dance now," she commanded. "Then you can toss these here," Granny said, reaching for Jean's flowers. "Denise and I'll scrap for 'em. An' may the best man win, Denise, 'cause I been mighty lonesome since Granddaddy passed."

After two nights' honeymoon in a cheap Savannah hotel, Mr. and Mrs. Robert Renfrew took off. Bobby'd enlisted as a mechanic, and the Air Force gave him x-ray eyes for aircraft and healing hands for their tangled electromechanical innards. Soon he could read a schematic like a story. Six months in, Bobby shot up to six-foot-two, and Jean got pregnant with Lorna.

Once Bobby made crew chief, Jean's folks took the marriage better. Or maybe Granny worked on them. By the time Susie followed Lorna two years later, Granny was blind and sick. She told Jean's mother she had to meet those babies before she went. So, five years after leaving, Bobby and Jean brought the girls back for Christmas in Georgia. Granny saw the children with her hands, and the two families met and made peace, everyone falling in love with those funny-looking half-breeds who turned out to be clever beauties.

Except for Bobby's back-to-back hitches in Vietnam, Jean and the girls went where he did, Wiesbaden, El Toro, Lackland, Eglin, Ramstein. And even after Granny died, and Jean and Bobby's parents, even after Lorna and Susie were grown, they all came back to Georgia. Denise and Charles lived there. So did Bobby and Jean after Bobby retired.

At 10:30, three hours after Bobby usually left, Jean reached a person. Bobby lit a cigarette—one of six he allowed himself daily—not because he wanted one, but for a smokescreen. Jean wouldn't want him staring when she heard. Bobby knows so much about Jean, but there's more he doesn't know. She still has her boundaries, places even Bobby can't go. She helps him out, though, she tells him things. That's how he knows so much. He feels privileged when she tells him.

"But if it's cancer, isn't it cancer now?" Jean asked. "My mother and grandmother died. My sister just finished chemo." Watchful waiting, the doctor said. Bobby couldn't hear that part, all he heard was that word. Jean listened. Then she talked. Then she waited. The silence stretched out. Bobby was on hold now, too.

Jean frowned, and the laugh lines around her mouth furrowed. "OK," she said. "When?" Then she groped unseeing across the table for a pen, the way Bobby remembered Jean's grandmother feeling around for things, and she curled her fingers around it carefully, as if it were fragile, or she was.

Jean's cool-headed. That's stayed the same, too. All over the world, it was Jean who scooped up hysterical mothers and their gashed, bleeding, or broken-armed kids and took them to sick-call. Always PTA president, always balancing the household budget to make not-quite-enough into plenty more. While she was at it, Jean finished college and started teaching.

Three years ago, Susie got engaged stateside, and Jean said, "It's time, Bobby," putting Bobby's thoughts into words at the kitchen table. Laying things out, like she was doing on the phone for the doctor, and for Bobby, too, when she said cancer.

After thirty years in, Bobby was ready for another line of work. On that year's Christmas trip, they looked at Georgia. Charles ran a siding outfit near the Marshes of Glynn, and he took Bobby on some jobs. When the Air Force gave Bobby his papers, he bought in with Charles and went out with the crew. Once Bobby got so he could wrap woodwork with the best of them, Charles moved Bobby into sales—years of training airmen to fix planes had taught Bobby to explain complicated jobs.

Jean wrote something and said goodbye, and Bobby exhaled a cloud of smoke. "He'll do a biopsy and operate," she said, looking away. She stood up so fast she knocked the pen and paper to the floor. "In a week," she said, bending to retrieve them. "A whole week." Then she came banging around the table—Jean, who was grace itself. The cups wallowed in the saucers, coffee splashed out, and she stood over Bobby, breathing hard. She plucked out his cigarette and stubbed it. Then she pulled him to his feet.

"Hold me, baby," she said. Then she laughed into his shoulder and said, in the mechanical voice of the tape, "Please continue to hold." After they'd stood there a good while, when she could breathe again, she sent him to work.

Then Jean went to the supermarket. She didn't bring a list, she just drifted around for an hour. The white lights beat down, the chill from the meat case spread across the store, and piped-in tunes glazed the aisles. Jean hummed along to those she knew, an old Eurythmics song and "Tracks of My Tears." She picked things up, inspecting them absently—bagged oranges from California and Florida, Dutch cocoa, milk, sugar, whipping cream, a thick bar of bittersweet Swiss chocolate. She put the oranges back but laid the other things in the cart like priceless breakables.

While she and Elton John sang "Benny and the Jets," Jean rolled through frozen foods. Jean didn't think about groceries, though. She thought about lumps, although she tried not to. Hers didn't feel like anything. Bobby found it. He told her afterward and took her hand to the place. Feeling it was like finding a fat blood-filled tick someplace no tick should be.

Before Jean and Bobby came back with the kids, blind Granny'd felt one, too. She didn't do anything because she knew. And knew that people in hospitals never came out. Months later, when the lump became an ulcer that oozed and stank, Leona found out.

"Don't want no doctors comin' at me with knives," Granny said. "They'll cut your life away." The doctors took Granny's breast to stop the rotting, but her cancer was like termites. Riddled Granny's bones, which broke when she coughed. Infested Granny's liver, which swelled like an obscene pregnancy. Ate Granny's lungs, which drowned her at last.

Leona was still teaching, but Willy'd retired. They put a hospital bed in the living room, tucked Granny in, and hired a nurse. Granny sank but didn't surrender; she listened to the TV and joked with the nurse. At sundown, she took a tot of bourbon with Willy and talked about whist, all the hands she'd played and won. Then her lungs went.

"Daddy threw me in the crick up home," she whispered to Willy. "Roped my waist and said, 'Swim, baby,' an' I did. He took me to the ocean oncet and flew me on those breakers all day. These here ones, though, they're over my head." That was all she said. She hung on three more long quiet days. Then the tide came in.

After the funeral, but before the truck returned for the bed, Leona stood in the shower mourning her mother, washing tears away with the soap. She stopped crying and felt of it again, then turned up the hot because she'd gone cold. She dressed for work and told Willy, "Don't give back the bed."

How did she know? But she did. In six months, she'd joined Granny. Willy took care of her; he didn't want a nurse between them, he wanted her company, just hers. Leona's went mainly to the bones. They had her on morphine, but she was glad to go.

After she died, Willy kept renting the bed. Denise and Charles couldn't get him to give it back. He had a tot of bourbon at night for his girls, then he crawled into it and slept. Living became a job, and he started having more than one tot. Three years later, when dogwood blossoms ghosted the woods behind the house, Willy had another bourbon, climbed into the hospital bed, and fell asleep to join his girls.

Denise found hers six years ago at a spa in Atlanta. When they put on the thick white bathrobe, her hand brushed the spot. Do everything, Denise told the doctors. They removed her breast, blasted her with x-rays, and pushed poison into her through a port. She lost weight with the nausea, and when her hair fell out, she got a real-hair wig, straighter and darker than her own. Cancer did a better make-over than any spa, she said. Last year, they said she was cured. "But you know what?" Denise said. "You're cured if you die of something else."

At the cashier, Jean awoke. She wrote a check for the groceries, surprised at this cartful of food from places she'd lived, surprised, too, at the way her handwriting stood on the lines, steady and familiar when nothing else was. As she carried out the groceries, she wondered idly if she'd be around to finish them.

She remembered cleaning out their mother's cabinets with Denise before selling the house. The gifts Jean and Bobby had brought—saffron, Rhine wine, that fine-ground German coffee—stood untouched, labeled with the year in Leona's schoolteacher writing.

Six days later, Jean finished the supper dishes and the hospital forms, and put a Post-It on the fridge so she wouldn't eat breakfast. Then she took a long bath and came out in purple-flowered silk, long and graceful. Bobby, sprawled on the bed, followed her with his eyes. She still looked like a queen, dark and shining. He'd taken off his workboots, but, on purpose and as usual, hadn't turned down the spread.

She lifted his heels and folded it. Usually she said something funny; Bobby's ignorance of bedspread behavior is a standing joke. "I thought about doing that," he said. "You've tried so hard to teach me to act civilized that I almost am." Jean smiled, a smile she had to work at, but didn't answer.

They thought about other things they'd taught each other. Then Jean really smiled, and Bobby did, too, although behind that thought was another, that tomorrow they might find out they'd learned and taught all they had time for. "Come to bed, baby," Jean said, already under the covers. She didn't have to coax him.

He was beat. Catch-up all week from the morning he'd missed, re-do's backed into next month. Not counting tomorrow. Bobby brushed his teeth, shucked his clothes, and crawled in. Then, as he crashed into sleep, Jean kissed him, the subtle signal that's all the long-married really need. "How you feelin'?" she asked.

He felt nothing, but he couldn't say so. Or he felt like he'd felt over Ramstein when the wheels of a C5A he was hitchhiking on locked up, and he had to help the green young pilot land. The cockpit was so quiet Bobby could hear his own heartbeat; he thought he could hear himself sweat. Though he felt like puking or praying, he spoke to the pilot evenly, confidently, the way Jean had talked to those football players. He knew the end would be fire and death. Knew it was all his fault, too: maybe his crew had missed a loose bolt or a slow leak.

His crew, hell; his crew was him, he was chief. He was responsible. Meanwhile, the pilot answered Bobby's questions, his voice cracking. Bobby could already see and hear them hitting the ground. He helped the kid keep the gauges straight while he prepared an apology for his posthumous court-martial. Then the gear came down, and the kid steered them out of the sky.

It took Bobby a week to stop waiting for a reprimand and a month to realize it was over. The wheels had just hung, a gremlin they could never replicate. Finally they replaced the hydraulics, gave her a shot of grease, and topped up the fluids. Damn thing never hesitated again.

This felt like that time in the air in the dark. And Bobby felt like that pilot. "We won't tell the girls till we know something," Jean decreed. But Bobby already knew something. He knew he had to prepare for the worst. Some part of him had already thought it through: get her to the hospital tomorrow, buy her casket, plan the service, pick the plot, pay the preacher, thoughts he drove away that wouldn't stay away.

He saw Jean's father sitting in his chair waiting three years to die and join Leona. Three years. He saw his own father throwing himself across his mother's coffin at the funeral home, crying and begging her to come back. He saw Willy giving Leona a back rub when you could count every rib. He remembered his father saying he couldn't do without his mother, saying she shouldn't have died first. He saw Willy feeding Leona one gray December afternoon, spooning grits into her because that was all she would eat. He remembered his father apologizing for letting his mother die.

He saw Willy carrying Leona to the bathroom. He saw Willy reaching around the sheets to give Leona a sponge bath, holding the sheets high to preserve her modesty because they were all there for Christmas, and she couldn't get up and work the shower and stand under it.

Bobby embraced Jean, brushed her forehead with his lips and put his hands on her in various places, trying to please her and also trying to see if he could manage to feel anything at all that would help him out. The new nightgown was good. Jean smelled like flowers. She was damp here and there from her bath, warm where he held her.

But Bobby just couldn't. Couldn't think about how to touch her, couldn't get started himself. It seemed wrong to have a good time the night before. "I can't, honey," he said, not saying the rest, why give her his worries on top of her own?

"I need you, Bobby," she said, muffled against his chest. "Tonight I need you. I want one night I was all there, one last night." This didn't help.

"I can't," Bobby said. "I want to, but I can't. Don't take it personal, Jean. You know you're not alone with this, don't you?"

"I know, Bobby," Jean said. But then she turned away, and he wasn't so sure. He didn't know that she turned away because even being near him kept her going, because it was better to cool off alone than simmer pointlessly, touching his sweet skin. She needed rest.

Hours later, though, Jean was still awake. She knew Bobby was, too; there is a sound, or a silence, your sleepless partner makes in the dark. She got up and pulled on her old flannel robe—purple silk was no protection from the lingering late-spring chill—and padded barefoot to the kitchen. She rummaged through the cabinets and rattled pots.

"Hey, Bobby," she said into the dark bedroom fifteen minutes later. "You still awake?" Knowing the answer, of course. "Brought you something." Bobby sat up, jammed a pillow behind his neck, and glanced at his service watch's cold green dial. Two-forty.

"I am," he said. "Against my better judgment."

"Me, too. Maybe this will help," she said, handing him a mug that spread heat into his hands.

"Careful," she said. "Spill it and you'll wish you believed in pajamas."

"Coffee?" he asked. Then he smelled the steam, correcting himself just as she answered, so they said together: "Hot chocolate."

"Real hot," he said. Then his mouth ran into something airy and odd. "What the hell?" he said. She cut on the light, laughing, and pointed at him in the dresser mirror, bearded with whipped cream and chocolate shavings. He licked his lips, laughing, too. She doused the light and kissed off the rest in the dark, wondering if that counted as eating after midnight. Then she sat beside him while he drank, watching, although she couldn't see.

"Mighty good," he said, imitating her slow drawl.

"Yeah," she said, and the way she answered made him know she'd heard his joke. "Old school. Hot milk and cocoa and sugar in a saucepan."

"Where's yours?"

"Can't."

"Oh, yeah." Her tombstone flashed before him, polished gray granite with deep black letters and dates, the year this year.

"Hot milk's supposed to help you sleep."

"I'll let you know. Or maybe I won't. If it works, I won't let you know, OK?"

She laughed again. The cocoa was rich and sweet, full of overtones and complication. Much better than that instant stuff. He'd forgotten how much better, hadn't had the real stuff since she brought it to him in bed those bitter early mornings in Germany.

Except then they'd had kids, and no time for shaved chocolate and whipped cream.

She sat Indian-style beside him on the bed, watching him, he felt it, instead of drinking with him as she had then. Wiesbaden or Ramstein? He couldn't remember. Then he could: Ramstein. The first time she did it was the day after he'd talked the kid down, after he'd bolted up in a sweat from the crash-and-burn nightmare that went on for weeks, always just before dawn and always the same.

Jean took the empty mug back and washed it, an ordinary daily thing she'd done a million times. While the mug drained, she cleaned the saucepan and wondered how many ordinary daily days they had after this one. By the time she came back to bed, Bobby was asleep, down deep and snoring. She pressed close and pulled his arm across her, his touch finally bearable.

They arrived early at a cold fluorescent waiting room decorated in stainproof blues and beiges and full of bright fake flowers and straggling houseplants. Then a nurse brought an ID bracelet and gown and took Jean through a steel door. Bobby got out and paced the parking lot.

He smoked fifteen of his half-dozen daily cigarettes and picked out funeral music. He thought about hospital beds, visiting nurses, deliveries of drugs and supplies. It was the rest he couldn't do, the things Jean would do if he got sick. She wouldn't mind how hard it went, how bad he looked, she'd go through it all, broth, bedpans, back rubs, and drugged naps. She'd make conversation, matter-of-fact and normal, or maybe even funny, instead of wordlessly mourning the whole time.

He remembered Leona crying in pain after surgery, her arm swollen and terrible because they'd cut away the nodes and muscles. The nurse murmured about exercises, and Leona refused. Then Willy pulled up his chair and talked her through them, using that teacher's tone, that coach's voice. Something else Bobby knew he couldn't do.

Jean had friends, women Bobby'd never met. Mrs. Fulbright was probably one. They'd help out, that's what women did. Leona's friends had come around even more at the end. They came to say goodbye, but they never said it. They made her laugh about old times instead. They brought flowers, but not too many. Not so many it looked like a funeral.

When Leona quit eating, they knew, but they still fed Willy. He ate the ladies' food and washed the containers. He thanked them constantly—when they picked up the containers, and when they brought them back refilled.

"They're great, but I can't talk to them," Willy said to Bobby one night when Leona drowsed on her drip. Jean and the girls were in Woodbine buying Easter clothes; Bobby'd gotten compassionate leave.

Willy's friends were all men, retired teachers like him. They never talked about anything personal. He didn't even know their wives' and girlfriends' names because they called them *the wife,* or *my girl.* "I can't talk to anybody but Leona about her dying," Willy said hoarsely. "And what would I say? Don't go? I know it hurts to stay, but don't go?"

The pollen-yellowed spring air caught in Bobby's throat, making his eyes and nose run, and he stepped inside for water. The room was still grim. He watched the nurses put people on hold and shuffle papers and wondered what would become of him and Jean, how they would make it through all the waiting rooms, much less the rest of it.

Bobby and Jean had been together longer now than anyone they knew. They didn't think alike, they didn't look alike, they didn't act alike, but they belonged to each other. They'd stuck it out through low pay, long labors, bad housing, world crises, teething, and teenagers. They loved each other, which meant a million things from *take out the trash* to *scratch my back* to *tell the truth.*

People talked about love as if it were a perfume that vanished when the other person left the room. People called marriage something to work at, which always made Bobby and Jean laugh when they heard it from some anorexic blonde actress or talk-show therapist.

"Yeah, hon," Bobby always said. "It's a *relationship.* You've got to work at those. Now get going, sweetie," he'd continue, swatting Jean on the butt. "Your work is to bring me food." And Jean swatted his butt right back and told him to get his own. He grinned at the thought.

Then the steel door swung open, revealing Jean. When she got close, she opened her shirt to show the bandage across her breast, too white on her brown skin, and said, "All gone." Before starting the biopsy, the doctor inserted a tube and threaded a wire, and the lump, a harmless cyst, collapsed like a leaky balloon.

"The girls would've worried for nothing," Jean said. But her voice wasn't right, her lips quivered. She came into his arms then, and he tried to be careful as he held her, sure that getting poked in such a sensitive place must hurt, sure that Jean would feel frailer than before. But she didn't, she felt just like herself, solid and sure.

Two nights later, Bobby sat up late, tweaking the estimate on a Dutch Colonial: Mrs. Fulbright's neighbor had seen his truck and called. After midnight, when he finally got to bed, Jean was still awake. "Bobby, are you all right?" she asked. They'd been tiptoeing around each other since the hospital.

She'd said she was fine now, but she wasn't. And Bobby couldn't stand down that quick, either. He was still in the ready-room, suited up. Worry's like smoking, easy to start and hard to quit. He was up to ten a day now and struggling.

"Are *you?*" he asked back. "I can't get over it," he said.

"Give yourself time," she answered, and Bobby grunted to say he was going to. "I'm right here, Bobby," Jean said. "It's OK."

Bobby said he knew that and turned over. At two a.m., though, he snapped out of another burial dream back into the familiar unfamiliar darkness of their room. She felt it in her sleep. She'd set her mind on him now, the way she used to set it on the girls when they were sick so she could get up before they called.

Bobby had battled back the dream's black smoke and sparks and undertakers. Then Jean's headstone appeared. When he moved close to read the second date, the dream evaporated, thank God. He shook his head, but the nightmare stayed stuck behind his eyes. He quit fighting it and got up. He poured himself some milk and sat at the kitchen table, wishing she'd join him.

The milk was cold and so was the kitchen. Goose bumps rose all over Bobby, who thought maybe pajamas wouldn't be so bad. The overhead light that fell bright on him darkened the table's scars and turned Bobby's bare hide sickly, bleaching the places his clothes usually covered, his unsunned shoulders, crotch, and thighs, and turning the milk anemic.

When Jean came looking for him, the light was low and warm. He'd lit an emergency candle and stuck it in a saucer. As she stepped up behind him, her flannel robe floated open. Underneath was her skin. She wound her left hand around his waist and put her right hand over his to help him stir. He could feel her everywhere, her breathing warmth, the muscles in her arm flexing against his as their two hands turned slow and steady.

The cocoa steamed and sent its fragrance into them; she put her chin over Bobby's shoulder to nuzzle his neck and scratchy cheek. Then he stopped stirring and turned to hold her, leaving her the wooden spoon, with which she continued stirring. She held him against her, stirring him, too. The robe slipped off, and he moved to catch it but missed. "Leave it," she whispered.

The candle lit and shadowed her, this beautiful geography he'd explored but would never finish learning. He thought of everything they'd passed across the table, newspapers, coffee cups, small talk, jokes, spats, laughter, trouble, the lingering looks longtime lovers give each other but can hardly bear to face, they see so much, they're so unguarded. They had to discuss it. He had to warn Jean he wasn't up to the job, he's not the man her father was. "I know that," she said. "That's why I married you."

"What're you talking about?"

"Oh, Daddy, he had his ideas. He went to college, where he met and married Mama, but college didn't teach him much about women—wives or daughters, either one. He didn't want Mama working, as if we could spare what she made. He didn't want Denise and me dating at all, much less low-class white boys," she said, shooting him a look and laughing.

"They never worked it out between them, how to be married. They fought all the time when we were growing up. Daddy was always waiting to start something.

"That's what I liked about you, Bobby. You weren't looking to fight. And even when you *had* to fight, you stayed calm."

"Calm? I was *scared.*"

"Maybe, but it didn't show. Remember that night in the field?"

"I couldn't believe you got out of the car."

"I couldn't believe you stayed so still and held me. That night was your night. I thought, 'I hope I can live up to this guy.'"

"God help us!" he said, laughing. "I thought I'd piss my pants. And then you went out and talked them down."

"It was easy once I knew them," she said. "I was scared, too, till then. It's what we don't know, Bobby," she said, putting her hand over his again, and, at last, looking into his eyes.

"I meant I don't think I could take care of you if you got sick," he said. "Like your father."

"I know what you meant, Bobby. But you could. I found out you could that night," she said. "I'll teach you the rest. Give you household skills that'll make your next wife very happy. I'm a teacher, after all."

"Don't talk like that," he said.

"I have to, Bobby. Taking care of someone isn't making the bed and cooking the food. That's easy. It's loving them and helping them lie easy until they leave. You can do that, Bobby. You've been doing it."

"Jean," he said. "You are my life."

"And you are mine," she said. "And one day we will lose each other. But not yet."

He filled her mug and threw a fistful of chocolate shreds on the whipped cream. "Real hot," he said, handing it over, but she drank anyway, burned her tongue, and fussed. Then he served himself.

"Bobby, don't. It's boiling," Jean said, touching his arm. "Let it cool." She set his mug beside hers and led him to bed. It wasn't sex any more, this reached Bobby like a premonition or revelation as they began. It was something that included skin but went beyond skin, and it had been so between them a long time.

When they came back from the beautiful bedroom, the mugs were just above body heat, the chocolate sweet and dusky. They sat and drank, and then they washed the dishes, standing side by side at the sink in a period of silence.

It was time to sleep. Jean fell down fast, one arm across the soon-to-follow Bobby, and Bobby slid into a good dream that didn't break. His life whispered something. They continued to hold.

Pour creme de menthe on the skin and add chocolate.

SHELLEY
JACKSON

The Marquis de Wonka

Shelley Jackson is the author of the short story collection The Melancholy of Anatomy, *the* hypertext classic Patchwork Girl, *several children's books, and* "Skin," *a story published in tattoos on the skin of 2,095 volunteers. Her first novel,* Half Life, *is forthcoming from HarperCollins. She lives in Brooklyn, New York, and teaches at the New School.*

I stand on the crumbling ramparts of the chocolate factory. Candyland stretches before me under a coppery sky, the chocolate plains striped with lengthening shadows. The gingerbread houses look a little tawdry in this light, the candy canes are gummy and pitted with age and warm weather. The climate has changed in recent years. Everything is on the verge of melting, every building slumps. The air reeks of cocoa and burnt sugar. The big rock candy mountain in the distance is a dark shadow behind the haze that rises from the valley. It is so hot that cinnamon bears leave sticky red tracks and herd animals like the gummy bears wake up glued together into one parti-colored mass that must be rolled into the river and sent downstream as a horror not to be borne, despite the peeping cries of the bears on the periphery. Almost more horrible are the dumb stares of those in the center watching us through the luminous forms of their mothers and brothers.

I hear the confused murmur of the crowd outside the gates, which never disperses, night or day. Willy Wonka is dead, they say, the chocolate factory is shut down, the universe is grinding to a halt. Willy Wonka is dead, his goatee points to the stars, and we are all alone.

231

■

We had stood outside the heavy gates, eyeing one another covertly. "He has a thing for little kids," remarked Veruca, our woman of the world. It was a strange thing to say, since we—the select—were all grown men and women (though youthful enough beside the elders who accompanied us). But no one uttered a protest. Indeed, there was something of the child about each of us. Veruca herself, older than the rest of us, was strangely attired in a stiff frock that rode up under her arms, baring her bitterly thin white legs. With her sour bony face she looked like an ill-tempered twelve-year-old. Stocky Violet presented a much different figure, yet the braids bouncing energetically around her shoulders gave her the appearance of an oversized toddler. Like a child, she was always playing with her mouth; anything handed her would find its way to that glossy orifice. Her eyes dreamy, she would taste the object, bite it gently, press its edges against her lips. Her fingers were always wet, the corners of her books were always bitten, the ends of her braids were sucked into points and left wet patches on her clothes. Then there was squat, energetic Mike Teavee, who wore a ten-gallon hat, Souvenir Of Texas, which was slightly too big for him and bent his ears out. Anyone taking in the crown of his hat and his diminutive red sneakers might give him a parental pat. Augustus Gloop, on the other hand, was even bigger than his stout parents, but he had such a soft, rosy, hairless complexion and small rosebud mouth that he looked more like a baby than a grown man. We made an interesting contrast, he and I, Charlie: thin, pale skinned and virginal.

■

A candy factory: what could be more innocent, more wholesome? Despite its dark towers, its menacing height, the narrow, inscrutable windows, the heavy, heavy gate with the heavy lock. "Come inside, my dears, you are welcome." One does not turn down an invitation from the factory. The Marquis was an odd but elegant figure in old-fashioned attire. Short and spry, capering nimbly about as he made his courtesy to us, he was not a figure to inspire alarm, yet there was something wayward in his eye that alerted me to some danger. What it was I could not imagine. The doors grated shut behind us and I jumped. My fellow guests—prisoners?—did not seem afraid. They chattered among themselves. "This way for the tour," chirped Wonka. We followed him. I was aware of a multitude behind and around us, but out of sight. Behind the scene, a steady powerful throbbing at the threshold of hearing.

∎

We hurried down pink serpentine corridors, passing countless doors, most closed, some ajar and affording glimpses of tall pipes and glistening machinery. I had the impression that something was continually being whisked out of sight as we approached. I quickly lost all sense of direction. The others giggled and jogged after the Marquis, puffing a little. Uncle Joe, shedding his years, seemed indefatigable, his hoary chin pointing like a compass at the flapping velvet tails through every twist and turn.

At length we arrived at a great arboretum, whose glass roof sheltered lush gardens and field grazed by chocolate bunnies (some of them very large!). A brown river surged between the green banks. My companions murmured and cooed, the Marquis bowed, and hurried on. More doors, more machines.

∎

I was shown to my room, which was a confection of pink and brown, with a mosaic floor of candy hearts. The stucco-seeming walls, with their rich powdery colors, turned out to be marzipan. Candy canes hooked the drapes to either side of the hard-candy windows, which let in a swirled light but did not disclose a view. I could not even tell, after the twists and turns of the corridor, whether my window faced out, or gave on to the central courtyard. Somehow this mattered to me.

I went to Uncle Joe's room, which was next door, and sat on his bed while he pottered about the room, plucking cotton candy from the bedding, licking the walls. "How can you?" I exclaimed. "Doesn't something in you rebel against this luxury? Can't you see this place is rotten, rank and rotten? And Wonka! An organ-grinder's monkey, grinning and shitting!"

"I'm sure you exaggerate," said Uncle Joe idly, gnawing a bed knob. "Why don't you accept your good fortune? It's all in fun, and it tastes good." I rose, he held the door open for my exit, saying, "Have you sampled the hinges? They're very nice."

I left his room in a temper, but by the time I gained my own, my fever had subsided. Uncle Joe was as fond of novelties as a child, but the dazzle would fade and he would see what I had glimpsed at once, that all the sweetness concealed something terrible.

∎

We gathered the next day in the arboretum for the continuation of our tour. We have finally met the workers: chocolate santas, teeming and identical. They are scantily dressed in their foil wrappers, many of which are torn away in part, revealing the smooth brown flanks with their greasy sheen and even at times (though I look away) their rudimentary genitals, which they take no pains to conceal. Violet leaned over and kissed a santa on the forehead, as if he were a child, and I saw her tongue slip out to taste him.

∎

I have learned that the chocolate river is directed throughout the factory, and bears away the waste products of fudge-making, taffy-pulling, lolly-pop-pouring, and all. A stream of offal, brown with streaks and thickenings of other colors and little scuds of malt and marshmallow surges foaming out of great pipes in the factory wall, and winds away downhill until it dissipates in the stinking marsh at the bottom of the valley. In fact, while we were looking at the current, there was a disturbance downstream, and a number of santas detached themselves from our party and hurried that way. Apparently poachers from outside sometimes plunge into the stream of offal and make their way against the tide through the great pipes, pulling themselves through with metal hooks they drive into the sides. There is usually a little air at the top of the pipe; not always. Sometimes they drown or succumb to the curious gases this fluid gives off, and their bodies come floating out again, but those that make it inside find rich hunting grounds, and may easily fill their bags and make the quicker trip back out to their families. I do not know what happens to those caught poaching the chocolate bunnies. The santas seize them and bind them, and they are carried off into the remote parts of the factory. Wonka will not say what becomes of them.

∎

I am distressed by the indiscriminate appetite of my comrades. The Marquis has not invited us to sample his wares—indeed, he says very little, but watches us closely—yet they taste everything, yea, chew the very walls! And have grown too familiar with the santas, who seem to be a race without decency.

∎

Augustus lumbered though the candy plants, snapping off the tips and putting them in his mouth. I had the impulse to stop him, but a great languor kept me where I was. I had the feeling this had all already happened, and there was nothing that would stop it. I looked at the Marquis. He had risen to his toes, alert as a bird. His eyes burned as Augustus stooped to the river.

∎

Wonka was showing us the stained rock candy windows. Disturbing scenes were depicted there, pink and brown bodies writhing in obscene embrace. Veruca giggled. I averted my eyes from the windows and studied the colored light on the floor beneath. My reverie was interrupted by a colossal roar. Wonka paused, his finger in the air, and then continued to speak, though we could hear shrill cries in the distance. Someone came pattering down the hallway, opening doors. A santa entered and scurried up to Wonka. "Ah!" the Marquis exclaimed brightly, rising to the tips of his toes as he pirouetted to face us. "The south wing has collapsed. Please excuse me." And with a wink and a secret smile, he strode out of the room, coattails busily flapping, the santa scurrying after him.

"One might almost think he wanted the wing to collapse," said Mr. Teavee, dourly. "The man's not well."

"Maybe he did," said Uncle Joe, "Maybe it is all part of his plan. How can we know what the Marquis is thinking?"

Mr. Teavee snorted and turned away, adjusting his crotch.

We were left to find our own way out of that portion of the factory. When we at last shuffled outside, or rather, into the arboretum, the air was thick with chocolate powder and we all began to cough. We judged it best to retire to our rooms, and all did so.

∎

We were selected. Why? The santas gossip and titter over me, but as yet, they leave me alone. Yet I have heard strange noises, seen strange things. I am well fed. Fed, perhaps, a little too well—on candy, what else? Surfeited, I crave the cabbage and potato soup of my childhood. My flesh grows meltingly soft. I have never been so fat. Yet I am malnourished. My hair falls out. It is as though it has nothing solid to hold onto anymore in this body of ooze and sludge.

∎

Thick, delicious smells rim our nostrils with fuchsia and brown. When I blow my nose at night, I lay two substantial cords into my handkerchief, swirled with colors like candy canes.

∎

Where has Wonka gone? Something strange is happening. The interrupted tour has never been resumed. The dust that lay so thick on everything for days, a soft bed that remade itself every night, has long since washed away in the regular rains (synthetic, of course). For days, cocoa rivulets in the gutters, wending their way through the garden to the river. I later found that small collapses often occur in the factory, which is very old. A roof caves in, a wall topples. A few workers may be killed; they are duly mourned, but production continues, the turbines roll, the baths seethe, the great teeth grind; the factory pulses with vitality. Yet Wonka does not return, and in his absence, the others grow complacent and riotous.

∎

If they could, they would eat the very walls, and leave nothing to hold the roof up! I partake of the chocolate, there is nothing else to eat, but I ready myself and sit down to it as to a regular meal, and eat neatly and quickly, then rise and go on my way. I say on my way: I take daily walks. I am trying to learn my way around the factory. Oddly, I always find myself back in the arboretum. There is no order to the building that I can discover.

∎

There is a funny light in Uncle Joe's eyes and red spots in his cheeks. He is more antic than ever, asking questions about everything, trying to interest me in the workings of the factory, which by now has ceased to arouse even mild curiosity—I loathe it and explore it only to find the way out. The only subject which still holds some interest for me is that of the Marquis himself.

∎

On one of my nightly perambulations, I found Veruca's parents standing side by side on a shelf, dressed in clingy metallic suits like the santas and wrapped in tinted cellophane, big bows over their heads. I slashed the cellophane and pulled them out, only to be berated violently for my pains. I don't understand.

∎

Something has occurred which has proved my fears about the Marquis all too well-founded, and has thrown me into miserable confusion. It was evening, I was restless and, wanting company, yet finding Uncle Joe not in his quarters, as so often these days, I set out in search of him. A santa darted past me in the hallway; I stopped him and asked, but received only a giggle in return. I followed him, nonetheless, and found myself in a room full of glass piping like many others. But what a sight met my eyes! There was Wonka, at last, but something else claimed my attention. Uncle Joe was naked and spread-eagled, tied at wrists and ankles to two glass pipes full of cherry syrup, the meager flesh on his buttocks sagging on the bone. The santas kneaded his buttocks, their tiny hard fingers leaving deep prints in the flesh, which sprung back only slowly. The Marquis approached. They spread Uncle Joe's buttocks. Wonka used a peppermint stick to part the wisps of gray hair, then lodged the tip against Uncle Joe's asshole.

"Stop!" I shouted, and stepped boldly into the room. "For shame! To use an old man so. Stand back!" I commanded, slapping the santas aside and striding through the crowd. "And you, sir! How dare you!" Wonka said nothing, but watched me with a curious expression. I felt a certain pride (how briefly!) as I snapped Uncle Joe's bonds with one tug—it was surprisingly easy—and wrapped my pajama shirt tenderly around his old shoulders. With what astonishment did I see the look of rage he turned on me as he threw off the shirt! He castigated me thoroughly for my "intrusion," as he called it, into his private affairs. The upshot was that I, Charlie, had to do up the ties again around my dear old uncle's wrists and ankles. The peppermint stick returned to its post; too slow to avert my eyes, I witnessed its surprisingly smooth entry. I hurried through the jostling crowd, pinched and patted into a state of shame. I fell once and one of the number yanked down my pajamas, revealing my condition to Wonka's gaze, and it was to his giggle that I scrambled up, fastening my pants, and reeled out of the room.

I understand nothing. Does Uncle Joe owe some private debt to Wonka, which he must repay by debasing himself? What crime could such a mild old man commit, to deserve such punishment?

∎

One by one my companions have abandoned their regular dress. I alone am fully clothed, though I confess the sultry air in this dungeon makes clothing hard to bear. I alone? I forget Wonka. He is always neatly attired.

∎

I sit writing late at night in my little cubbyhole, from which I have removed all frippery of sugared pansies, jimmies, and nonpareils, and pause from time to time to listen to one of the strange noises (a low laugh, a throaty gulping) that penetrates my remote corner of the chocolate factory. The floor of my room trembles incessantly. I rarely see Uncle Joe anymore. Why do I resist, when everyone else has yielded with all signs of happiness? Why am I here? I rise from my desk and leave my room.

∎

Augustus Gloop spends all his time soaking in the lukewarm shallows of the chocolate river, almost submerged and snorting like a hippopotamus, or standing and spewing brown showers into the air, which fall like rain on the streaked globe of his naked body. He has mud fights with the santas. Or chases the gummi fish and comes up with them wriggling in his teeth. I think he has forgotten how to speak. His mother and father sit under a picnic umbrella in the sugar garden. They offer one another bonbons, take sips of lemonade. They put me in mind of a music box or a wind-up clock. The frequent (timed) storms of rain and rock candy hail have shredded the picnic umbrella, which in any case was made of frilled paper, so that only the tines stand out, from which snippets of damp tissue sadly droop, and Mr. and Mrs. Gloop are regularly watered down. Their hair, their skin sparkles (rather prettily) with sugar crystals, and every time it rains the crystals melt a little, then harden again into a glassy veneer that is perceptibly thicker every time I go by. I tap the glass and see an irritable look sweep over Mrs. Gloop's face; she never had time for me, and she does not want to be interrupted. The Gloops are becoming candy pops. Do they know what is happening to their son? I am worried about him; I suspect unspeakable things. I have seen him drag his huge mass onto the shore, and lie there on his stomach, his Himalayan buttocks propped up, looking back over his shoulder (at whom? at what?) with a look I hesitate to interpret, lest I do him an injustice, but in which I can only read expectancy, and the most unabridged lust. I have seen strange prints in the mud, not human ones.

■

Looking around me, I am appalled by our fatted faces. We are pink and wrinkled as the soft pile of a sleeping man's genitals. Or swollen like Gloop *père*, who resembles a diseased apple, with glossy cheeks and a nose like a blob of matter forced out through a small hole under pressure from the fermenting pulp within, then plumped. His eyebrow hairs are singly erect; the eyes recessed and dull, glancing anxiously but unfocusedly about. All this increasingly difficult to make out, of course, behind the hard candy coating whose transparency is impaired by a multitude of cracks, each bearing some reflected fragment of Mr. Gloop's sad face.

■

They whisper about me.

■

A brown fountain sports in the center of a lawn. Chocolate bunnies hop across the unnaturally even grass, dipping their sealed muzzles to the blades in pantomime. Veruca sits naked, all angles, in a giant tulip, its thick blades curving around her. She seems to be made of white chocolate. Despite the rich food, her hard limbs, in which muscle and bone may easily be distinguished, have barely softened. As I approach, I see she holds a squirrel to her teats; its defanged jaw is fastened on her nipples, which are unexpectedly large and spongy on her boyish chest. Another squirrel comes flouncing across the lawn and lands neatly on her lap, attaching itself to her other nipple. Veruca sits upright; I believe she fancies herself a queen on her throne.

■

One dark night, attracted by the light, I came upon Mike Teavee shooting one of his videos. Mr. Gloop lay helpless while Violet sucked on his candy-coated cock. This was before all such small protuberances were smoothed over by his thick, glassy crust.

■

Even I have yielded to Violet. In an empty hallway, on one of my nocturnal walks, I came upon her. Her eyes had a purple glint and her mouth worked incessantly on her gum. Her lips were elastic and gleaming. I should not have stopped, but I was lonely, why not admit it—where is Uncle Joe?—and in a second she had fallen to her plump knees in the corridor. Eyes shining, she spit her gum into her hand, stuck it behind her ear, and unzipped my fly. Those jaws! She sucked the very soul out of my astonished organ and for a second my entire being seemed aligned like an arrow and poised to plunge between those purple lips. I yielded up my sum of sperm and more; I thought she would suck my balls up through my cock, but she opened her mouth and let my stretched tube spring back. Then she popped her gum in her mouth again, and sauntered away. I returned to my room, and alone in my bed, cradling my shrunken testicles in confusion and remorse, I wept.

∎

Gloop can no longer support himself, on the rare occasions he pulls himself out of the chocolate river, but slithers along the wall, leaving rich brown streaks behind him, as if he were wearing away his own considerable substance.

∎

One figure passes through these halls unsullied. I have never seen a smudge of chocolate on the hem of his velvet coat, and I know without looking that the dusting of snow on his shoulders is dandruff, not powdered sugar. Seeing what has become of us here, I esteem him, now, for the very qualities that at first made me uneasy. His briskness, his brusqueness, the sudden swerves of his wit only deepen my admiration for him, here where everything is languid and slow. As for what passed between Wonka and Uncle Joe, well, I know my uncle better now. Here in the factory, we all get what we deserve.

∎

I awoke from a dream and looked about me wildly. "We don't need to force you," the chocolate santas had said, in their shimmering metallic whispers. "You will yield of your own accord."

∎

The sights I have seen this night! Woken by a storm that by now I knew was inside, not outside the factory, I descended the stairs into the arboretum. Twice as I made my way down the wind whirled up against me and drove me against the wall; clinging to the stones, I made my way through clouds of whipped cream, my face and hands lacerated by sugar crystals. At the bottom of the stairs the winds suddenly ceased, though when I looked up I could see the storm still raging, and varicolored blobs and sparkling whole crystals fell around me as I forced a path through the sticky greenery. The scene was dimly and generally illuminated by the factory lights far above, but sporadic flashes of lightning disclosed peculiar tableaux. Every hollow and grotto in the bushes was occupied by santas, masturbating, lashing one another with licorice whips, inserting gum balls in various orifices and popping them out into one another's mouths, stuffing fondant up their fundaments and shitting candy rose petals and leaves with practiced apertures. They paid no attention to me and I did my best to pay none in return, though the fading prints on my startled retinas were hard to ignore.

I gained the river, and parted the brush, looking for Augustus. I saw him at last. Massive as he was, the black figure that stood over him dwarfed him. The tell-tale bifurcated silhouette of its long ears identified the figure at once: it was a chocolate bunny. Again and again it thrust against Gloop's mountainous rump.

∎

Violet's parents, always meek, have rolled themselves in the mud by the river until they were brown all over, then gone and crouched very still in the grass with the other bunnies. I believe they were bagged by poachers, who must have had a nasty shock on Easter morning.

∎

One tries to make sense of things; one tries, I don't know why, to hold something together. I feel more prim and pedantic than ever, taking notes in my antiquated script, pulling each letter tight. I feel like a kind of crystal: hard, clear, regular, discrete. "Rock candy," suggests Uncle Joe. No.

∎

I have tried to speak to Veruca, but when I get too close to her the squirrels chase me away.

■

I came upon one of Mike's videos playing to a roomful of quiet santas. Close-up: Violet lifted her head, her chin smeared with chocolate. Mrs. Teavee's thighs were coated with syrup; hot fudge rolled down her crack and flowed from between her knees, a slow black satiny river. Mrs. Teavee spurted a black jet, gouts of chocolate bursting reluctantly from her piss-hole and spattering Violet's face. Violet clamped her mouth over the fountain and drank.

Cut: Violet propelled chocolate-covered malt balls from her cunt into Mrs. Teavee's mouth, then strapped on a chocolate bar, knobbly with nuts and oozing caramel, and rammed it down Mr. Teavee's throat. The santas sighed and pawed one another. I fled to my room, and lay on my bed, chewing my pillow, for hours. I shall do without one in the future.

■

Augustus floats by in the chocolate river, his paws resting on his chest like a sea otter's, his body decaying slowly but peaceably. Chocolate already runs in his veins, forms sweet dark clots in his arteries. He is bigger than ever, a human island, spongy and barely solid, no more than a swampy, stringy thickening in the cocoa. The santas gather giggling on the shore. They begin hurling hard candies at Augustus, striped red-and-white bonbons, and these embed themselves in his side while he utters weird weak coos of protest, soft sounds like baby laughter, and bleeds slow blobs of nougat chunky with what looks like candied fruit. Gummy fish sluggishly surface and lick up the nougat with lazy passes of their tongues.

■

I have only to imagine fleeing the factory (floating out on the river, dropping off the ramparts onto a cushion of cotton candy) to know there is no real escape. The people outside are no different from us, they just have a little more room for dessert.

Beyond the factory is still the factory. Everyone's looking for the golden ticket.

∎

One night in a remote corridor, I rounded a corner and saw Wonka's small figure hurrying ahead of me. A band of santas hastened after him. Perhaps he had another collapse to attend to; the walls seemed to be caving in everywhere. Often the fondant foundations would shift and a trickle of chocolate powder would spill out of a crevice and fall in a plume toward the floor. Poachers had been seen more frequently as well, and there were cracks in the ceiling of the arboretum. Yet I made bold to stop him. "Sir," I said, "Let me be blunt. Terrible things happen here, of which I would like to believe you know nothing. I throw myself at your feet in supplication. Please, do not take a young man's innocence, and leave him with nothing, do not let him be forced into atrocities whose temptations he loathes, despite the example set by others. I am hard pressed. Give me some sign that you approve my efforts!"

The face he turned to me was strained. A tic transfigured it at intervals. "I have very little time," he said. I made my apologies again. "You don't understand," he said. A tear stood in his eye—not, I thought, a tear of sadness, but of profound weariness. With a quick movement he caught it on a fingertip and held it out to me. "Taste it," he said. "It's sweet!" He capered about, exposing his pointed dick to the santas and giggling. They drew back, and looked at him strangely.

∎

A new sound has joined the throbbing of the machines. The people are pounding on the gate. The murmur of their voices rises and falls. Word of the outside world has reached us, I don't know how, and the news is strange. Swedish fish practice to be piranhas, grinning at bathers. Gummy mice are grown furtive;

they roll in dirt to dull their jewel tones and dig burrows in the fields of chocolate. They sneak into kitchens, scavenging chips of peppermint candy for purposes of their own. Candyland is astir, fecund, its motley inhabitants complaining, confiding, buying and selling in a hundred accents. A woman has given birth to a chocolate bunny. It is said she was startled by an Easter basket. Sluggish chocolate rain begins to fall, oozing off the bottom of chocolate clouds. All the candy animals are restless, the gummy worms coil and uncoil in the cellophane grass, and marshmallow Peeps have been found strangled to death, worms knotted around their yellow throats.

■

There are skirmishes. The santas foray beyond the walls and come to grips with the townspeople, and there are casualties. I have found my way to the ramparts, and from the walls I can see a corpse, a vulture's beak buried deep in its chocolate entrails. Candy engines putt-putt, dropping candy shrapnel; the santas are knee-deep in chocolate mud and flak. Here within, the santas are restive, and Wonka has disappeared again. For the first time, the great machines stop. They are silent for hours, and everyone is nervous and unhappy—yes, even I—until the rumble begins again.

■

Uncle Joe joined me as I stood on the walls, watching the crowd below. As the sun set, a restless, jostling crowd formed around a giant chocolate bunny. It was hollow. There were flames spurting out of its eyes, the smell of burnt chocolate on the air, and between its paws, a glowing aperture. By this gate stood a dark-chocolate santa—filled, I surmised, with liqueur—who coaxed a drop out of his nether spigot into each supplicating mouth as it passed through. The air was thick with a fog that stained cloth and coiled oilily around my legs. It was hard to breathe. The warm air seemed on the verge of setting at any minute, and had already solidified at the edges of the scene. Renegade santas in torn wrappers, triangular shreds of foil still stuck in their melting flesh, shouldered through the crowd, pressing people into line.

Then faces began to turn our way. A wave went through the crowd, and it began moving toward us. I took a step back, looking about me. Uncle Joe seized my arm and pointed.

Wonka stood on the dark ramparts, his small penis exposed and erect, its peculiarly pointed head silhouetted against the stormy skies. He looked like a sort of gargoyle. He spoke giddily and inaudibly, jigged a little on the worn princess heels of his boots, laughed. Suddenly, he ejaculated, a few marshmallow gobbets that the wind unreeled stickily and whisked away. I felt something burning under my ribs. It might have been pity. It might have been indigestion.

∎

I had admired Willy Wonka. I had loathed the factory. But Wonka *was* the factory. If there was evil in the factory, it was in him; if there was good in him, it was in the factory as well. The factory was no farther from Wonka than the answer from the question, the servant from the master, the candy from the tooth. Temptation and judgment, submission and mastery, were two sides of one gumdrop. No baited the trap for yes, yes lay down with no and gave birth to pretty please with sugar on top and all its unappetizing permutations. Fair was foul and foul was fair and it was the one on top who cried uncle. There was no virtue. My innocence was grossly knowing, my resistance nothing but an invitation. A golden ticket—which had brought me, precisely, this.

∎

Balancing on the wall, the Marquis teetered toward me. "The chocolate factory will use you up, Charlie," he said, quelling a tic with a monstrous effort. "You will burn, like the filament of a bulb. As I have done. Its demands are imperious. It is afire with libertine fancies, brimming with invention, knocking and seething with production. It has been my pleasure to think myself its master. It will now be my pleasure to give way." He giggled. "Last night a bunny buggered me," he said, "And I liked it."

"Resist!" I said, catching his hands in mine. "Oh, sir, resist!"

He freed his hands. "Resistance and submission both have their pleasures, and it is the masters of the one who are the virtuosos of the other. But you know that already." Behind us, the santas were gathering, a muttering throng blocking our retreat.

The Marquis looked back at the santas, a half-smile on his face. "It is time." He handed me his cane. He stripped hastily and plunged among the jostling santas, a pale, saintly figure gliding unsteadily in a hip-high sea. Then the Marquis de Wonka disappeared with his workers into the bowels of the factory.

■

The crowd below sways back and forth. An unearthly wail rises to my ears. "Seize the factory!" I hear. "Wonka is dead!" "He's mad!" "He's gone! Storm the gates!"

■

Santas gather on all sides of me, tugging on my pants and shirttail. They are chanting. I catch snatches of rhyming syllables but no sense. I stagger to and fro, laughing, and place my hand on two of the indistinguishable heads, paternally, but also to keep my balance. I feel like Gulliver. They begin to undress me.

Uncle Joe mounted the ramparts. "Gone, my people? Wonka gone? Why, of course not," shouted Uncle Joe. Behind him, two santas were working the diminutive coat over my shoulders, while two more plied a shoehorn and wedged me into the tight shoes.

I took the hat myself and set it on my head. Then they drew me to the ramparts.

The crowd hushed.

CHERYL A.
TOWNSEND

The Silk Blouse

Cheryl A. Townsend was the editor of Impetus *magazine and owner of Cat's Impetuous Books & stuff in Kent, Ohio (www.the-hold.com/impetus/index. html). Now she reads her back stock and engages in drive-by shootings with her camera. Her poetry and photography appear regularly on* The Hold *and* Thunder Sandwich *ezine sites. She recently starred in the art film* Jesus & Her Gospel of Yes, *which won the Best Experimental Film Award in the Las Vegas leg of the New York Film Festival. She is much heavier than in her last bio.*

He saw it as soon as he walked through the doors. A blouse. Facing the aisle that led to his reason for being there. That blouse. It made him forget his reason. It made him remember her. She wore a blouse just like it last night. He started thinking about last night as he stood in the aisle. He was staring at the blouse. It was staring back. With her eyes. With her hair down on it. With her laughter filling it. He touched it. Felt the softness of the silk. Felt the softness he knew was hers. He imagined touching her. He wished he had. He was smiling at the blouse, standing in the aisle. His hand rubbing the material. Smiling. He felt as intoxicated with the memory as he did when she was there. When she sat across from him. Drinking coffee and eating chocolate cheesecake. She swore it was the best chocolate cheesecake she had ever eaten. It was the way she slid that fork full of chocolate in. She just held it there. Like a wine taster would their wine. She savored it. Closing her eyes. Kittenly content. He was enthralled at watching her. It was so innocent. So sexual. He wanted to touch her.

Touch her arm. Her cheek. Just to touch her. Just to feel a piece of that euphoria. To share something so sweetly decadent. To share her. He watched her. He felt a strange longing he had never experienced before. Feeling so at ease in this simple delight they were, somehow, sharing. Realizing he had never been so intimate with a woman as then. Marveling at how naïve she was at the effect of her abandonment. Her enjoyment. The silkiness of the blouse felt like the smoothness of the cheesecake. He fantasized hand feeding it to her. How his fingers would feel in her mouth. His finger with all the creamy chocolate. That warm, soft, delightfully moist cheesecake. Her eyes closed. Enjoying it. His finger. Cheesecake. Her mouth.

"Is there something I can help you with, sir?"

He was standing in the aisle. He had an erection. He was fondling a blouse.

He was caught.

He couldn't wait to tell her.

from # Bogeywoman

Jaimy Gordon's third novel, Bogeywoman, *was published by Sun & Moon in 1999. In 1991, she won an Academy-Institute Award for her fiction from the American Academy of Arts and Letters. Her other works include the book* She Drove Without Stopping *(Algonquin), the novella* Circumspections from an Equestrian Statue *(Burning Deck), a narrative poem,* The Bend, The Lip, The Kid *(Sun), and the underground classic* Shamp of the City-Solo *(McPherson & Co.). With Peter Bickle, she translates from the German, most recently* Hermine: An Animal Life, *a novel by Maria Beig (New Issues Poetry and Prose, 2004).*

In Crazyland the craziest is queen, in Hare-Rohring adolescent wing everybody loved the see-through princess best, including me. And not just because Emily was Miss Dying Popularity. Talk about ugly-cute—she was the ugly-cutest of all the world's cute-uglies, something between a bug and a baby bird, with those thready limbs and great big eyes shining out of their boneholes, a no-nose with yellow freckles on it and bucked teeth that pushed the short upper lip out of her tight face like a little beak. The starving whiteness around her freckles made her skin sort of shine, and I never detected in her—it takes one to know one, so believe me I looked—one flyspeck of showmanship in her sincere desire to disappear. She was more like the embarrassed usherette at her own crazy play—things had gotten out of hand, if she'd known she would never have invited herself to be born. Artless is what she was. I call her my see-through princess because you sort of had the feeling you could gaze into her and see every lump and

251

bubble, see all the organs where they lay and the heart where it clenched and relaxed, clenched and gave up the fight again. Every few weeks they carried her off to her bed and locked her in there and fed her through a tube. She was patient with this treatment.

She was brave and good, old Emily, and though refusal was her middle name, her starved muscles somehow held up their end when we Bug Motels went on mission. She was like Joan of Arc compared to the fuddy boys in our set. She had only this one problem, that food so disgusted her she was doomed to starve herself to death. And when they rolled her off to her bed once a month or so to forcefeed her, her limbs hung over the edge of the gurney like long wax tapers that had been left too long in the heat. She glowed in the dark, the white and yellow curls nodded around her small face like petals of some rakish compositae, and the first time this happened, I mean the first time they ever rolled her by me which happened to be the first time I ever saw her, though her neck was too weak to hold up her head, the little beak in her cute-ugly bug face opened and she smiled at me. She smiled at me I can only say hopefully, though we hadn't been introduced. For some reason old Emily loved me at first sight. And she didn't even need me—she had cooing nurses to throw away.

So I knew she wouldn't scream or snitch or throw me out. Still it wasn't that easy to get in to her, if the Regicide wouldn't help. I had to stand behind my own door, holding a potted cactus that Merlin had accidentally sent with my stuff—now I was glad I'd kept the thing—and from there I peered through the crack between the hinges in the direction of Emily's room, number 307, until the nurse's aide, Delilah not Reggie, came out of it pushing the big rattlybones housekeeping cart with the dirty linen bin trailing behind it, and turned east. I winged the cactus in a perfect blooper pitch over her head so it crashed off her starboard bow, went rolling off in three prickly balls and she froze and stared up at the ceiling—and meanwhile I ran like hell (in my silent tracker's moccasins) to slip through Emily's door before its hydraulic moan came to an end.

How Love Got Me Out of There

She lay there exactly like a wasting princess in some fairy-tale, right down to the snowy counterpane with her pipecleaner elbows on it. Her bottom half, where it went under the crackling sheets, made hardly a bump, and under the bunched-around skirt of her quilted pink I ♥ CHOCOLATE bathrobe (a present from the nurses) she was like one of those half-dollies that housewives freakish for chintz use to cover the toaster—I mean she was there to the waist and nothing underneath, not even the blank crotch that drives you to distraction in a plastic dolly when you finally get alone with her and take a look. So let it be declared that, from the first mingling with Emily, who I believe had a strong crush on me, mine was a respectfully crotchless love for her crotchless self, you'd be afraid of breaking that Popsicle stick body just by jiggling the bed next to it, let alone lying down on top of it. True, I always had designs on Emily, but they were on her mind not her body. I mean she wasn't quite twelve, her bug face was more ugly than cute when you really looked into its caves, and her body was not even there. All the same I wanted to finger the wolfram filament of her incandescence, wanted to know to its hot wire core her amazing lack of appetite. Piggery I have always understood, especially in the famine of sex, but not that other thing, the pure *want* of hunger, a click in the throat and disgusted blank in the gut like a caterpillar who unless it lands on a muskmelon leaf doesn't even know the world is food.

"Hey Em, how you doing?" I whispered as the door whooshed shut behind me. "Ursie!" she peeped, her beak opened up a crack and I could tell she was glad to see me. "Say Em, want me to sneak you up sumpm? How bout a comic or a, er, a Three Musketeers or sumpm?" I whispered. I would have been glad to crawl through enemy fire on my belly to the card and candy shop in the lobby and give up my last nickel to see her fall; I didn't want to believe in her purity unless I absolutely had to. But she was as ashamed of not eating as I was jealous of it, which gave me a funny feeling it might be true.

Emily's face crumpled in a smile that pulled the pale freckles even wider over her little bulb of a nose. "That would be nice since it was from you but I prolly couldn't eat it," she said sheepishly, and the tops of her ears pinked up, which was something to see, against the yarzeit-candle color of the rest of her.

"They're going to keep you here till you eat. You better eat. How come you don't eat?" I asked bluntly.

"It looks good but then it don't go down," she said, describing more of life's favors than she knew. "At first it tastes like a hamburger or whatever it is, but then it gets sticky, real sticky like I'm eating…" Her voice got thin as a piece of spaghetti just talking about it and then I heard a soft click—her throat closed, her lips pulled back and I could see all her rotten little teeth. "And I got to spit it out," she finally said, "or throw up."

I shouldn't have asked for more but I couldn't help it: "Like you're eating *what*?" "Like I'm eating b.m.," she whispered. "Oooo," I said. I saw a human dumpling glowing on a plate where a hamburger just had squatted, and, like that, her case looked hopeless. But then I recognized the object I was staring at. "A Baby Ruth could be a poop," I said. "And nothing looks better than that. Hey, that's what makes you want to eat it—cause it looks like a nice piece of poop." Emily laughed, her big eyes widened like happy clams in their red rims and I thought I was getting somewhere.

"Sure," I argued. "You know it's true. O'Henrys too. Must be everybody wants to eat something that looks like poop. You better not tell Foofer I said that." "I wouldn't never," Emily said. She stared up at me and got that grave little soap flake of light in each eye like Joan of Arc in the classic comic. "Tootsie Rolls too," I pursued. "And Mounds." Emily nodded. "And Fifth Avenue." Emily twisted her nosebulb and shook her head—"Not so poopy," she said. She never ever went along with a queer idea for the sake of the conversation, not even to save her skinny life. "Oh come on—if it's chocolate in a bar it's poop. You gotta admit." Her head was still fanning stubbornly back and forth on its baby-bird neck but she was grinning a little.

"Come on, say it. When I eat a Clark Bar I'm thinking poop, umm umm good, and so are you, so is everybody. Now listen, Emily, never mind Foofer, if you tell any dreambox mechanic in this whole joint I said that, I'll never speak to you again." "I wouldn't never." "Cause I'm getting a new one." Emily blinked at me. "A new dreambox mechanic. Well, anyhow I'm going to ask for her." I waited for Emily to ask me who, but she didn't. "You know, the one you brought to Bertie's bathroom when O got her head stuck. What was her name." Emily didn't choose to tell me. "Er, Doctor Zuk," I craftily answered myself.

"You can't just ask for somebody," Emily said. "Why not?" "You're sposed to work with who you got. Like in O.U.S.O.B. Besides I think Doctor Zuk don't have no regular patients." "How come?" "She just goes around talking to you and writing stuff down. I think maybe she's famous." *No dreambox adjustor too beautiful on her horse*—she was famous. Why do they say *My head swam*—my head drowned, wave-dragged, glug glug, over stone shoals of hunger, sodden sponges of disgust. She was famous. I was never going to get her or be her. Her swirling bluegreen atmospheres of confidence, that equestrienne spotlight she rode in, the mermaid spangles on her brassiere—it all made sense now that she was famous. I double drowned for envy: she had greatness, and she was studying other people, not me.

"How d'you know all that?" "I ast." *My head swam*—my dreambox bobbed emptily on the waves, like a bait float. "Why'd you ask?" (Emily Nix Peabody, refusal was her middle name, never asked anything she didn't really want to know.) "She's old but she's so purty. I never saw anyone like her before." "What's she famous for? Is she a dreambox adjustor?" "I din't ask." "Didn't ask!" I stared at Emily so severely that she added, "Prolly," in a small scared voice. "She's from Europe," Emily recollected, "—or somewhere—" I suddenly recalled, for my part, I was here to save my see-through princess, not to bully her. My ears itched hotly for shame.

Yes I was here to feed my seventy-nine-pound princess as well as to milk her. I loved her. I always meant to fatten her up, no mistake about that. "Hey Em. Don't you ever want to put sumpm in your mouth?" I asked, "just to suck it? Not to eat it?" She wrinkled her little spotty-toadstool nose. "Sure," I said, "like some things just say *put me in your mouth* as soon as you look at them. You don't know what I mean? Honest?"

I looked around the room for the perfect thing. Kitchens are best for suckable stuff, bakelite spoon handles and Pyrex thermometers and marble pestles. Even a writing desk has silky pens and crunchy pencils, but a room in the bughouse is a desert to the mouth, everything fixed down or flimsy white plastic made to throwaway. The only thing I saw was the maraschino cherry buttons of Emily's I ♥ CHOCOLATE—thank God nurses have pets, I thought, though it's kind of awkward to suck another girl's bathrobe buttons, even if you're *looth*—especially when she's wearing the thing. Emily and me, we weren't that far along, but we weren't that innocent either, I couldn't just suck her buttons I mean.

And all of a sudden I saw it, just what I needed: Emily's pink-pearl plastic three-piece toilet set, maybe the one thing she had from home, with a sort of shoehorn of suckable handle on the hairbrush, an ordinary L-shaped comb and a mirror like a wreath of pinky lips that twisted to a pink scepter, positively mouth watering, at one end. "Yum," I said, picking up the pink comb and smoking it rakishly. I handed the hairbrush to Emily. I wanted her to notice that mirror handle herself and ask for it. But no, refusal was her middle name. "I wanna smoke like you," she piped up. "Sure, OK," I shrugged, and gave her the comb and took back the hairbrush, but then I smoked its fat handle like a big pink cigar. Use your imagination, Peabody, I was trying to say. We smoked her hair set peacefully for a time. Two little kites of spit started glinting in Emily's mouth corners and I thought I was onto something big.

"Next you gotta try bubble gum," I said, although I poisonally hate bubble gum. "Hey," Emily whispered. "Let's smoke real cigarettes." "Real cigarettes?" I said, uneasily. What else could I say?—my Pall Malls and matches were in plain view, squaring my breast pocket. "Real cigarettes? What for?"

I've told you we teenage mental patients weren't given to foiling each other's stupid schemes. Heads were for dreambox mechanics to fix. We were young and set in our ways; it was our job to be crazy, not to be fixed. Time would change us, not our doctors in their wildest dreams, if we were in their wildest dreams, which I doubt. I mean, mental patience is a culture like the one it's wrapped in; its sameness doesn't stay the same or it rots. Fresh bad ideas were not to be sniffed at. And anyhow everybody smokes in a mental hospital; it's like drinking wine in France. If my see-through princess wanted a cigarette, it was my job to whip out the smokes, but I didn't... just yet.

"You're not even twelve years old," I said. "You're gonna puke if you smoke. You puke all the time anyway. That's why you're here. You can't afford to lose even one more calorie or you'll croak." "I smoked awready." Emily said, "my brother Barney showed me." "Brother Barney," I sneered, "what an example. When was this?" "They let him home for Christmas when I was ten." (Barney was in reform school.) "I bet he pushed one in your mouth and made you smoke." Emily was no snitch, but she didn't deny it. Instead she said proudly: "We smoked Kools." "OK, I'll give you a cigarette if you promise not to throw up." "OK." "Swear." "I swear."

I believed her. In fact suddenly I was afraid she would choke back her puke and die trying, for this was another way of being pure. Things were getting out of hand, it was like she was going down the laundry chute head first again, and this was not what I'd had in mind for my see-through princess at all. "Also you have to eat a coddy," I stipulated. "I'll throw up." "So smoke *and* eat a coddy and you won't throw up. *You swore.*"

There was a nub of logic there and you could see her circling it, circling it, looking for a place to land. Luckily I had a coddy on me as I often did in those days. I took a puck of damp white napkin out of my pocket and spread it open and there was my rusty round coddy, fifteen cents at the snack bar in the lobby, and next to it I laid a cellophane two-pack of saltines, a squirt-tube of mustard, a Pall Mall and a pack of matches, which said under the profile of a smiling girl with a nose like a rose thorn: *Can you draw me?*

"You gotta eat, Peabody, or you'll never get out of here," I said. Now that was limp for none of us Bug Motels exactly wanted out of here. "I mean out of this room," I added. "OK." "You swear." "I swear." She took up the coddy in one hand and the cigarette in the other, and I tore off a match.

And now I ignited and she nibbled and puffed, gulped and hacked and fizzed and choked. The cigarette smoke steamed whitely out of the yellow baby-bird angles of her beak, curled like chicken feathers around those agonized callouses where the rough little lips came together, and all at once two worms of something worm-white gleamed in the corners of her mouth, regurgitated coddy I guess—

"I'm not gonna gag I'm not I'm not I'm not," I muttered, and whirled around to put my back to her and grabbed the first thing that stuck out—an old dry sink on the wall was what it was, about the most disgusting thing you could bump into, which you thought was a urinal until you really looked. I threw back my head and gasped for air and accidentally caught sight of Emily in the mirror over the sink. She was waxier white than the pillow behind her head, her ugly-cute forehead dented with worry and

areve

the two worms of coddy still curled in her mouth corners. Gluey boiling down my gut but I refused to be a rotten influence, that was that, there we were, truce, no puking, she lay I stood and we both hicked like old pumps in a barnyard.

"You don't have to eat anything," I gave in. "I can't save you if you're going to do like that." "S'purty good," she said meekly. "Kinda dry." "Aw spit it out," I said. "Or I might puke myself." "S'kinda sharp. I mean it tastes kinda sharp, when I'm chewing and the smoke goes up my nose. Like chewing needles or sumpm." "Oooo, that does sound good. Much better than poop," I said bitterly. "I thought you liked poop," Emily said. "I said *everybody* liked poop, not me." "Ain't you everybody? One of em I mean?" "I guess so," I sighed.

"You could still save me," Emily said, plaintively yet sportingly, the way a kid wheedles you to keep playing. Only, old Emily would never say I could save her just to keep me playing. I sneaked a glance at her in the mirror. Her cute-ugly mug was peaceful against the white pillow. The back of her hand smeared over her mouth in an almost satisfied way. "Whatcha do with the coddy?" I demanded. "I eat it." "Aw come on, Emily!" "Yeah. Honest. It was good."

I squinted at her suspiciously. Her fingers, as short and skinny as birthday candles, lay on the coverlet and half a cigarette still stuck up from them like a play smokestack, fuming. There were ashes in every direction: black smears on the pillowcases, pale gray drifts down the front of her I ♥ CHOCOLATE bathrobe. But nothing worse.

"You didn't puke?" "Unh-unh. *I swore.*" "You're not really going to smoke that thing to the end, are you, Emily?" "I like it with a coddy." "You swear you ate that coddy? I'm going to get you another one and see." "Don't go. Pretty please don't go. Let's play fish." Why couldn't I stop? "Only if you eat a coddy," I bullied. "I ain't hungry no more. Don't go." "Swear you'll eat a coddy and I'll come right back." "I swear. But don't go. They won't let you in," she said, and the bottom lip of her little buggy mouth trembled.

"Don't worry, I can get in. I can get in any time I want. I'll stay till you stop eating coddies, I swear. Hey, wanna split a Hollywood Bar?" She gave me a sickish smile—her lip curled back on her bucked bad teeth in friendly, bashful disgust. "Unh-unh. Too poopy," she said.

How Love Got Me Out of There

The door hadn't quite hissed shut behind me when I hit the dayroom, running. "Gimme fifteen cents," I panted at the Bug Motels' card table. "I got her to eat a coddy." The whole place was smoking like an Indian encampment—there were around ninety little aluminum foil ashtrays in that room, and every ashtray had its mental patient—and O and Dion sat together in the whirly, cobwebby light, in a rubble of gum wrappers and potato chip bags, slapping their cards against the table. "Come on, gimme fifteen cents," I repeated, "she ate a coddy, the whole thing." Laughter burped out of the TV.

Dion lazily shoved a dollar at me. "Who ya talking about, Emily? She ate?" "She ate." "She ate! So what do you need fifteen cents for?" "Another coddy." "You think she's gonna eat another one? Today? Geez, Koderer, you're doing better than Buzzey, maybe you should open up your own bughouse," Dion said, snickering. Let him mock. I was proud. I was Karen Horney. I was Margaret Mead. I was Doctor Zuk after all. "So how'd you do it?" O spooky-fluted, one smudgy green eye narrowing at me suspiciously, almost reproachfully, the other hidden under the blueblack dip of her forelock. I wondered then, I wonder now, why a dark billow of hair over one eye makes a woman look beautiful and dangerous, what sort of pirate's-eye-patch effect that is, as if half-blind were alluring, and why O, blindfolded by that Dragon Lady ripple of hair, still held me with eyes that calmly said, *Walk the plank.* "So how'd you get her to eat?" O asked again, without smiling. She was bristling mad, I could tell, and suddenly I didn't think I should go into that just now. "Tell you later," I huffed, snatching up the dollar.

"Hey, pick me up a coddy too," Dion said, "while you're down there. And a pack of Luckies." He laid another dollar on the table. "Get me a coddy and a chocolate snowball and ten pieces of Bazooka," someone else chimed in, scooping over a pile of change. "Five pretzels. And a strawberry Turkish Taffy for Mrs. Wilcox." "A dime's worth of banana BB Bats and a pack of peanut butter crackers." Pretty soon half the nuts in the dayroom were putting in their orders. "Forget it," I shouted, "I'm just buying for the Bug Motels today, you guys'll have to get your own stuff." "Yeah, all you grownup mental patients ever do is sit on your fat asses all day and watch TV and fart," Bertie tactfully assisted me. "That doesn't represent my sentiments," I announced to the dayroom, since I was Karen Horney. "I just have an urgent mission to execute today and can't take on anything else." Under my breath: "Goddamn you, Bertie, don't stir up the mental patients, I'm in a hurry and this is a matter of life or death." Bertie laughed. "We could grow up into mental patients ourselves," I hissed. "We *are* mental patients," O reminded me. "Yeah, well we're not hopeless cases yet," I said under my breath. I took a step toward the seventh floor landing where the elevators were, put my hand on the ward door and felt O's pirate eye peg-leg it up my back. *You're not loving me and me alone the way you promised*, it told me telepathically. *You're no beauty but you'll pay.* I turned around reluctantly. This was when I saw that O was insanely jealous (I do not speak figuratively, we *were* in the bughouse), and like all insanely jealous people she was clairvoyant. It doesn't take a wizard—I mean everybody's dreambox is a pantry of such stuff, hungers, lost loves, unobtainable oinks, etc. Now she was peering into my dreambox and sniffing another woman in my life and I was making haste to cut Doctor Zuk out of my thoughts with a can opener. "Emily's organs are rotting," I parried weakly—but everybody knew that already. "Er, how bout you, O?" "How bout me?" she echoed icily. "You want anything from downstairs?" She didn't even answer me. "How bout a Hollywood Bar?" "I can get what I want myself," she replied. She was scary but—well I'll ring her up a cherry snowball I thought—just lemme feed old Emily first.

Snowballs sweating in a cardboard six-pack, pretzel rods like a row of cigars in breast pocket, candy bars crackling low in my overalls, soft warm coddies swinging in a small white bag from my teeth. And one of Dion's Luckies fuming away between my knuckles. I had had to ask an intern for a light. Ironically, when Emily was ready to eat, it was the world's lunchtime; the line had stretched from the snack bar to the newspaper kiosk all the way across the lobby. Where had I left my own cigarettes, my matches, even my 250-wrapper Mr. Peanut lighter? Godzilla's sakes—on Emily's bed—fifty-three minutes ago. The first, the second floor sank away, beaten-looking people, broken-off chunks of families, got on and off. Yes I'd lost my perfect fix on Emily's rescue by funding this expedition with Bug Motels' candy money, that was a mistake, my fault for flouncing around pretending I was Karen Horney, but now I was on my way back to her cute-ugly, spindly self.

Then the elevator stopped dead and jerked to perfect blackness and stillness and right away I started to be very very sorry just like O had telepathically said I would. I never doubted O was at the bottom of it, I knew she had the power—some electrician or maintenance guy or orderly she had oinked, or who was praying to oink her next week—she *had* to stop thinking of men that way. There was an emergency phone under the buttonboard in all these elevators. When I felt around for the receiver and clapped it to my ear, O spooky-fluted out of the earpiece: "You're standup as boiled spaghetti, Koderer, and now you're gonna get it," and hung up. In the black elevator sweat started to trickle under my dirty bangs, and my armpits itched madly. Suddenly it came back to me, a queer story I'd heard about how O first got to Hare-Rohring—there was that about working the Pratt Street bars from the age of twelve, and busting out her stepfather's bathroom window where they'd locked her in and climbing down and never coming back, and ten foster homes and fifteen shows in juvenile court and three years' probation later—but what I remembered was the judge finally kicking her case to Hare-Rohring after she pinned her little foster sister, *who she liked better than anybody*, that was the part I particularly remembered, to the bathroom door with an oyster knife. Presumably an act of overzealous babysitting... Had she thrown the knife like Flavia the Slavegirl on *Super Circus*? I wondered uneasily—who walked on the knives in her hands, her back arched like a bow. Just then the elevator lurched into motion, seemed to sink (it was too dark to see) more floors than the hospital had floors, into the sewers beneath Broadway. It grounded like a submarine; I could practically hear it scrape gravel. The doors sprang open, some kind of spotlight beamed into my eyes and I couldn't see a thing—and then something boinked against the wall behind me. I turned around. The spotlight picked out its edges. A jeweled dagger (of course it was just a garish letter opener filched from one of the royals) stuck there in the padding a second or two and fell to the floor, clunk. I leaned down and picked it up and squinted into the blackness. "Is that you, O?" "What if it is," she spooky-fluted from a few feet away. "Well, heck," I said—I was impressed; the sweat rolled steadily, copiously out of my armpits—"if you don't end up in the bughouse for life, you could get a job in a circus. Maybe Merlin would even hire you." I thought better of that. "But for Merlin's World Tour you'd have to be nonviolent. I don't think you qualify." "I could plead insanity if I killed you," O trilled darkly, out of the darkness. "Besides I'm still a juvenile. I betcha I'd get off," she speculated. I tried my best to ignore this line of thought. "Ain't you gonna ask me what you did wrong?" O

spooky-fluted. "No," I replied, but on she went. "You said you'd
be mine all mine. I oughta cut your nose right off, you dirty jew
bull dagger." I stared into the blackness, imagining her ratted
hair like rapids in a black stream and her wild raccoony eyes
ringed with black and a little too close together, sparkling. This
was a side of beauty I'd never seen. Could you sink your face in
her nuzzies after she called you that, even if she asked you to? Of
course I didn't know yet exactly what a bull dagger was. "Takes
one to know one," I ventured recklessly. "Anyway I never said I'd
be yours all yours" "I oughta cut your lying lips off too. You love
that skeleton baby—you love her more than me. You sneaked into
Emily's room, you dirty liar." "You love Emily as much as I do," I
pointed out, gesturing into the blind dark with my bag of coddies,
for O was deeply sentimental when she wasn't throwing knives.
"That don't make me no bull dagger," she growled. "Maybe you
wouldn't mind telling me," I croaked out carefully, "what a bull
dagger is?" Something about that was going too far: O bloomed
out of darkness, furious, grabbing at my hair and glasses and
shedding great wet sobs: "Go eat yourself, you jew jasper—"
She could throw a knife but not a punch I guess. Or maybe she
didn't really want to hurt me. I held the jeweled letter opener
firmly behind my back and let her bite and scratch. Toothmarks
on my neck might add a certain cachet… vaporized that idea,
think of Emily, Emily! My poor see-through princess who even ate
for me, I had to see that she truly loved me, loved me more than
she loved any of them, and now where was I when she needed
me? It had been well over an hour. Suddenly the lights came up,
with a lurch we started to move, *3B, 2B, 1B,* through the base-
ments. O's face was still in my face, only we were drenched with
fluorescent light. You'd think I wouldn't be able to see beauty so
close up, all hair roots and blackheads and tiny red threads in
the eyeballs, but tears webbed her gunky eyelashes like dew in
the grass at night and even her sweat was flowers. When the kiss
came it was hot and dry, then hot and wet, it sucked in all bodily

terrains, a southwestern national park of a kiss and I forgot to notice if it was any different because the other one kissing had just called me a dirty jew.

Chocolate is good for three things. Two of 'em cannot be mentioned on public television.

ROBERT BIXBY

Living on Television

Robert Bixby is publisher of March Street Books (www.marchstreetpress-com), editor of the semiannual Parting Gifts, *and facilitator of Cranbrook Writers' Conference. He has published in* Gargoyle, Washington Review, Greensboro Review, Carolina Quarterly, Redbook, Omni, *and other magazines. He can be contacted at rbixby@earthlink.net.*

Clayton and his son Adam liked to watch network movies that had already been on HBO to try to pick out the scenes that were altered for broadcast. Adam liked it because it gave him license to use curse words at will. Each time the actor said "What an animal," Adam would cry out "What an ASSHOLE!"

Clayton liked it because the films were subtly altered, like memory, only in the opposite direction. The women who had been naked now wore bikinis. Now the camera cut away a split second before the wild sex, a split second before the bad guy's pistol blew a man's crotch into a lumpy stew of cock and balls.

How different his marriage would have been if the networks got hold of it. He imagined a neighborhood full of muddle-headed neighbors coming over to borrow things and utter funny malapropisms at his door. He and Karen getting into crazy situations, but every half-hour reaching a charming resolution based on traditional values of honesty and hard work. Maybe coming out of the house at the end to wave, like the Nelsons when he was a kid.

The censors would cut out the fights. The ambulance would never come. No sleeping around.

The car in the pool? It probably would still happen, but the night would have ended peacefully sometime before every pane of glass in the house was smashed. Maybe it would have had some lovemaking. Not sex, but lovemaking *à la* Donna Reed. Kissing. Smooching.

The water had boiled up through holes in the firewall under the dashboard. He rolled down a window to escape and was almost crushed by the water rushing in. The side of the pool was hard by the window, so he had to push the still-floating car toward the center of the pool.

When the wrecker came, he dived in himself to attach the cable to the bumper. He paid the wrecker driver an extra fifty not to tell the police. Nothing was really hurt but the groceries in the back seat and a little masonry at the edge of the pool. And the car smelled like bleach forever after. When the divorce came through, he was happy to sign it over to her. He still couldn't believe he'd got off so easily.

There were too many complications for a half-hour sitcom, he decided. Maybe a made-for-TV movie. In it, he would have a terrible drinking problem made worse by his wife's slow deterioration from the disease of the week. If only his wife could have contracted a disease of the week. She could have died heroically in a way that ennobled all around her.

And yet driving the car into the pool had been the quickest and easiest way to get the blood off. The fence could be replaced. The car could be dried out. The sheer outrageousness of driving into the pool would distract anyone's attention from the fact that there had been a hit-and-run death that night.

Suddenly he had a hot desire for a beer. Or two. But he couldn't. If Karen found out, she'd take him to court and he wouldn't even get to see Adam on weekends.

He got up to get himself a Coke. Tomorrow was Monday. He would drop Adam off at his school and be alone for five days. Then he'd have a beer. He could be dry for a weekend for his son's sake. "'SHITHEAD!'" cried Adam's voice from the next room. "His voice said 'Simpleton,' but his mouth said, 'SHITHEAD!'"

The neighbor's yard light stood tall over the privacy fence between the backyards. He watched the flickering blue form irregular curves on the pool's surface. Mild. December. The cold, black, California desert sky. This might be a long night, he decided. Then he turned to the living room. "How about some popper corn?"

Adam appeared at the door, a tiny version of Clayton, but still beautiful, still possessed of hair. Ten years ago Adam had installed himself as Clayton's self-worth. At his birth, Clayton decided that anyone who could put life into something so perfect couldn't be all bad.

"Caramel?" said Adam, those syllables holding all the hopes in the world.

"Caramel it is," he said, pulling down the box. When he turned around, he was alone again.

He had got drunker the night the car took its bath, sitting out on the patio watching blue water drip off and out of the Olds. Seeing the man's face through the windshield the split second before impact. Like a photograph that grew sharper over time. A face he carried with him still, and recalled at odd moments like this.

He couldn't really remember what happened to the windows. The next morning they were just gone, along with Karen and Adam.

The phone rang in the middle of the popcorn.

"Hello?"

"They're turning all the God damns into DAMNS," Adam cried with delight. "The guys look like they're stuttering."

"I was going to ask if Adam was there but I can hear him."

"He's in the other room." It was Joanie.

"He must be watching a war movie. I can hear the machine guns."

"I wish you could be here," he said.

"Tomorrow. When Adam's gone. I can't let go with a kid in the house."

"I can't remember what your breasts taste like."

"Lemon meringue."

"That's right. Lemon meringue." They had high-calorie telephone sex when there couldn't be any other kind. "I want to cover them with whipped egg whites." In the microwave the last few maidens gave up and popped. He turned the oven off and pulled out the bag. "No. Not whipped egg whites," he said, opening the popping bag. The blast of steam fogged his glasses. "I want to cover them with caramel." He cut the caramel pouch on three sides and laid the cake of caramel on the top of the corn.

"Caramel," she said. She liked him to be creative.

He folded the bag shut and shoved it back in the microwave. "And as I shove it in, your heat makes the caramel melt." He could hear her breathing on the other end of the wire. He set the microwave timer.

"What's that beeping?"

"It's my watch."

"Throw it in the sink. It's distracting." He could hear her settling back into her bed. The sound of naked skin on satin. He was getting an erection. Maybe the night wouldn't be so bad, after all.

"Dad," Adam called. "They completely bleeped COCKSUCKER. Just cut it out." He could hear her breathing on the telephone.

"What next?"

The timer had counted down to a few seconds, so he turned off the oven and pulled the bag out. "I pull it out," he said, "and I spread you on aluminum foil to cool."

"Foil?" she said. "Foil? But I don't want to cool."

"And then I begin to eat you."

"All at once or little bit at a time?"

"In little bites everywhere. But at first, you're too hot. I nibble a little around the edges, but still I burn my mouth."

"I'm on fire."

"You're so hot steam is rising off of you."

"I want you. Take me. All of me."

"No. Just little bites. So there will be something to share with others."

"Others?"

He put the caramel corn in a Tupperware dish and set it on the floor by Adam in front of the television, dragging the telephone cord behind him. Two men were holding guns to a woman's head. He waited for the explosion, but they cut to the Doublemint twins. They were wearing little mint-green skating outfits, giving each other significant glances, buying at a concession stand that sold nothing but Doublemint gum.

"Now we're in a car," he said, out of ideas. The car always came into it. "We're in a grocery store parking lot. It's raining. You don't have anything on under your raincoat." He thought if he ran through it just one more time, he might cut out the bad parts, make the night come out right.

"No, Clayton. Not that one."

"You're buying avocados." He tried a new tack—she usually craved Dutch chocolate cream. He knew he was out of control. "You buy two avocados. One for you and one for me. Men keep looking at you. They can tell you're naked under your raincoat. You stare back and they look away. Your nipples are hard."

"I don't want this one."

"This time will be different. When you step out, the wind is blowing. You have to hold your raincoat down. You get in the car and we start to drive. You want to come to my house, but my wife is home. I want to go to your house, but your husband is due back any time and you don't know when to expect him. We decide to do it in the car in the rain. But you have to stop by your house to get your diaphragm. You always forget your diaphragm."

"This is no good. Don't do this," she said. He thought she was crying. Crying. Naked on satin sheets. Why didn't she hang up if it was no good?

"And you get your diaphragm and we drive away. Your husband isn't anywhere around. Still in Denver looking over the building site. We don't see anyone."

"No one sees us."

"No one sees us." He thought for a second. How would it have been? "We go to a school parking lot. Next to the football stadium. It's dark. You pull the avocados out of your raincoat pockets. They're big and waxy. I peel one with a knife."

"Then what?" She was with him now.

"I put the skin on your belly." He turned out the kitchen light and looked out at the stars. Through the clear air, he could see Mars near the moon. It looked very close. His own personal planet. Not red, exactly, but yellowish white. Not very different from a star to the naked eye. "And I mash the flesh with my hands and rub it all over you. Your raincoat is open. I can see your white skin in the starlight. The windows are all steamed. But I can see shapes moving outside. Someone is out there watching."

"Who?"

"We never find out. Who could it be, standing there watching me spread avocado over you?"

"A bum off the street. A stranger. A high school kid who just got done smashing out windows in the school."

He wished she hadn't mentioned that. His hand had been bloody, covered with cuts the next day. He could feel them solid for an instant against his knuckles, then nothing but shards raining down on the sill. "A stranger is watching. He puts his hand around his eyes. He can't see who we are, but he can see what we're doing."

"Then you make love to me."

"Yes." Smooching, but he doesn't say that. In his mind, as soon as they had avoided the meeting with her husband, it had turned into an R-rated version of Donna Reed. He licked off the avocado. Alligator pear. He realized he hadn't heard any curse words out of the living room and he looked up. Adam was standing in the door. He covered the mouthpiece. "Do you need something?"

"Aren't you going to watch the rest of the movie?"

"I'll be in in a second. Did they get to the shoot-out yet?" On the other end of the wire he could hear Joanie's heavy breathing. He could almost feel her body wrench under him.

"No." Adam said. "What's a diaphragm?"

"It's like a showercap. Go on in and call me for the shoot-out. I want to see how the censor screws it up." Adam went back into the room blue with television light.

After a few seconds, Joanie moaned softly into the telephone.

"I'm lighting two cigarettes," Clayton said, striking a lighter near the phone. "How was it for you?"

"A steamroller. Like a cement mixer." Her husband had been in construction. "A jackhammer."

"Here's your cigarette."

"Thanks." He heard her light a cigarette, only of course, it was a joint. She always smoked dope after sex. Sometimes before, too. Sometimes during.

"You'd better take a shower and wash off that avocado."

"It's good for my skin." She yawned into the telephone. It was late. "I can't wait to see you tomorrow."

"Here it comes," Adam called from the other room.

They sat for a minute more, listening to the distant crackle on the line. "Come over early." Clayton said. "I'll make you supper."

"Can I bring anything?"

"You've got to be kidding."

She said. "I love you."

"Look out. She's sneaking up on you," Adam called through the television to the drug czar.

"I—have to go. Adam. See you tomorrow." He hung up. He went into the next room. Adam had eaten all the caramel corn.

Good guys and villains were shooting. People were falling the-
atrically.

"They left out the part, where that guy…" Adam trailed off,
involved in something else going on. One of the bullets caught a
man and his head spun around. The camera cut to some other
action, missing the deluge of brains they had both been waiting
for. "Did you see that?" Adam said.

"No. I didn't see anything."

"They cut out the whole brain thing."

Adam begged to watch *Friday the 13th*, which came on at
eleven. "Which one is it?" Clayton said.

"Four or six. Which one has the V first?"

"It's late. Get dressed for bed. I'll make up a bed on the couch.
But I don't want any trouble out of you in the morning. One gripe
and we'll have a set bedtime on Sunday night."

He put a sheet and pillow on the couch and when Adam came
back in, he covered him with a blanket. Then he sat down on the
floor to watch the slaughter. Adam fell asleep a few minutes into
the movie. Clayton watched for a while. Blood rained down the
far side of the glass, never really touching him, never making him
feel he had to do anything about it.

DENISE DUHAMEL

Sex for Chocolate in New York

Denise Duhamel is the author of ten books and chapbooks of poetry. Her most recent titles are The Star-Spangled Banner *(winner of the Crab Orchard Award in Poetry, Southern Illinois Press, 1999),* Exquisite Politics *(a collaborative work with Maureen Seaton (Tia Chucha Press, 1997),* Kinky *(Orchises Press, 1997),* Girl Soldier *(Garden Street Press, 1996), and* How the Sky Fell *(winner of Pearl Editions chapbook contest, 1996).*

Just because Lulu was plump, her tricks thought she enjoyed going down on them.

"No way," she'd tell them. "That'll cost you an extra two bars…"

Most of them would whine for a minute, then say something like, "OK, Lulu baby, but only because you look so damn fine…" Each would reach into the grocery bag he kept in the back seat, or into his glove compartment, and pull out a couple of Snickers.

She started off accepting only Godiva or Lindt, but now that she was a full-blown addict—selling herself in the Meat District, snorting Nesquik in the crowded bathrooms of The Vault—anything chocolate would do.

She'd adjust her snug white leather bustier and get to work, one eye always on the candy waiting on the car seat or night stand.

It hadn't always been this way, she'd tell the occasional john who wanted to help her, the ones who threw in a bunch of carrots or a couple of packets of Ramen noodles with her chocolate pay. She was raised upstate in a macrobiotic household. Her mother actually made Lulu's baby food in a blender so that she had no sugar or additives until she was four. Until Uncle Ralph came to visit. She tried to block him from her memory—the way he sat her on his knee, the way he slipped her a Hershey's Kiss when her healthy parents were out at the food co-op shopping for organic vegetables.

"The problem was I liked it!" she whimpered, resting her head on an elderly man's shoulder. "I can still taste that little lump melting in my mouth. I feel so ashamed."

"That bastard!" they'd say about her Uncle Ralph.

Once a widowed gentleman took her to Moon Struck Diner and tried to feed her scrambled eggs.

"Just a few bites, Lulu," he said, but anyone could tell her heart wasn't in it.

She was busy eyeing the Black Forest cake that spun slowly on display in a glass tube-shaped case.

She went home at sunrise, a pack of Little Debbie Snack Cakes under her arm.

She didn't get along so well with the other girls, who were all hooked on coke or heroin. On the corner of 11th Avenue and 16th Street, she'd suck on a chocolate cigarette as the others smoked their Virginia Slims.

"Where did you get those?" Sheila, a recent runaway, asked one evening. "I thought they were outlawed. You know, a bad influence for kids and all…"

"They're only illegal in the States," Lulu said, chomping off her cigarette's end. "There's a guy on 9th Avenue who gets them for me from a candy factory in South America… You interested?"

"Hey, Lulu, you should go easy, baby, on that chocolate," Wendy chimed in. "And keep your nasty habit to yourself. Don't go trying to corrupt this sweet little girl…"

Lulu hated that judgmental Wendy.

"It's OK," Sheila said. "I can take care of myself. Besides, I don't want to get fat."

"Speaking of fat…" Wendy zoomed in on Lulu's thighs.

"Not all our tricks like sticks!" Lulu said. "Besides, I'm just a little bloated…You know, PMS…"

She was relieved that one of her regulars pulled up shortly after. Lulu smirked toward Wendy as she slid into the beat-up Buick as if to say, "Ha ha, I was chosen first."

There was no chocolate rehab. No cop to pick her up for possession of Mounds bars. People, Lulu figured, were ignorant about chocolate. A steady customer actually tried to pay her in white chocolate one night. She threw the bars in his face, forcing him to read the ingredients aloud.

"Do you see the word cocoa there?" she snapped. "Do you see the word chocolate listed as any ingredient at all?"

"I just thought you'd like a change," he whimpered, like a dutiful husband.

"Get me *real* chocolate!" Lulu growled.

"I just assumed white chocolate was a form of chocolate. I mean it says chocolate right here on the front of the wrapper."

"Find yourself a new girl, you ignoramus! Never come near me again!"

The man started to cry.

Lulu hated herself. She was out of control.

She ate Santas at Christmas, hollow bunnies at Easter. She ate chocolate coins whenever she could get her hands on them. She ate canned frosting through *Rosie O'Donnell* and *Oprah*. She couldn't fall asleep during the day anymore because of all the caffeine. She'd let her membership to PONY's lapse. Sometimes she was too full and exhausted to even work at night. Her pimp was on the verge of firing her when she ran into Uncle Ralph on 23rd Street, on her way to have her black leather shorts dry cleaned.

He didn't seem to recognize her.

"It's me!" she said, "Your niece. Little Lulu. What the hell are you doing in Manhattan?"

She forgot that she hated him. She was in a chocolate haze.

Uncle Ralph scooped her up into his arms, then put his hands on her shoulders.

"Lulu, everyone in Woodstock is worried sick about you. Your mother's herb garden is overrun with weeds…Your father's stopped going away with his Iron John men's group. The other night I saw them watching *David Letterman* and drinking Pepsi. Imagine your folks drinking? Their hearts are broken, Lulu."

Lulu burst into tears and let her ridiculous shorts fall to the ground. She buried her face in Uncle Ralph's chest. Then, she picked up her prostitute hot pants and threw them into the trash.

"They were getting too tight anyway," she said to Uncle Ralph.

"Lulu, I'm just in town overnight. A Goober convention…"

Lulu's anger hit her. She remember the silver-wrapped Kiss, their little secret.

"What do you say you pack up your things and I can drive you home tomorrow?" asked Uncle Ralph.

"A Goober convention? You degenerate! You pervert!"

"That's my job, Lulu. I'm a candy retailer. You knew that, didn't you?"

"You sick twisted fuck…"

She started to run away, but Uncle Ralph caught her. She squirmed in his grasp.

"What is it, Lulu? What's the matter?"

She punched and she kicked. Even though Uncle Ralph was an old man now, he held his own. Passersby stared but kept on walking.

"Are you on drugs or something?" he asked.

The sun streamed through Uncle Ralph's windshield. Lulu thought it was strange to be in a car that was driving to somewhere other than a hotel. She fiddled with the buttons on the radio and kept pushing the back windows up and down like she was a little kid. Uncle Ralph's gray sideburns reminded her of some of her tricks.

"I'm so sorry," Uncle Ralph said. "I got the candy wholesale. I was just trying to show off. You know, I was just in town that one weekend. I never had any kids of my own. I didn't know... I mean, I just thought my sister was too restrictive with your diet. But I can see now it was none of my business—"

"It's OK," Lulu said. "I mean, I would have had chocolate sooner or later, right? There's school and the other kids..."

It was the first day of her cure. Her temples pounded the steady beat of withdrawal. She was like Gretel, climbing out of the witch's window ledge, escaping the city. She didn't tell Uncle Ralph what she'd hidden in her purse. She'd snatched a sample kit of Milk Duds and Raisinettes from his trunk, just in case.

Forget love... I'd rather fall in chocolate!

NANCY
LUDMERER

Eavesdropping

Nancy Ludmerer writes fiction and practices law in New York City. Her fiction has recently appeared in The Kenyon Review, Cimmaron Review, Snake Nation Review, Sou'wester, North American Review, *and elsewhere. Her flash fiction has won prizes from* Grain *and* Night Train, *and her short-short* "Bar Mitzvah" *was recently read on* Word by Word, *a literary arts radio program that airs on KRCB, a California-based NPR affiliate.*

After the yellow roses and the Chablis Premier Cru and the buttery Chilean sea bass (let's forget it's nearly extinct for one night, darling), after the kisses shivering the back of my neck and hands parting my silk robe, after the Thelonius Monk and the Fauchon chocolate and the robe falling and the taut sheets, and after my hot mouth singeing the soft, bristly, chocolatey hairs of his belly, there is the baby monitor.

"I'll go," I say, pushing myself up with force. The wailing means she's wet. We have learned her different cries, learned them all.

"No, you stay here. I'll go."

I am lying face down uncovered. My ass, when I turn to look at it, is white and round and to him, I know, perfect and complete, a world unto itself, even if I think it's too big.

"Whatsa matter, baby?" I hear him over the baby monitor. "Whatsa matter? Daddy's here." There is the noise of Velcro ripping and diaper gel oozing. "Oh, what a pretty tushy, what a wet pretty tushy." He begins to sing: "Daddy's gonna dry it, yes I am, Lizzie's gotta diet, chub-wub-ham!"

The wailing stops. "That's a good Lizzie," he croons. When he comes back, I'm on my side with the sheet and quilt over me.

He puts his arms around me from behind. Before Lizzie, there were no yellow roses, no Chablis Premier Cru, no nightgowns, no Monk. Before, there was just us.

"You're a prince," I whisper. He massages my shoulders and I feel him rising against my ass, and it's different now, with my back turned, and after his hand drops below my waist, and after he strives against me and after my resistance flags and after our breathing sounds like nothing we've breathed before, there's the baby monitor.

"Shit."

"No," he says. "Not shit; it's the wrong cry." He's right, this is the hungry, stick-your-tit-in-my-face, cry.

"Me," I say. He tries to hold me back, but I slide naked out of bed and run angrily into her room. "All right, all right," I say and take her and sit in the rocker. The wicker is rough against my naked back but she is warm against my breast and when she sucks hard, it feels better than good.

"Oh," I cry. "Oh. Oh."

Right into the baby monitor.

R R Angell

French Twist

R R Angell is a graduate of the Clarion West Writers' Workshop and a Virginia Center for the Creative Arts fellow. He is a Maryland State Arts Council grant recipient, and his writing has won several awards, including the Dana Award for Speculative Fiction and the Jenny McKean Moore Writer's Award. His work has appeared in The Baltimore Review, Fantastic Stories of the Imagination, Gargoyle, Scorched Earth, Fishnet, Astounding Tales, *and* Asimov's Science Fiction Magazine, *among others. He has recently completed a novel-in-stories, "Bay Window," a temporally bilateral tale of the complete life of Stephen Learner. His website is www.rrangell.com.*

During the week, the courtyard across the street was used as a children's playpen between the hours of eleven a.m. and two p.m. On those very hot and sunny Paris days in early June the noise was almost as unbearable as the heat of the old city, whose every surface seemed tinged with lampblack accumulated over hundreds of years. Even the hot pavement of my street had stretch marks and had, in some places, crumbled away to reveal stained and decaying bricks. At least the kids had chestnut trees to protect them from the soot and the sun; the clustered leaves formed thousands of natural parasols protecting their porcelain, Marlene Dietrich skin.

It wasn't that I minded much, not having that same protection. I was, after all, at treetop level on the top floor of a five-story walk-up near St Denis (the best and worst part of the place was the circular staircase with its delicate wooden-capped banister that defined a cylinder of air from the skylight all the way down to the hard black-and-white-tiled entrance hall where a bank of brassy mailboxes greeted those descending), *le quatrième étage* to be exact; a little French quirk to disguise the fact that you were farther from ground level than it sounded, possibly making it easier to rent the tiny studio apartment to unsuspecting foreigners, Americans like me, struggling to reconnect with their college French and escape, trade really, one slick advertising-driven culture for another. At least this one was in another language, and the novelty of it made it infinitely more appealing.

All said, I should have probably stayed in Boston, bought a little red Miata, and hopped into the singles bar scene instead of taking a six-month leave of absence. My girlfriend, Kim (ex-girlfriend now), accused me of having early mid-life problems. At twenty-nine, I knew I was too young for mid-life problems, even though my dad died at age fifty-seven a few years back in a car accident, so nothing medical there. Kim and I had a convenient life together for three, almost four, years; a great apartment overlooking the Charles River at the top of one of those old four-story, dried-blood brick affairs. We had enough space, at least at first. Our parents wanted us to marry. Kim wanted children. Recently, that had been all she wanted to talk about.

One Sunday, her fat tabby turned over the kitchen trash while Kim was out running. As I was cleaning up after the fur ball, I found a month's worth of birth control pills under gnawed and mostly licked-clean Chinese takeout containers. That afternoon I avoided her, watched her from across the room. That night I pulled out the Trojans and she got upset, but more so that I had caught on.

Not long afterwards, I really did catch on. It would have been OK in the long run had I stuck it out, but I figured that, to be certain, I'd have to demand a DNA test of her, and I just couldn't handle that kind of garbage. There are some things for which you should not be in competition. That's just the way I was raised. She wanted the apartment too, so I moved back to West Concord with my mom for a few months and socked away the bucks until I couldn't stand it anymore.

Then the wind changed and I got the correspondence from Jean Christophe about his apartment. A dirt-cheap sublet. I had been missing a little romance, kind of hard to get any this far out in the 'burbs, especially at your mother's where even a little everyday sin was enough to cause nagging guilt. Mother apologized, saying she worried that I wouldn't meet someone, fall in love, maybe get married if I lived at home much longer. She was probably right. That's OK, that's what Paris is for, especially in the spring they say. Too bad I had missed that, too.

At the top of the stairwell, across from my door, was a little closet-sized *pissoir*. Not that there wasn't a tiny low-flow shower and a toilet that sucked its contents out with such force (also using minimal water) that you felt it would take you with it. I had all I needed there: the bathroom, a college-sized refrigerator next to a two-burner stove that housed the smallest oven I'd ever seen, and, *bien sûr*, the requisite kitchen sink. So I didn't need the *pissoir* across the hall until I got the first water bill, and changed my mind about using that public closet.

There was one on every floor, left over from ancient times when plumbing was more rudimentary. You could lose a cat that way; it could fall in and slip right down five stories and no one would never know. Kind of makes you paranoid, but I no longer had a cat. My *pissoir* was different, slightly bigger, and the hole in the floor went straight down into the blackness of hell, whereas the others' soil pipes sloped back toward the main shaft. You find these things out when you stumble home at three a.m. on a Saturday night and suddenly need to lose the greasy bistro meal (it had been a good idea on the way home at the time) when almost halfway up the spinning stairs to home.

But that was another night, a small orientation to the solitude of a foreign city, your vulnerability protected like ganache by only the thinnest chocolate shell, before the uniform crust of

days clads you in stone, transforming you into a living gargoyle
that peers endlessly down through chestnut leaves to an abandoned playpen where you could envision your three-year-old
(if you had one) enjoying himself in dappled sunlight. Then the
children would flood the yard, *alors*, and you recoiled from the
iron-railed window set in the slate-gray mansard roof, and pulled
the windows shut like doors, to cut down the noise and keep the
sweating heat inside.

To pass those hours I would throw on Club Music CDs left
there by my friend Jean Christophe, then try to lose myself in
a couple of freelance assignments coding C++ software utilities
for my old job. Yeah, my old job. That's how I thought about it
at that point. Who takes a leave of absence, in Paris no less, and
expects not to change enough never to return? Who wants to be
the same person at the end of it all?

As weeks wore on, it became increasingly difficult to stay in
that shuttered apartment. In Paris in the summer you lived for
the night. In the daytime the subways were too hot, like steam
tunnels, so you walked or biked everywhere in the shade or took
a cab. Jean Christophe had left me an old bicycle. At least while
you were riding you had a breeze. That was my preferred mode
of transportation until it got stolen outside Les Jardins des Lux-
embourg on the other side of the river where I was cultivating
the habit of reading the midday away in grassy shade.

St Denis, as the tortoiseshell *plan de Paris* goes, is in the tenth
arrondissement, not a bad place, not too far to places you'd want
to see if you were still a tourist. I had done most of it in the first
idle weeks, the cool weeks when the Metro was tolerable, and I was
halfway adjusted to above-ground navigation thanks to the bike.

But I was not a tourist. Not anymore. I went to the market. I
cooked my own meals. Sometimes it was just soup and a baguette
or a hunk of cheese (or even spaghetti with ketchup, a cheap-
eats trick Jean Christophe showed me once a decade before
when I was touring after college and he was still an engineering

student in Orléans) when I didn't feel like ferreting out a *prix fixe* meal in some hole-in-the-wall. I saved my money for drinks, the exorbitant cover charges at loud, Montmartre technobars, cab fare home, and later, the girl in the air-conditioned *pâtisserie* on the corner.

The *pâtisserie* was two doors down from the *boulangerie* at the end of my block where I got my daily baguette. The doors were elegant, cut-glass oak affairs behind two plain columns set on small checkered tile, the door so beautifully carved that your hand lingered there, brushed gently, as you pushed your way inside, a golden tinkling bell announcing you to the glistening, illuminated cases, and the little marble tables against the plate glass, and standing willowy behind the cases, Valerie. It was then that I realized that this was the one place in the entire *arrondissement* that Jean Christophe had not told me about, so I had not been looking for it, even though it had been there like a glowing Christmas ornament all the time.

"*Bon après-midi, monsieur*," *elle a dit*, her hair jet black and short, cut in the style of the day, the tiny white apron wrapped twice, it seemed, around the slenderest body.

It was the eyebrows that would fascinate me later, shading the darkest of eyes, a slender nose, full petite lips, moist as they glossed over my own in the closeness of that first kiss. Each individual black hair emerged from a perfect alabaster so transparent that its blue root appeared to sink into its depth, becoming the shadow of an adjacent hair. They arranged themselves to form a perfect artist's arch, not truncated like children's brows or those plucked *femme fatales'*, but naturally thinning to an extended point around the ridge of *les yeux*, yes, because that's what those eyes were; completely frank and irresistible invitations.

"*Je veux chercher*," I said haltingly, wincing from the headache that came from concentrating all day in another language.

"Well, you have found me," she said, not switching to English like every other Parisian with whom I had come in contact.

"Not you, I meant that I want to search," I explained, taking a deep breath.

"Ah. You search for your lifetime, do you not?" She cocked her head and leaned against the large case beside the register, her arm stretched across the top so that her hand dangled in the air beyond the glass. No ring. "Perhaps you would like to *look* here for a while, and take a break from your searching?"

"Yes, look," I said, feeling my earlobes warm at her words. The voice was hard edged, her words well delineated and precise; easy for me to discern.

She poured back into herself and floated down the glass counter, reaching into the case, pulling out a dark cube.

"Try this one. It is a favorite of mine."

The piece was displayed on a sliver of waxed paper across her flattened hand, offered like a sugar cube or an apple to a horse in a manner that avoids an accidental bite by blind teeth. As I was almost touching it, she closed her hand and flipped it over.

"No. Not for you, yet," she said, and moistened her lips. "This one, I think, for you."

Her hand turned over again slowly, revealing a white chocolate piece shaped like a plump oyster, an exquisite work.

"I have never seen such a thing," I said, meaning both the magic trick and the candy.

"Seashells, aside from pastry, they are a specialty of the house. This one has an almost liquid center, tainted with vanilla," she said, pushing it closer. "Take it," she demanded. "Welcome to Paris. Will you be long here?"

"A few months more," I said, reaching for the oyster, hesitating, then extracting it from her palm. I half-expected her to snatch it back, change it to something else. "My friend has gone to Vietnam for an extended vacation," I explained.

"The food Vietnamese is very good. Everyone goes there for the food."

"I've never been."

"No. But Jean Christophe loves food, as do we all."

"How do you know Jean Christophe?"

"We met here. His apartment is just across from the little park by the school, in the building with all the morning cats."

It was true. By eight a.m., every wrought-iron balcony on that side of the building held a pampered and self-indulgent cat lounging in the morning sun. I looked down on them as I sat in my own window with my morning coffee, made in an American pot I had brought since Jean Christophe, and most of the French, seemed to prefer hot chocolate in oversized cups for breakfast. The coffee here was espresso, black, or with too much milk. All the stairs made it too difficult to go for coffee on the street, so I made my own, American-style, and watched the tenants from my perch leave for work in black dresses and leather handbags while the cats lazed and stretched in the sun.

"Are they neutered, these cats behind bars, do you think?" she asked, looking from the shell to my eyes.

"Yes, I think they must be."

"I hope," she said, stretching her neck and arms, "that all the window cats are not."

She had two little moles there that had me thinking of vampires, and I was jealous and realized I needed to go.

"No, I..." As I started to shrug, the shell slipped away and I grabbed for it, catching it and snapping it in half. The filling oozed into the cup of my hand and I looked for napkins, then to her as she watched me, amused, offering no assistance. There was nothing else to be done, so I picked the shells out and ate them, then licked the spilled center from my palm, finding a small, hard-candy pearl.

"An authentic oyster," I said, as she handed me a damp cloth. My headache was gone.

"Yes," she said. "I am called Valerie."

"Roger," I told her. "Roger Brinkman. I live just...," I said, turning to point, but then, we had already had that conversation.

"I know, Roger. But now I must close." She smiled. "I will see you tomorrow, yes?"

"Yes. We will... of course." I handed back the towel and stumbled out onto the sidewalk with my thoughts. When I looked back, the closed sign was in the window and the lights were already off. There was no sign of Valerie, just the hum of the air conditioner and the blare of rushing cars reflected in the glass, and I began to feel the heat of the late afternoon.

Nothing worked for me the rest of the day. I was flushed with her and came back to her with every tangential thought. The window and my door were open until the wind shifted and the stench of the *pissoir* (someone had left the door open again) wafted in through the door of my apartment. I lay down on the futon and dozed, slipping through images of her, her hands shifting back and forth, the sound of startled pigeons, her smooth skin cool as virgin marble.

The sun was setting when I woke to my neighbor cursing herself after dropping something out on the landing, fumbling with her keys. The rest of my baguette became a cheese sandwich with one slice of ham. I ate the last of the *cornichons*, plucking them from the pickle-water in the little jar and sucking the juice from my fingers. Tomorrow was grocery day at the *hypermarket*, for I was also out of dental paste and toilet paper. A few more bottles of *vin de table* would help, but I dreaded lugging too much up the stairs.

By the time the sun was down and the lights of the city glared at the sky, I was ready. The apartment was too confining and I needed some physical motion. Le Club Metro didn't have a line yet, but it was early, and the door-boy was bored as he stamped my hand with black-light ink, looking at me with contempt reserved for those he recognized. Inside the black corridor I put the foam earplugs in and felt the pulse of music against my chest. I entered the flashing black-lit cavern, the music too loud without enough people on the floor to absorb it, and climbed the short stairs past clutches of leather boys to the bar and my usual gin and tonic, the lime glowing darkly among fluorescing ice cubes.

Just after midnight, I was on my second G&T and things were picking up. Clusters of dancers had formed their meditative clumps. The music picked up and the pacifiers came out, and they ground their teeth just the same. I itched to get out there, to move, but I wanted a denser crowd where I could get lost in the tapestry of the dance, so I leaned against the railing and looked out over the parastolic crowd, waiting.

The hand firmly grasped the back of my neck. Another hand slipped palm down in front of my face, closed into a fist, turned and opened to reveal another oyster as her body pressed against me. She released my neck and I took the candy, turning to her.

"It is tomorrow, so now I can see you," she shouted.

"So what does this mean?" I held up the white chocolate shell which glowed vaguely purple until a red searchlight from the dance floor washed over us, flashing from the chrome buckles on identical leather jackets worn by two pale males close behind her. They were grinding their teeth, watching me, and vibrating with rhythm. They crowded closer, and I saw that below her smooth white jaw line she was also in leather. Tight leather.

"Eat it," she ordered. "Dance with me."

That was the easy part.

■

Valerie turned to me in front of my mailbox, leaning her chest into me, letting her head fall back as if for a kiss. I licked the moles on her smooth neck, feeling them under my tongue. She pushed away as I moved to embrace her, then ran up the stairs, not pausing to look back or ask which floor was mine. When I reached her, my heart was pounding in my chest and I was sweating into my still-damp clothes, not all from the climb.

The key slipped easily into the lock. She slipped her hands around my hips and into my pockets before the door was even open, reaching deep and pulling me against her, then holding me back.

We walked in like that. I dropped my keys on the bookcase and reached back over her head to shut the door as she undid my belt, sliding it from the loops and spinning me around to face her. She looped the belt around my neck.

"You look good in a collar," she husked, working on my top button, then sliding the zipper slowly, inch by inch. My hands were on her shoulders, working under the straps of her leather knapsack and trying to figure out how to get it off her without interrupting her momentum. She pushed my pants down, then backed away, peeling off the pack, looking at me.

"Take off your boots," she said. "Where are your glasses?"

"Cabinet," I said, pointing, then dropped into my only chair to unlace.

She took a large glass and put ice in it, then filled it and drank while looking under the sink. I slipped off my pants and saw her retrieve a large bowl. She poured the remaining ice water into the bowl, then filled it, placing it in the center of the floor.

"What's that for?"

"You'll see; I am an artist."

Valerie unbuttoned her black shirt, throwing it on my work-table. I expected leather, not black lace with a tiny pink bow between the cups. Very French. I started to rise, and she pushed me down.

"Wait." She opened her pack and pulled out a handful of leather thongs. "I like you in the chair. Take off your shirt and your bikini. Leave the belt on your neck."

She watched, unembarrassed, smiling at the right moment. The drying sweat chilled me even as I felt flushed. Then she tied my arms to the arms of the chair, palms up. Likewise, she tied my ankles. With the belt, she looped it around the back support and my neck, then cinched it, preventing me from leaning forward as I watched her slip off her shoes, then her slacks.

I don't know why I trusted her. Maybe it was being alone in the City of Lights, maybe I knew I would leave someday. Maybe it was being far from home, the liberating distance, or the romantic and oversexed notions I had of Parisians that all this somehow reinforced. I don't know why I trusted her and her instinctual way of doing things, like she already knew I wouldn't mind. So when she straddled my hand and reached for me with her lips, I was wide awake and aware of her skin, saw the few faded freckles, traced her eyebrows in extreme close-up, licking them, and feeling each snake-smooth hair as I tasted the salt from our dancing, and knew the softness of her just as I closed my eyes.

She slid away from me, back to her pack, and pulled out a dark squeeze bottle that she placed between my legs on the chair. It was cold to the touch and I shrank back, intensely aware of it as she removed the black lace.

Small moles like dark constellations patterned across her chest, a few down the sides of her traceable stomach. I could taste my tongue on each one. She took the bottle, squeezed liquid chocolate above her breast. The drips flowed down, dividing around the hardening nipple to accumulate on the tip from behind, just enough to hang there, a nipple of its own, a slow, thick quiver in front of my eyes. I stretched for it, my tongue straining, my head restrained, and I tried to wag it toward me by curling my tongue in repeated air licks. She shifted to the other, an even bigger drip, and she began to hum between deep breaths, dropping down to kiss me, dropping down again to smell me, her breath hot and controlled. I could feel the vibrations as she hummed, almost touching.

Valerie stood and, holding the bottle at her pelvis, squirted me, a V from nipple to nipple. It ran like thick blood down my chest, my stomach, then she started covering me with the chocolate, matting my hair, drizzling on me and around me, then smoothing it with her hand until I was covered.

"This will not harden on such a hot man," she whispered, then she was washing me with ice cubes, the chocolate hardening around me, then more chocolate, more ice, layering me up. She backed away, admiring her work, then slipped out of her panties and untied me.

"Do not move unless I move you," she commanded, then climbed onto me, taking me into her, licking my chocolate-stained lips. "Now, slowly. Do not break the shell."

I melted into her.

∎

It went on like that for a while, a couple of weeks maybe, well into July. Every day I would escape the children and sit out under the small trees at a café near the Beaubourg, little finches flitting in and out, beggars all, while the giant red lips of the fountain moved up and down spraying water before a bright fantasy scarecrow that stood against the backdrop of a dirty cathedral. The tourists arrived late, in snapping herds, but passed by my little café in favor of standing in line across the plaza at the Centre Pompidou while I passed time until the afternoon reading the paper, tending to a coffee, a pastry, then finally wine and a sandwich (with the salad, as they say).

Then it would get too hot to stay, and I returned, ducking inside the cool *pâtisserie* to browse glinting cases of temptation until there was a lull in customers. She would hand me a shell if we could be together that night, always a little magic act, always a little oyster until she leaned across the counter one day to pull something from my ear. Valerie had been showing signs of boredom, and I was terrified that she would dismiss me in favor of one of her leather-wrapped androgyns, leaving me to watch her moves across a glittering floor with someone else. But the novelty of her was wearing off, the sublime and dangerous falling into routine.

Behind my ear she found a razor clam, sharply detailed and
fragrant with black chocolate mud on painted marzipan. She
dragged it across my upper lip. I chased it with my mouth, biting
off the end in what I hoped was toothy sexiness. In her strongly
delicate fingers the end remained in front of me, the center a sunset pink nested in bright red like a drawn heart lying on its side. In
my mouth, almond and chocolate mixed with vanilla overtones. I
cupped her elbow, tracing her forearm to her wrist and the cross
of light blue veins there, pausing at the pulse against my fingertips, then grasped the stump of the clam and took it from her.
Her eyes skipped across my face, then cut away as a customer
entered, the delicate bell annoying the air between us.

"I'll call first," Valerie said, dismissing me. She smiled and
turned away.

∎

The phone rang at sunset, waking me.

"I bring something for you tonight," she said, then an ambulance went by wherever she was, drowning her out. I leaned
toward the open window, hoping she was nearby, but only the
twilight twitter of birds fluffing the chestnut leaves floated into
my hearing. On the phone she sighed, then said, "Tonight, we
eat cake," and hung up.

Not long afterward (she must have taken a cab), her leather-
gloved knock came on the door. Even in all the heat, she didn't
sweat much, just enough to moisten her skin with scent and
saltiness, but I knew her heartbeat, strong like a pile driver, an
underlying bass insistence that permeated her when I was near,
syncing with my own when I checked, my ear against her chest,
her throat. I could hear it sometimes even in her wrist, and now,
in my doorway, as she handed me two gold-striped boxes done
up in string, I thought there were other places I should place my
ear and listen.

She was in a simple lime-green blouse, a black wrap-around skirt with an almost invisible pattern. Her hair slicked back and glossy. I could feel my hands running through it, like otter's fur.

"You look hungry, Roger."

"There's that," I said. "Drink?"

"In my backpack," she said, turning to allow me access.

I removed it from her back and retrieved a light-green bottle etched on the outside, like glass after a long time in the surf. There was no label, but it was unopened. As I pulled the cork, she stood at the window looking down at the streetlight, her arms pulled up to her chest like a little girl, hopeful. We could hear people moving by the building, an occasional shout. A bottle shattered on the street below. I wanted to turn the light off, see her head silhouetted against the moonlit sky, her body against dark leaves, almost invisible.

"Turn out the light," she whispered, swaying in the window.

The moon would be full in a few days and the light was strong. The leaves took on greater definition and her silhouette deepened and glowed around the edge. Fireworks broke into the night, popping and washing the window jamb with faint color, flashing from the glass. I brushed her shoulders with my fingers, then ran my hand down her neck, playing the scales of her vertebra past her shoulders, down the indent of her spine, to the wrapping of the skirt. Valerie turned, my hand sliding across her lower back, catching in the cloth that loosened, and fell.

She held two shotglasses against her chest, a cube of ice in each, and she extended her arms, gently pushing me back. I had forgotten the bottle. It glowed blue in the moonlight as I poured, the liquid clouding in the glass.

"What is it?"

"Absinthe," she whispered to me, the word sounding obscene and alluring. "Drink." She guided the glass to my mouth and tipped it up. "Now it is my turn."

She put her glass down on the sill, devoting both hands to unbuttoning my shirt, stroking down my chest, her fingernails tickling my stomach, then reversing upward, becoming fingers again on my pectorals, her hands sliding under the fabric of my shirt, over my shoulders. I allowed the shirt to fall, her to peel the sleeves down my arms, and off. She took her drink and tossed it back, offering the glass for more, and I retrieved the bottle and poured for us both. A distant double bang resonated in the night and a lone voice on the street shouted in reply.

Her blouse slipped like water over her head, her arms stretched upward in a dive, then drifted down like angel's wings in a dream. She was in a two-piece something, dark and silky, almost glossy. I bent to kiss her, and she moved back just enough to hand me the glass.

"We must observe the rules," she said.

It was her turn. She tickled around my waist then stroked my arm, arriving at my watch and unbuckling it. She drank. I removed her boots, she my socks, all one at a time, with each piece a shot. The moon was higher, the light stronger, and her skin glowed as I embraced her, looking down her star-washed back. I slid my hand down smooth skin, slippery cloth.

"My turn," she said, grasping my jeans and pushing me back. "Look up," she commanded.

I looked at the ceiling, the cracking and falling plaster around the window, reaching up as hands slipped down my sides and the sky spun as the world evaporated.

Then I was flat out on the bed, naked, a curious sense of delayed touch, dulled senses. There was a tightness around me and I raised up on my elbows to look, and found her at the window.

"Do not move, or we will both be sad," she said, turning to me. Behind her head the edge of a golden chrysanthemum sparked in the sky, turning blood red and dissolving.

She had slipped a small spring-loaded guillotine around me, a snug fit, getting snugger.

"Valerie?"

"We celebrate liberation by applying the guillotine to tyrants."

She flowed toward me, knelt, and kissed me, pressing me back with her lips. I could smell the dark sweetness on her breath, taste it on her tongue. She slid across my chest, to sit there and peer down at me; sparks in the window caught my eye.

"Listen to me," she whispered, coming closer, her breath and lips next to my ear. "You must hold out against release, until I am finished with you, or it will be mine, and your last."

"Last what?" I said stupidly, hoping this is what she loved in me, an innocence worth preserving perhaps, as she backed down on me. But I knew, and I saw it in her eyes, that hungry spark beckoning the fuse to draw nearer, coaxing the pressure to build, then setting the charge in heaven to explode with radiating brilliance.

She pulled my fingers to her, leaning into the support, soft warmth in the palms of my eager hands. Moving, moving, ever moving against me as I remained the rock-solid base, eager immobility, trying not to feel her heat, not to smell her glistening skin, not to close my eyes but to stare toward the window for shimmering shards to arch into view, explode into white light and thunder, one after another, until the distance was indistinguishable from the room, the light indistinguishable from dark, the pleasure indistinguishable from the pain and the flood, snapping when she fell against me, her lips bruising themselves against my numb and bloodless face. Then she pushed off, pulling up her hands now covered wet and dark, and she fell beside me.

I reached for the darkness in my lap, my hand moving through an eternity, my sense of touch distant as if touching another. There were fragments there, bone and blood, and I withdrew to cover my face, plummeting from ecstasy to despair as my heart rang in my chest. Then the smell was there, and I pulled my hand from my face, and tasted. The guillotine had shattered, melted and smeared between us, and it was all a trick. In my relief I wanted to kiss her, to share my happiness. Instead, I fell back against sweated sheets. Kim would never have done this.

But neither would I, and that's the point. My graduation from plain routine seemed complete. There were these new heights, undreamed of even in my silent and staid adolescence, that made me mourn for simpler times, lost as I was now on that endless ladder. Dreams of Valerie and a life together were sharply cut off. There was danger in women I'd rather not know about. Perhaps that was her plan; keep it all recreational.

She rolled against me, draping her arm and snuggling. Very inconsistent.

"Five times," she breathed into my ear. "A record."

Recreational was good, but I was no Houdini. This escalation was not good. An ambulance sped by without the siren, its lights bright against the window. Could have been mine, if she had called. I could never have conceived that she would do something like this. Valerie was already fast asleep.

I listened to the crowds stumble home in the darkness.

∎

I didn't see her for four days, though she phoned every one, leaving message after message. Come to the club tonight, we missed you last evening. Valerie knew I was resting, adjusting. But she also knew I wanted more, and so did I. I picked up the phone.

"Hello, this is Jean Christophe," came the voice. "Roger?"

"Yes. How are you?"

"I am very fine, thank you."

"How is Vietnam?" I asked, looking down at the rumple of sheets.

"Oh, the food is good, you know. But I have just arrived here in Ho Chi Minh. How is my apartment?"

"Oh, Jean Christophe, the sex is good here, you know."

In the empty phone I could almost hear the ocean roar.

"Valerie." He made a statement.

"Yes," I said after a time, alert now to all the spaces in his voice.

"I see," he said. "Roger?"

"Yes?"

"I have something to say. Don't take this the wrong way, *mon ami*."

"No."

Static surged on the line and we waited it out.

"I have been all this time at, how you say, sanitarium."

"For your health?"

"Yes, exactly. No loony bin here, although she drove me crazy." He paused, and I waited for him to go on. "You understand?" he said. "She is not good for...for..."

"Experience?"

"*Exactement*. She is not good exposure for Paris."

"I see."

"Too much sugar, it excites too far. One loses one's taste for... for...normal living. She will give you dreams, that one, and take things from you."

"What does she want?"

"She wants the apartment. Has she asked you for a key yet?"

"No. Why would she want this place," I quipped. "No offense, Jean Christophe."

"Ah, she wants to live there, for the children across the street. It is a neighborhood center for the children."

"Is one of them hers?" I asked. Time stretched again into static. I waited for him to speak. "Yours?" I probed.

I could hear him shrug half a world away.

"No." He coughed. "I don't know. Certainly not mine." The static was back. "I must go," he said. "Maybe you should go on a trip, get away. Amsterdam, perhaps, though it is the wrong time of year to vacation."

He told me he was due for tea with a Buddhist monk. Soon we hung up.

I went to the French window and opened it to sun and the children playing below. The breeze felt good. The children jostled each other for a position on the jungle gym.

It was past eleven a.m. The *pâtisserie* had been open an hour. Thin women in black dresses and pearls stood before the cases, tiny purses with long straps hung from slight shoulders. Some carried paper shopping bags with rope handles and the designs out, and all their faces were dusted with arrogance, indifferent to each other.

A solid and pudgy woman in a streaked apron, bags under her eyes, moved behind the counter, handing over a small gold-striped box, punching buttons on the register. From the back room, Valerie appeared with a large box, shot me a glance, and showed a woman the cake inside before stretching a gold ribbon around the corners of the box. The pudgy woman worked the register while the customer searched through her purse.

"A sample, sir," Valerie said, extending her palm. On it was a simple dome of dark chocolate, a circle around the top. "These are my favorite," she said, "and I'd like for you to have one now."

The pudgy woman stepped over, turning her back to me as the other woman slipped through to the street, and whispered something to Valerie as she untied her apron. Valerie nodded vigorously, twice, and the pudgy woman, pulling the apron over her head, went into the back room.

"She's gone to piss, so we have a moment."

I took the sample and popped it into my mouth. The cherry liqueur burst onto my tongue; the candied fruit inside was perfect.

"Tonight, a group is getting together early at the club. I will pick you up at six p.m. We will have dinner first. Does that work for you?"

"No oysters, or any other shells, today?" I was curious about the evening.

"No," she said, the hint of a smile appearing. "I am out of them, for now."

■

I took a taxi to Les Jardins and found some shade. Lying there, I stared up into the tree, and through it to blue specks of sky which opened and closed in the light breeze that had blessedly appeared. There were no squirrels there, or in any park in Paris I had learned, so I had nothing to watch skip through the manicured branches except birds, and they were too fast for my mood. As it was I didn't feel like reading, so I laid the open book on my chest and closed my eyes. I missed the squirrels.

"That is not good for the spine," a voice said above me among the chatter of birds.

My eyes opened on a thin pretty-boy with full lips. I didn't recognize him at first, without the leather, dressed as he was in a purple shirt and baggy pants. Even then he had to prompt me.

"You are Valerie's," he said. "I am Cheve."

"Ah, yes," I said, sitting up. "Won't you join me?"

"I prefer to stand."

"What are you doing here?"

"I am just looking," he said, scanning the rows of trees. "Are you joining us tonight?" he asked presently, eyeing me peripherally.

"I think so."

"It's important that you come," he said, collapsing cross-legged on the grass.

"Why?" I asked.

"You got the cherry today, didn't you?" He licked his lips, leaving a secret smile, and glanced off into the trees.

"Yes, so what?"

"I want you to come. We all do, but especially I want that." He absentmindedly smoothed the grass between us, then stretched out in front of me. The curve of space between his hip and ribs told me just how thin he kept himself, and the skin that appeared there was clear but for a single mole that pulled at my eyes, hypnotic, like hers.

"You do?" I said.

"We could go now, if you desire it." The shirt rose a little more.

"We could?"

"Yes. I am called Cheve. That is short for horse, you know?"

He sat up when I laughed, pulling his shirt back down and pouting.

"Thank you, Cheval," I said. "But I don't do that sort of thing with boys."

"She can make anyone do anything, or anything do anyone." He went back to smoothing the grass.

"Shall I tell her you said so?" I didn't doubt him, but I wondered where he figured in all of this.

"No," he said. Then, "It doesn't matter." His hand waved away the annoying thought. "But I will tell you." He stared at me, his eyes a brilliant blue, too blue for anything but contact lenses, and he leaned forward. "It is driving us crazy, all this talk of you," he hissed. "The time is ripe for her in the month. You understand? Give her what she wants, then give her back to us. I beg you."

"What are you talking about?"

"She hasn't told you?" It was his turn to laugh.

■

The long walk back did nothing to clear my head. Images of skin and ice overlaid memories of Kim in the jungle of my thoughts. On my street I stumbled where the pavement had peeled away, revealing old and crumbling bricks. The cats in the window boxes watched me passively in the sun.

The phone was ringing when I made the landing. Then it stopped, and I caught my breath against the stench of the open *pissoir* behind me. Sweat beaded my forehead, dripped down against my ear, clean sweat. The key shook in my hand, and it took three attempts before I was able to insert it into the lock. Behind the door, Jean Christophe's phone started ringing again, and ice gripped the pit of my stomach.

I pulled out, throwing the keys down the *pissoir*, and felt the sweet wind rising as I raced back down the stairs and out past the empty playground.

LYNDA SCHOR

The Meaning of Chocolate

Lynda Schor is the author of three collections of short fiction. Her latest is
The Body Parts Shop, *published by the Fiction Collective Two (FC2). Her
stories and articles have been published in many magazines and anthologies. She has been nominated for an O. Henry Award, and has received
two Maryland State Arts Council grants and other prizes. She lives in New
York City and teaches at the Lang College of The New School. She's the
fiction editor of the online literary magazine* Salt River Review.

It's evening. My husband Al and I feel sweaty and sloppy, the
way I always feel when I'm with any of my family. We are seated
at a large glass table on a lovely landscaped terrace, drinking
chocolate martinis. Above the bushes lining the marble terrace,
the pillars of a huge white and brick porticoed mansion loom in
the brownish dusk. We are at Hershey House, in Hershey, PA. My
sister Isabella, her husband Elias, and their daughter Olivia are
also here. My other sister, Elena, her husband Gert, and their two
kids will be arriving tomorrow. In spite of hating these tourist
amusement parks, Al and I find the chocolate martinis delicious,
suitably ruinous to our diets, and are becoming slightly woozy.
Which is good, as neither of us wants to be there.

We're here because Elena and Isabella made us feel guilty, as
usual, for not wanting to join this small family reunion, as none
of them live in or near New York City, where Al and I live.

"Why can't they ever come visit us?" we always say to each
other. "Other people who have kids travel." "They can afford to
stay in any hotel in NYC," we say.

Isabella and Elias are very wealthy. He owns a Greek shipping company. But Isabella's always complaining she doesn't have enough money. What can't she afford? Isn't a five-million-dollar home in the hills of Los Angeles, with a pool, enough? And Elena's husband owns a world-renowned bedding company called Fluff-eroo.

Meanwhile, Al and I are the only ones who can't afford to stay at Hershey House. We had to rush right off to find some crummy tenement-like motel in the slummy section of Hershey—or maybe it's not Hershey, but some outskirt—where the chocolate-making slaves had to live. Because, as Isabella said, "this is an extremely popular place."

Though Al and I would never come here if we could help it, we saw right away that most Americans feel differently, and it is, indeed, popular, teeming with enormous families wearing shorts and striped shirts, with chocolate stains around their mouths.

After driving for hours we found our overpriced tenement motel about five miles on the outskirts of Chocolate Town. It was right behind a huge Ramada Inn and is called Ramada Outhouse.

Olivia, who is exhausted, as it's after eight-thirty p.m., and she's been on rides all day at the Amusement Park, and has been in the chocolate pool, slumps over the table, her head held up by her chocolate-stained hand. Her shorts and shirt look worn out too, limp, her shirt off one of her small, smooth white shoulders, a large chocolate stain resembling a bib surrounding her neckline. She perks up though at having some new people to talk to.

"I went on the roller coaster, and I wasn't even scared," she says, brushing her pale chocolate bangs back with chocolate-stained puffy fingers. "I went on the Chocolate Factory tour, and I saw how chocolate is made, and we floated on a chocolate sea, and they took a picture of us. And they gave us some free chocolate on the way out."

"Me, me, me," says Elias, who is balder than when I saw him last. He is wearing some pale flax Greek ceremonial shirt with red safari shorts.

"She's only a kid," says Isabella, who looks very much like me, yet looks totally different from me at the same time.

"Yeah," Isabella continued Olivia's story, "they showed us how Mr. Hershey tasted chocolate while on a fun trip in South America. It was a bitter cocoa drink made from cacao beans, and he thought he'd import the beans cheaply, and make chocolate here."

Olivia places her filthy fingers over her mother's mouth to stop the flow of words. I can smell her chocolatey fingers from across the table.

"Where's our food," says Al. I've ordered chicken in chocolate sauce, and Al has ordered steak in chocolate sauce. We're starving but feeling happier by the moment. Isabella orders more chocolate martinis for all.

Olivia holds up a photo she's pulled out of a grubby brown plastic bag she's been clutching. It's of Olivia, Isabella, and Elias, seated in an open tram car—Olivia and Isabella holding hands over the safety bar in the front seat, Elias looking over their faces, in the seat behind. They are smiling, though they seem somewhat surprised by the flash. Behind Elias sits an outsize fuzzy brown chocolate bar, wearing clothing, red shirt and shorts (is that an open fly?) that seem slightly awry.

"They take a photo of everyone who goes through the factory," says Olivia, her pale blue eyes glowing, "and then they give it to you."

"You have to buy it or you don't get it," says Isabella.

"That's business," says Elias, who talks about three things, money, business, and computers. Because he's a Republican we don't speak to each other much. "You have to admire the commercial chocolate empire Hershey has built here."

I don't tell him about the article I'm writing about the Hershey empire, for the magazine *Imperialist*, for which I'll be paid, if they like it, fifty dollars. "And then," I say, "Hershey got slaves, Indians from South America, to plant his chocolate beans and pick them, too, on the land he stole from them in Peru and Ecuador, and then he brought some slaves over here to mix the chocolate in his factory."

"He paid them," said Elias. "Is it his fault they needed the money so badly they'd work for practically nothing? Is it his fault that two cents a day looked good to them? Is it his fault they needed the money so much they'd work twenty-four hours a day? Hershey, like any good American businessman, only took advantage of the situation."

"This house, and the entire gorgeous Hershey gardens, was a gift from Hershey to his wife," says Isabella, flashing her twenty-four-carat diamond ring. Why her not me, just has to come into every woman's mind when they find that out. And it slips into mine.

Our food arrives. Isabella gets her chocolate truffles and mashed potatoes with chocolate sauce.

"I didn't order this," whines Olivia, throwing over her large glass of chocolate milk, which splashes into everyone's food, and our clothes, including my pale blue jeans.

"OK, OK," mollifies Isabella, wiping everywhere with whatever napkins she can find. "Just don't drink it. You can order something else."

"You're spoiling her," says Elias. "Don't order anything else for her."

Al and I observe the scene while mopping our clothes. For the first time in years we are on Elias's side. I sip my martini. I'm feeling somewhat smashed as I gaze into the candle on our table.

"Yes, yes," shouts Olivia, "I wanted the Chocolate Bean Champagne." She spits at the waiter, who flinches, looking like a flashbulb went off in his face. Al and I say nothing, though we'd love to see Isabella give Olivia a great big smack.

Elena too would have a hard time watching this. She is incredibly organized (she might be German—who knows—I thought I was adopted for a while), her house in Lake Forest, Illinois, is always spotless and her kids are always on schedule, neatly dressed, and very polite. If they forget to thank someone or to say goodbye, they are always reminded, either by Elena, or by her husband Gert, who IS German. "Is Elena really the way she seems or has she absorbed Gert's personality like part of some cult?" Isabella will ask me when we get home from some family gathering. Meanwhile Elena will call me complaining about Isabella's parenting of Olivia, who, Elena thinks, needs a regular bedtime and to be made to see the consequences of her acts rather than being indulged. "Talk to Isabella," says Elena. "No, you," I say, wondering whether keeping silent is the right thing. I guess they all get together and complain about me too.

"Olivia, apologize to the waiter," says Isabella tentatively.

"Nooo!" screams Olivia.

Al and I use our napkins to wipe the blood and lymphatic fluid from our necks from our burst eardrums, and watch incredulously as Isabella puts her arms around Olivia to comfort her for her screaming fit. Everyone else in the entire restaurant has turned toward us. Though we can't hear yet, we can see Isabella is offering Olivia five different possibilities of chocolate drinks.

"She needs to go to bed," says Elias, placing his arm hopefully around Isabella's shoulders.

Isabella removes Elias's arm by shrugging hard. "There's nothing less sexy than kids," says Isabella to me and Al, implying that, because we are artists, we are probably enjoying unimaginable sexual activities and experiences. I want her to think that to make up for the low regard she has of our commitment to writing and to being artists. But this isn't a sexy time for me either. All we seem to be doing is figuring out how to pay our rent, and how we can subsidize our writing-for-nothing habit. In fact, instead of thinking about Al and me throwing each other across our bed in our hideous motel room, I'm wondering who's going to pay the bill for all the chocolate drinks and food.

"Chocolate is an aphrodisiac," says Elias.

"Well this kid vacationland doesn't turn me on," says Isabella. She continues, "Why are you suddenly interested? We haven't screwed in four years."

Al looks alarmed when I offer to take Olivia back to the chocolate store so she can see the life-sized chocolate creatures parade for the last time today and to give Elias and Isabella some time alone together. Though at home in LA they have three nannies. Olivia takes my hand. Elias pays the bill.

At the chocolate store we wander the aisles and counters looking at chocolate cars, animals, books, and plain chocolate bars in every size, including one the size of a small TV set. There are Hershey Kisses in every size too—tiny ones, or ones as big as a baby.

I'm ready to drop. I'm just getting up the courage to suggest to Olivia that we bring her back to her parents, when people dressed as chocolate bars in clothing, and huge Hershey Kisses, aluminum foil covering their torsos, come marching out of some door and mingle with the kids, posing with them, while their parents take photos.

"Is this town racist?" asks Al. "I can't find dark chocolate anywhere."

"Do you want us to take your picture with that walking chocolate bar?" I ask Olivia. "Or that huge Hershey Kiss?" The Kiss has his round belly dressed in aluminum foil. He's wearing red tights on his skinny legs. The chocolate bar is obviously a woman, with lovely yellow legs and pretty, long, sienna hair.

Olivia looks horrified, and jumps back four feet. I bend down to talk to her, holding her around her waist. She studies the large creatures. "They're just people in there like you and me, wearing costumes," she reassures herself. "They're just people," she repeats, shrinking back more. This sounds like something her mother must have told her. I know she really believes they are enormous walking and talking chocolate items. Last year I watched her posing with huge Little Mermaids and a bigger-than-life-size Minnie Mouse at Disneyland in Orlando—that hellhole. We were there because we were made to feel guilty enough by Isabella and Elena to pay what a trip to Florence for two weeks would cost, for a crummy hotel a long bus ride from all the rides. And I know she thought they were real and not just people in costumes—she even got their autographs.

"Let's take her on the last ride of the day," says Al. I'm still feeling woozy from the chocolate martinis. I'm dizzy, and colors seem especially bright. But I'm game. Olivia, her shirt dripping off her shoulders, face and hands brown with dirt and chocolate, her shopping bag full of all sorts of chocolates, manages to run with us to where the tour train begins its Chocolate Factory tour. We are gingerly stepping into the open car, Al holding our bags, me hanging onto her elbow, when four giant Hershey Kisses, one with a red cloth mask around his/her face, grabs Olivia, who gives one of her heaven-splitting screams. I drop her arm as I raise my hands involuntarily over my ears. But maybe that was me screaming. The Kiss is carrying Olivia off, kicking and screaming, while the three other huge Kisses grab me and Al, and holding us, pull the lever to start the ride. In the background I hear a drone about Mr. Hershey discovering chocolate. We seem to be speeding forward in the open tram. One of the huge Kisses is tying my hands behind me with some soft purple ropes. Al, already cuffed in pink silk, is being undressed by a huge Kiss with long, bare legs that look human, and so do her pale bulbous breasts bursting from her foil wrap. Al's arms, pulled back by his cuffs, show up his slinky biceps, his triceps. I'm still struggling, but Al isn't. Two sexy female Kisses are slowly undressing him, and he seems to be enjoying it immensely. I wonder for a second how these heavy-bottomed Kisses can be sexy, but they are. I hear Al's ragged breathing. When, together, they pull down his Eddie

Bauer gray briefs, he gasps and I see that he's very excited. He's flushed and moves around as if attempting to escape, his swollen penis leading the way.

For a minute I feel betrayed, then realize I'm incredibly turned on too, and that jealousy has always excited me. Now a male Kiss is undressing me slowly while another, sex indeterminate, but who looks male sometimes, who has smooth slender arms, but seems to possess a long, thin penis, lifts my shirt, circling around my hardening nipples with delicate chocolate fingers, then blows hot breath on them. I feel my nipples harden and watch the large male Kiss slowly pull aside his foil wrap. I've never liked chocolate Kisses, but now I'm completely moist; I feel like I'm melting. For one second I remember Olivia. "Where's my niece?" I ask. But my anxiety just makes me hotter—the sense of danger can be heady. Moist and swollen, I feel a tremendous urge to get closer to the expanse of chocolate belly. I want this Kiss so much I can weep. But he teases me, coming closer slowly, so slowly. The car clangs metallically as it moves and turns along its track, and the chocolate narrative drones on. Shadows of muscular workers grinding beans and mixing chocolate in vats surround us. "Eat me," says the Kiss, finally pressing his warm belly against my hot flushed face. His liquid brown eyes are eloquent. These are only people, I tell myself. I place my swollen lips on that huge chocolate expanse, and press. The Kiss moans, and presses closer now, and closer. I stick my tongue into the chocolate, and it feels liquid, like a suction whirlpool. Soon I feel completely enwrapped, surrounded, subsumed. I spread my legs, I spread anything I can spread, I want to become part of the chocolate, I don't know where the chocolate ends. I am the chocolate.

I'm filling even as I'm surrounded. I lick, and suck, and ingest. From the corner of my eye Al seems similarly enveloped. Meanwhile I'm boiling hot, and I feel completely open. I can't tell where I begin and the chocolate people end, or which one is doing what, nor do I care. My arms are still held behind me and waves of burning excitement shiver through me, becoming stronger and stronger. I'm about ready to burst, but my chocolate Kiss man—or woman—keeps things so slow, keeping me from coming. Beautiful chocolate torture. Smooth chocolate pours silkily across my nipples, my hair, my face, and passes along between my open spread legs. My mouth is ravenously engaged in sucking. In huge waves the chocolate becomes sweeter and sweeter. A groan from someone—my Kiss? Al?—sends me off into an incredible orgasmic spasm that reverberates throughout my entire boundary-less body. When it finally ends and I've stopped trembling, I feel like a huge puddle.

Suddenly there's a flash! Our tram has slowed, and locks into place with a click. I feel exhausted, disoriented, dizzy, and look around trying to get my bearings, running my hands through my damp, messy curls. This is like waking instantly from a long wet dream—the kind that takes place in a public space. Am I even dressed? I recall that I have to find Olivia. Or was the kidnapping just a nightmare? There's another flash.

In the photo they sell us, Al and I are seated in the tram alongside Olivia, who is in the middle, between us. She's smiling and holding tight to the safety bar. Al and I are looking very full, bellies burgeoning. We are dressed, and look extremely satisfied, our eyes half-closed, our mouths and hands covered with chocolate.

When my high school boyfriend French-kissed me with a Hershey's Kiss in his mouth, I realized there was a brand-new frontier in pleasure ahead of me.

Ice Cream Headaches

Eugene Stein was raised in the Bronx, New York. His novel, Straitjacket & Tie, *was published by Ticknor & Fields. His collection of short stories,* Touch and Go, *was published by William Morrow/Rob Weisbach Books. His stories have appeared in* Harper's, Gargoyle, Iowa Review, *and* Witness, *among other publications, and he has won a Pushcart Prize. He lives with his partner and their two daughters in Los Angeles.*

W endy wiped her mouth on her hand. "Stupid, the man lies on top of the woman."

"You're both right," Susan said with great authority. She was twelve, a year older than her sister Wendy, three years older than her sister Laura. She ate a Dixie cup of ice cream because she believed that licking a cone made her look childish. Their mother always ordered ice cream in a cup. It was a warm Saturday in June—so warm that their parents had given Susan money to buy a treat at the Baskin-Robbins around the block from their apartment building, even though they hadn't yet eaten lunch.

They had all asked for paper cups of water, because cold water was delicious with ice cream. Not everyone knew that.

"What way do Mommy and Daddy do it?" Laura asked, licking her cone contentedly.

Susan didn't know and therefore ignored the question. "Laur, let me taste your ice cream." Susan had bought pistachio ice cream, which Laura hated, but Laura had bought vanilla fudge ice cream, which Susan loved. Susan licked Laura's cone several times.

"Give it back!"

"You said I could taste it." She licked it again.

"Susan!"

"Stop being such a baby." Susan licked the cone before handing it back to Laura.

Wendy, worried that Susan would want to taste her cone, too, began eating her strawberry ice cream with great haste. She got a headache from the cold.

"How often do they do it?" Laura asked.

"A lot," Susan said.

"But how often?"

"Three times a week."

"How do you know that?" Wendy demanded. Her stomach felt queer. "You don't know that." She had never imagined it could be so often. She had thought it was perhaps once or twice a year.

Susan shrugged. "I'm estimating."

"What does that mean, estimating?" Laura asked.

A boy with straight dirty blonde hair, wearing shorts and an Elton John T-shirt—it was 1974—passed by outside the ice cream parlor, carrying a thin musical instrument case. He glanced inside, stopped for a moment, and then walked away.

Laura looked at the boy and then back at her sisters. "Susan, what does that mean, estimating?"

"He looked at us," Wendy whispered.

"No he didn't." Susan, looking down at her cup, scooped up the last of her ice cream.

"You like him!" Laura guessed.

"Don't be a jerk."

"He's cute," Wendy said.

"You like blonde hair," Laura insisted. She knew it was true, and now she was uneasy, because she didn't like blonde hair and she didn't like boys. And so Susan's interest in the blonde boy—an interest measured, Wendy and even Laura could tell, by the intensity with which Susan studied the bottom of her cup—had separated the sisters.

Susan decided to change the conversation. "Who are you going to marry, Laur?"

They had played this game before. "I'm going to marry—I'm going to marry—" Laura didn't know whom she was going to marry.

"I'm going to marry a doctor, so we can go to Bermuda on vacation," Wendy said. Their next-door neighbors, Dr. and Mrs. Wachtel, traveled often. The Lerner children watered their plants for them when they were gone. Dr. Wachtel was their pediatrician.

"I'm going to marry an artist, and live in Paris, and speak French, and eat snails," Susan told them.

"Yuck," Laura said. But the snails fascinated her...

The blonde boy walked back in front of the ice cream parlor and waved at them.

"He waved!" Laura cried.

Susan was nearly choking with anger. "Stop looking at him!"

"But he waved at us," Wendy said.

"It's rude to stare," Susan told her sisters. She chewed nervously on her wooden spoon, which resembled a miniature version of the tongue depressors Dr. Wachtel used. She had told her mother she didn't want to go to Dr. Wachtel's office anymore. She didn't want him to see her naked, not when he lived next door.

"He's coming in," Wendy whispered.

"He's looking at us!" Laura bounced with excitement in her chair.

"I know him," Susan said quietly, wiping her hands on a napkin.

The boy stood in front of their table and dropped the case at his side. "Hi."

"Hi," Susan said.

Laura was mesmerized by the boy and especially by his case. "What's in there?"

"My clarinet."

He was speaking to Laura but he was looking at Susan, and Wendy was jealous. She wanted to be as tall as Susan and draw as well as Susan, she wanted the boys to like her as much as—or more than—they liked Susan. She didn't want to marry a doctor, Wendy decided. She wanted to marry a musician.

"Can I see?" Laura pleaded.

"Just ignore her," Susan said.

"I'll show you." The boy opened the case, and the girls looked at the gleaming sections of his clarinet.

"Did you break it?" Laura asked.

"No. It fits together." He snapped the case shut. "You want to go to the schoolyard?" he asked Susan.

"Yeah." Susan got up from her seat. "Here." She gave Wendy a dollar bill. "You can get some more ice cream. But then go straight home."

Wendy bought a Dixie cup of ice cream this time. Laura ordered another cone and chewed the ice cream more than licked it. She loved the rich ribbons of chocolate.

"You'll get a headache," Wendy said.

Laura didn't care. She ate the ice cream quickly, because it was delicious and before it could be taken away.

■

At home, no one answered when Wendy knocked at the front door of the apartment. Wendy had already gotten out her key and was working it into the top lock when her mother opened the door. Barefoot, she was dressed in her terry cloth bathrobe, which she rarely wore. "I didn't hear you."

"We knocked," Wendy said.

"Mommy, your hair," Laura complained.

"I didn't have time to brush it. Where's Susan?"

Wendy moved past them into the living room, where her father was sitting in his boxer shorts, reading the newspaper. He usually wore an undershirt around the house, but now he was bare-chested. Earlier, at breakfast, he had worn his undershirt. And their mother had been in her nightgown. Her father's chest hairs were turning gray, Wendy noticed. In front of him, on a dish on the coffee table, was a thick slice of halvah, his favorite dessert.

"Daddy, you're not even dressed," Laura said.

Wendy's stomach knotted tight. She retreated to the bedroom she shared with Laura. It was too hot today. She pulled down her purple blanket, stripped off her shirt and shorts, and threw herself on her bed wearing only her underpants, lying against the cool of the sheets. She breathed into her pillow, then rolled over and cleaned lint out of her bellybutton.

She remembered, as a little girl, thinking that babies came out of the mother's navel.

Now she was thinking about something else. It was funny that her parents hadn't gotten dressed. Some mornings they liked to lie in bed.

They liked it. She had never understood that they might like it.

Her parents had converted the dining room of the apartment into a living room, and the original living room into a third bedroom, where they slept. Because the old living room had no door, her parents had installed an accordion door, which was usually folded open. Some mornings, when Wendy got up early, the accordion door was latched shut. Until now, she had never understood.

Her feet rubbed against the wool blanket at the foot of the bed; the wool itched but she liked it. *Her parents liked it.*

"Are you OK?" Her mother had come into the room and now she felt Wendy's forehead.

"No," Wendy lied.

"You don't feel warm."

She groaned. "I'm sick."

"Sweetheart, what's the matter? Is it your stomach?"

Her mother sat on the edge of the bed and Wendy crawled into her arms. She let her mother rock her. "You're my big girl," her mother said.

She stroked her mother's bathrobe. *Like this*, Wendy thought. This was how she liked her mother.

■

They stopped at a candy store on the way to the schoolyard and bought a Hershey's bar and split it, and Susan's hands were still sticky. Then they decided to go to the park instead of the schoolyard, and in the park she stopped to wash her fingers in the water fountain. Andy washed his hands too and their fingers touched under the water.

The shock of his hand, of his fingers touching her. His fingers were bigger than hers. Musical fingers. He said sometimes his fingers knew a piece better than he did.

He was older than she, a grade ahead and a year and a half older. He was starting to grow tall, and in the last few months Susan had watched his face change shape.

They had first met in the park, she playing with an older friend, he with a younger. They had paired off almost immediately, confusing their friends. She liked his fingers and he had held her hand. Sometimes they wouldn't see each other for a week or two because they went to different schools but now in the spring they saw each other more, meeting in the neighborhood or making plans to meet in the park. She was too young to date; her mother said she couldn't date yet, she wasn't even thirteen.

In the park they ran into friends of his and they ran in the woods. He put down his clarinet case and they ran. It was a game, he said, run catch kiss, the others had all played it before.

Delightful to run in the park between the trees, delightful to scare the squirrels and to laugh. She was laughing and breathing hard, he would try to grab her, she would run away.

To breathe hard, to feel him touch her, to smell the trees, to crunch the tree droppings underfoot, to hear his friends scream and laugh, to fall on the grass... Dizzy, dizzy running this way and that, falling...

He tackled her and she fell to the ground, she smelled the grass and the dirt, the beautiful loamy smell of the dirt and the green smell of the grass, she was laughing. The world rolled underneath her, the sky rose and her heart rose, the whole world was shiny. It was all so beautiful, *he said he would take her to a concert*. Now he kissed her and she tasted chocolate, wonderful chocolate, her chocolate mouth and his chocolate breath.

Andrew likes me.

∎

Laura told her parents she was leaving and ran out of the house before anyone could stop her. At night her mother wouldn't let her go outside alone but during the day she still could. She went to the schoolyard but they weren't there. She went back to the ice cream store but there were only families there, families eating ice cream for lunch, fat fathers licking ice cream cones with double scoops, small children with chocolate smeared across their faces. Her mother looked down on people like that, mothers who didn't feed their families well, but then she had sent them out for ice cream this morning. So everyone made exceptions. She couldn't find Susan anywhere. They might be here in the park but the park was too big. A hole in the fence led to the golf course and they could be anywhere on the golf course.

She walked down the path to a wooded part of the park. It was quieter here, darker and cooler. Sometimes, under the dark shade of the trees, the lights along the path would come on early, right in the middle of the afternoon. At least that's what Wendy had told her. Laura had walked here at night with her father and the lampposts buzzed like bees.

No one was here. She twirled around and around, like the tornado in *The Wizard of Oz*, making herself dizzy. She had eggs inside her but they weren't ready to hatch. Her mother had explained it all. "I'm estimating, I'm estimating!" she sang. The secret word thrilled her, she vibrated like the lampposts.

She didn't like boys.

She liked her friend Ellen.

She got tired and staggered over to a bench. She had a daydream that she frightened people with her amazingly accurate weather forecasts. She had another daydream that she predicted a tornado but no one would believe her.

Someone had dropped a Tootsie Roll on the ground, and the ants were swarming over it. She watched the ants for a long time and when she looked up, she realized that she had been hearing the sounds of boys and girls playing in the woods on the other side of the path. She edged closer to the woods. Through the trees, she could see girls running. Sometimes the girls ran fast, sometimes they screamed with happy terror. Sometimes they let themselves get caught and kissed by the boys. Laura liked looking at them. They were older than Susan, most of the girls, but Susan was there, too.

She heard Susan laughing. Her sister. Susan liked it, she liked the boy and she liked kissing him.

Laura sat back down on the bench and bowed her head, dizzy again. She didn't like boys like that. *Now she knew she would never change.*

The ants surged around the Tootsie Roll. They liked the sugar. They brought it back to their queen and the queen had babies. When she was a little girl she thought a man gave a woman a seed to eat and the woman ate the seed.

Laura picked up one of the ants on her finger. Ellen said that in South America they ate chocolate-covered ants. Laura loved the smell of Ellen's clothes and pillowcase—Ellen's mother used fabric softener. Laura liked smelling her girlfriends.

She wanted to marry—Ellen.

Ellen's sister said a boy could put his weenie in a girl's mouth, some girls liked that.

That's what it was like with a boy. Laura put the ant in her mouth. She pretended it was chocolate, but she could hardly taste it. She had chosen a small one.

"What are you doing?" Susan was yelling at her. "Are you crazy?" Susan was standing there, watching her. And the boy was with her.

Laura ran away, humiliated, crying. They had seen her eat the ant. Oh God, they had seen her eat the ant. She tried to spit it out, but it was too late. Now she knew she would never change. They had seen her and the ant was already inside her.

Chocolate, men, coffee— some things are better rich.

CHRISTY
SHEFFIELD
SANFORD

Dreams of Snakes, Chocolate and Men

Christy Sheffield Sanford won a 1999 Alden B. Dow Creativity Fellowship. She was also recently selected in international competition as the trAce Virtual Writer-in-Residence. In 1998, she was awarded The Well's prize for the Best Hyperlinked Work on the Web. Her online work has been published in Light and Dust, Enterzone, Ylem, Salt Hill, *and many other ezines and project sites. She has won a National Endowment for the Arts Fellowship and is the author of seven books, including* The H's: The Spasm of a Requiem, The Italian Smoking Piece, *and* Only the Nude Can Redeem the Landscape.

Snake On Captiva Island I sit on a ledge beside palmettos; a blue and green snake sticks its head through pine straw, I lift the reptile, thin as my ring finger, and it expands to a gray, puffy-cheeked, diamondback rattler the length of a bed. Trembling, I sling the snake onto snapping twigs.

Chocolate Bar Hmmm, my bittersweet addiction. A waiter serves me a dark, satiny chocolate bar, lumpy with peanuts like a Baby Ruth, but with a few bites missing. My teeth clamp on something hard. I try again. My jaws ache. I shove the confection off the table. The dessert plate breaks.

Snake,
Chocolate Bar

A viper slithers over an inedible candy bar. I tear aside the skin, do a cross section on the bar—discover only a teleidoscope of rich designs. Even under the microscope, candy looks alluring. Yet the surfaces within surfaces confound me.

Man,
Snake,
Chocolate Bar

A swarthy man wears a violet shirt and eats pink watermelon. A purple snake shifts in his black hair, slides across his chest, intertwines our legs. He peels a wrapper from his chocolate bar, munches the candy, passes it to me. I taste. "Theobroma—food of the gods," he whispers. A delicious spasm ripples through my pelvis.

Chocolate,
Snakes,
Man

Last night the chocolate factory exploded and burned. The smell of scorched chocolate permeated every room in my house. The lost, luscious promises. In the surrounding woods, some snakes fled underground; others died of smoke inhalation. And in the plant, a man eating watermelon on his break perished.

Chocolate,
Men,
Snakes

Even now in the Orinoco basin, harvesters with machetes reap cocoa pods for me. My brain still carries the chemicals chocolate and men trigger. All over the world, men in violet shirts split watermelons and toast me with their juicy sections. Racers, whips, cobras and kings wait, ready to weave through all my dreams.

Patrick Chapman

Return of the Empress

Patrick Chapman was born in 1968 and lives in Dublin. His poetry books are Jazztown *(Raven, 1991),* The New Pornography *(Salmon, 1996),* Touchpaper Star *(Lapwing, 2004), and* Breaking Hearts and Traffic Lights *(Salmon, due 2007). He was shortlisted for a Hennessy Award in 1995 and 1999. His story, "A Ghost," won first prize in the 2003 Cinescape Genre Literary Contest. Also in 2003, he wrote* Burning the Bed, *a film starring Gina McKee and Aidan Gillen. It was named Best Narrative Short at the 2004 DeadCenter Film Festival in Oklahoma.*

It was a Turkish Delight from La Maison du Chocolat that gave Clora Lynne the idea. She would become immortalized in her own special way. Certainly, she had been an icon of the small screen in Britain in the 1980s, but her star had faded. Nobody now remembered that she had once ruled the vast, totalitarian Human Empire that had radiated from Earth as far as seventy light years. They remembered her frocks, yes, and her high heels; her long, flowing red hair and her outrageous makeup. They vaguely remembered the character, Leonora, but not remotely did they remember the actor.

As far as Clora Lynne was concerned, she had been the most glamorous thing in that BBC TV show, *Raven's Rebels*. Her antagonist, the bitter anti-hero Raven, or, as the actor was called, Davison Ross, was another matter. He was still a minor celebrity and seemed these days to make a living on the convention circuit in the States. She had read on the Internet recently that he had just done a commercial for a hemorrhoid ointment.

Clora Lynne was above all that. She was beyond infinity, as it were. She could not bear to expose the aged whale that she had become to those young men for whom, thirty years earlier, she had been a masturbatory fantasy. Now, secluded in a luxurious Paris suite paid for by her divorce, Clora Lynne had turned her back on the world. Every one of her sixty years had gathered now, in the folds of her flesh hanging loose around her hips, in the deflated barrage balloons that had once been the most famous breasts in England, in the varicose tracery that seemed to hold her legs together, in the old, sagging skin that was more like a carrier bag for her body, tied up in her hair that, though still red and long, had streaks of gray in it. Someone, she thought, someone should tear that bag open and perhaps, just perhaps, they would find a gift inside it.

In her youth, she had appeared in a number of Hammer films, usually as a virgin deflowered by a witchfinder, or as sacrificial jailbait, or as a bride of Dracula. Christopher Lee had once asked her out on a date, but she had turned him down on the grounds that he was, being immortal, too old for her. A spell on ITV's police drama *Blue Light* had taken care of the rent for a while, but in those days, television actors were paid hardly anything and besides, she had been much more interested in religion, so she had walked. One of those utopian seventies cults had claimed her for a few months spent in a spartan commune on an island off Scotland. Though uplifted at first, she soon tired of the Exegesis therapy and discovered that the politics of the place were far from utopian. They were, in fact, enough to drive anyone insane, so insane she went: when she returned to the real world, she accepted a sudden marriage proposal from the American film producer Ed Wallace, eighteen years her senior and rich off the back of a few successful disaster movies.

Then came *Raven's Rebels* in 1979. Suggestions in the press of an affair with Davison Ross had almost endangered her marriage to Wallace, but he had let the rumors pass, without ever quite believing her protestations of innocence. The truth was that Ross had, on several occasions, propositioned her. He had persistently begged to fuck her, in character. Every time, Clora Lynne turned him down. After all, Ross was himself married, to the steadfast and ordinary Johanna Fitch, a makeup artist he had met in the 1960s, while he was in rep in Leeds and she was nightly transforming him, a white man from Somerset, into Othello.

As the show became a hit in the UK, with over ten million viewers tuning in regularly, Clora Lynne found herself in the public eye. She did not like the attention but whenever there was a camera or a reporter handy, she encouraged it. She also did not like the conditions in which she had to work. There was not much of a budget on that show, so for all her high heels and camp frocks, the production just looked cheap. Quarries doubled as alien worlds. Nuclear power stations were spaceports. The flats that formed the walls of her flagship used to wobble. The increasingly less salubrious guest artistes—at first the usual RSC types, and, in later years, high-profile stars of light entertainment who could not act, but would draw in jaded viewers as the ratings took a nosedive—began to give the show a patina of tinsel which she found depressing. Five years into the show, Ross was the bigger star. After a particularly gruesome evening out with the cast, at the end of which Ross put his hand on her ass and asked her to join him in the greenroom for a hand shandy, Clora Lynne refused him one last time, then threw a glass of Blue Nun in his face.

A week later, Ross had her fired. The producers informed her that at the end of the current run, she would be let go.

At least, Clora Lynne had thought, *they'll have to give me a spectacular exit. A dramatic death scene.*

Instead, they simply wrote her out. She did not even appear in the last couple of episodes of the fifth series. Early in the sixth, a minor character alluded to her arrest and imprisonment in a coup. Leonora was replaced with a younger vamp, played by Candace

Wells, a redhead who had once slept with Ross while they were both in a production of *Run for Your Wife!* in Scarborough.

However, at the end of the sixth series, *Raven's Rebels* itself was canceled. *The public missed me,* Clora Lynne often thought to herself. *That show was dead without me. I was Leonora, Empress of the Human Worlds, Lord Protector of the True Philosophy, High Admiral of All the Fleets, and Successor to the Glorious Founder. And they wrote me out.*

Three weeks after the show went off the air, a tabloid story involving herself, a young fan, and twenty gallons of drinking chocolate ended her career, her marriage, and her life in England.

These days, Clora Lynne knew, such a scandal would have meant that she would get her own chat show, a column in *The Independent on Sunday,* and a recording contract. Despite everything, Wallace had been generous. He had just produced a series of Hollywood space operas and had negotiated for himself a large cut of the merchandise. Her divorce settlement paid for the luxury suite on the Rue du Faubourg St-Honoré. It paid the staff to be courteous but not officious. It paid for chocolate, which she still liked, as befitted an Empress, to bathe in. She had the men downstairs blend gallons of drinking chocolate for her and bring it up in the elevator, in drums. They would pour the creamy liquid into the bath, then withdraw discreetly. They thought her mad, or at least eccentric, but this was Paris. You could do what you liked, if you had money. She never had visitors. She rarely went out. The telephone almost never rang. Twice, early on, the night porter, Lamargue, had tried to interest her in a gigolo, but she had declined and nobody had suggested such a thing again.

Instead, she read Proust, over and over, for eighteen years. "It seems to me," she once told the concierge, Ribaud, before she was confident enough to use French, "that if you are going to go the whole hog with Proust, you might as well do him the honor of taking as long to read it as he took to write it." It did not register with Ribaud that she was being amusing.

Neither did he guess that although she spoke with Received Pronunciation, she was actually from Carmarthen.

Alone in her room, with a freshly delivered bath of drinking chocolate waiting for her, Clora Lynne would take off her clothes and stand naked in the hotel room. Appraising her old flesh in the mirror, she imagined herself being eaten out by a succession of fanboys, all of whom had, in their own tiny minds, jerked off to the sound of her evil laughter, each of whom had, in her daydream, to stuff her mouth with delicacies from La Maison du Chocolat before she could come. Though standing, Clora Lynne would almost pass out with that fantasy of those little turd-burglars making love to her as she was now, rather than as they preferred her to be, before she would snap out of it and go to the bath and take care of herself. There, she would lie down, sinking in like a hippo, masturbating herself to a raucous orgasm. Often, she would gush. She would close her eyes as though succumbing to the deep, warm, anesthetic of a chocolate death by drowning. It was the ending she had not been given, the ending she desired, the ending—on more than one occasion of falling asleep briefly before her breath geysered out—that she very nearly had.

Twenty years of this. People had given up on her. The boy, the young fanboy, had grown up and was now running a web-site in honor of the show and the woman whose career he had destroyed. He once wrote on his site that Ross had put him up to it. Ross's lawyers had made him take that posting down, though they had not closed the site. That boy, Clora Lynne knew, was in love with the fictional character she had played, and vilified the real her as a fake for having not lived up to his ideal of the Empress. She sometimes read his site at the computer in her master bedroom and wondered what would happen if they actually met again. She might have to strangle the little scumbag. Scandal was something that Clora Lynne was less comfortable with than fame. How had it been? In her chocolate bath, she would reminisce.

Terrence Elliotte had seduced her. His little fanwank fantasy was to be caught naked with his Empress. And he had succeeded. Oh, he had known how to get under her skin. They had met at a fan convention in Chicago, the last one she ever attended. Elliotte—stupid name, she thought, for a stupid little fuckwit—had flown over from London to meet her. He had come up to her at a signing and got her to autograph the black-and-white ten-by-eight publicity photograph that showed her staring off into space, her hands around her throat. Appealing to her sense of vanity, he had bought her drinks that night at the convention's disco. He had bought her cigarettes. He had bought her expensive chocolates from a local boutique.

Elliotte had claimed to be nineteen and she had believed him. With sweet words she rarely heard in those days, he enticed her to bring him up to her hotel room. What he hadn't told her, and what she discovered suddenly as she lay naked in a bath of chocolate, expecting him to join her, was that he had also brought along a photographer from one of the London redtops.

The man burst in. Eight snaps later and she was finished. Her chocolate-covered breasts were all over *The Sun* a day later, accompanied by an interview with the boy who was now "in hiding for fear of reprisals by rabid fans." Even his worried parents did not know where he was, and the newspaper was not telling. On her return to England, reporters ambushed her at Arrivals in Heathrow. Back in her Kensington flat, there was a fax from L.A. It was Wallace, expressing disappointment in her poor taste and demanding a divorce.

The police called around but took the incident no further than a few questions. Quite literally, in England now, she could not get arrested.

Chocolate was the only means by which Clora Lynne could have an orgasm. It had started in her teens when she found that, on eating a Fry's Turkish Delight while masturbating, the intensity of her orgasms was magnified. If she had her mouth stuffed with this chocolate, she would gush like Niagara inverted. Soon, she could not come without it. Eventually, she had taken to bathing in drinking chocolate. At her divorce proceedings, Ed Wallace cited her chocolate addiction as grounds. She found that, at least, quite amusing. He also cited the incident in Chicago. And besides all of the above, there were the enormous cleaning bills.

A luxury hotel suite in Paris, even one as deliriously well appointed as this one, with its three bedrooms, two lounges, and ostentatious bathroom, all done in the style of Louis Quatorze, even a hotel suite in Paris with nine television sets, can be your very own Bastille.

Clora Lynne liked to watch television. Sometimes she would have a couple of sets in each room. Then, once in a while, she liked to watch all nine sets simultaneously, bringing them into the main bedroom, plugging them into a pair of extension cords, basking in cathode rays as though sunbathing in the light of fame.

When not taking chocolate baths, while chain-smoking Marlboro Lights, while cursing the terrible fortune that had brought her to this place and the enormous fortune that kept her here, she would revel in the horrors of European television. The French channels—with their subtitled crime capers, bad variety programs, and inept soap operas—made her think that, if she had still had a career, she could have landed a lead role in any one of them. The Italian channels, with their porn-inflected news programs, made her jealous of those slut housewives who were nobody until they exposed their breasts, whereas she had been nobody after she had done the same. On the German stations, all she could watch without laughing was *Raumschiff Enterprise: Das Nächste Jahrhundert.* It heartened her to see Patrick Stewart dubbed into very stiff German, as though a car salesman had taken over his voice. If only, Clora Lynne thought, if only I had auditioned for that show. I would have walked away with the part of Deanna Troi, who also liked chocolate. Given her then-status as *persona non grata*, she had not received the call. It had occurred to her that, having had one role in a hit space opera, she was considered too famous. She had been too good for *Star Trek*.

In her heart, she would have given anything to have that kind of exposure again. She would even have accepted the role of Beverly Crusher. Her own show never appeared on German television. In truth, Clora Lynne would not be able to watch the beautiful young woman she had been. The icon. The Empress. Still, they could have sent her a DVD, though she had not even been asked to do a commentary.

Now, as she rose, she felt for the first time odd that she had left all nine sets on with the sound down, flickering silently through the night. She could not sleep without being bathed in the cold glow of television, and she always left them on, but now, this morning, it was strange to her.

In the shower, she found a lump in her left breast. She spent the rest of the day sitting naked on her bed, almost catatonic, watching the blitzkrieg in Iraq, the bathycolpian Italian house-wives, the worst of French variety.

The following day, Clora Lynne decided to go out. It was a cold, crisp Wednesday morning in April, nearly eleven, when she rose from her bed where she had fallen asleep at some hour she could not remember. She did not order breakfast. She did not have a shower. Feeling her breast, she found the lump still there.

She went straight for the wardrobe and put on an elaborate black dress that had a starburst insignia on the front, and a high collar at the back. It was one that she used to be able to fit into easily but now it accentuated the flab around her belly and her legs. She did not put on knickers or a bra. Black shoes that pinched her feet, a pearl necklace that Wallace had given her, and a black Prada handbag completed her ensemble. In the bathroom mirror, she looked like an echo of someone powerful. *A deranged image of a glamour queen,* she thought. *Well, maybe that's what I am.* The dress was the one she had worn in Episode 48, in which Raven had nearly succeeded in blowing her up.

Downstairs in the lobby, she went over to the reception desk. There was only Ribaud on duty, and no bellboy, and a few residents coming and going. A sour-looking couple in what she took to be their twenties stood in front of the desk, checking in.

"Monsieur," Clora Lynne said, regardless, trying to get Ribaud's attention. He was a wiry man whose skin looked like he had stolen it from a chicken. In his seventies, uniformed, circumspect, he seemed to Clora Lynne to be every inch the indifferent Parisian. In fact, he was from a small village near Antibes.

"Un moment," said Ribaud.

"Monsieur!"

Ribaud ignored her. He smiled at the young couple, waiting as the man signed in. Then, Ribaud handed the key to the young woman. He did not call for anyone to help them with their bags, so they picked up their own luggage and dragged themselves over to the elevator.

By now, Clora Lynne had taken a pad of hotel stationery, written something on it with a hotel pen, and torn the page off. She held it up for him. Ribaud turned to her. *"Madame Lynne. Je vois qu'aujourd'hui vous êtes l'Empresse."* Impatiently, Clora Lynne gave him the piece of paper with her instructions on it. *"Je veux que vous obteniez ces articles pour moi. Chargez-les à ma pièce."*

"Certainement, Madame." He took the paper, glanced at it, and looked up at her with a wry smile at her stiff French.

As imperiously as she could manage, Clora Lynne turned on her heel and walked away toward the revolving front door.

Out on Rue du Faubourg St-Honoré, she headed for La Maison du Chocolat. As she walked, she observed the people: poor, stinking humanity. If Raven were here, with his powerful starship, *Emancipator*, he could take them all out with the push of a button. But he probably wouldn't. Even an anti-hero as bitter as he had nonetheless been the good guy.

Taking people out at the push of a button had been her job, until The Powers That Be had written her out. Halfway to the store, she stopped in the street to feel her left breast and although she could not detect the lump, she knew it was there. Perhaps, when she got to the shop, she could ask them to wrap it in hard chocolate and isolate it from the rest of her body.

La Maison du Chocolat was busy. They knew her there, but did not make that too obvious.

Every so often, Clora Lynne would turn up and buy a Boîte Maison, an artillery of intense bursts of pleasure: a variety of ganaches infused with the flavors of summer: apricot and lavender, melon and port, passion fruit and coriander. As she stood in the boutique, casting an avaricious eye over the displays, she tried to not notice other customers. They were in the way and this was her private paradise.

Today, she ordered something simple. She spotted five Turkish Delights, covered in dark chocolate, and immediately knew that she had to have them: one for every year she had been Empress.

Minutes after leaving La Maison du Chocolat, Clora Lynne was sitting outdoors at a small table, with a café latte and a glass of water in front of her. The waiter was, of course, rude, but the coffee was deliriously good. To her, French coffee was the best in the world. As she sipped, she deliberated on whether to have the chocolates all at once or to save them for later. One orgasm for each Turkish Delight. That was the plan.

She put down her coffee cup and decided. Reaching into her bag, she took out the tiny box and put it on the table. Then she opened it, picked up one of the chocolates, bit a corner off, and came, there in the street, quietly, without anyone noticing.

It took her minutes to regain her focus and when she did, she found herself staring at the chocolate, a brown square with a little corner of pink where she had bitten it.

In that moment, something changed in her. She knew now what she would do.

Later that day, as she lay in her room watching television, Ribaud telephoned and told her that the items she had ordered were ready. He sounded sad on the room's old, bakelite telephone. "I also have the number you wanted," he said, in English.

Clora Lynne wrote it down. Then she got up off the bed and went to her computer, where she emailed Terrence Elliotte to tell him what a little prick he was and that now she wanted payback for what he had done to her.

Davison Ross was at home when she called him that evening.

"What are you wearing?" he asked, after their awkward reintroduction and a few false apologies.

"Nothing," Clora Lynne said.

"My God, woman," Ross said. "Have you no shame?"

"You know I don't."

There was a pause. Ross broke the silence. "Clora, listen. Why are you calling me?"

"I wanted," she said, "I wanted to offer you something."

"Why now, when all those years ago, I couldn't have you even if I paid you?"

"I'm dying, Davison. I have cancer. I want...to see what it's like."

"I should think you'd hate me, after all the things I did to you."

"You want to fuck the Empress," Clora Lynne said. "I want to fuck Raven. Bring your costume."

"What's that you said?" asked Davison, suddenly registering an important fact.

"I want to fuck you in character."

"No, about the cancer."

"I have it. I don't know how long I'll have it, though. Cancer is like that."

"I'm...I'm sorry to hear that. Listen, I've got to go to Milton Keynes tomorrow to do a Q&A with the fan club. After that, I'm in Birmingham to shoot a training video."

"Do you want to fuck me or not?"

"Well, you're old now."

"So are you."

"I suppose...I suppose in character it would be all right."

"How's Johanna?"

"She's fine. Fine. And the cats are fine, too. She's out with the girls tonight. Bridge."

"Will you come?"

"That depends on what you do to me, you dirty wench."

"I hate you, Davison Ross. But I want this."

"Old girl," Ross said. "You were the only one who ever refused me. How could I resist, even if you are a fat old trout?"

"I'll fly you over. You can't be making much money from asshole cream."

"You heard about that? Well, it beats being on *EastEnders*."

Five evenings later, they sat having dinner in a dark little restaurant near La Bastille, Les Mouches. It was a cosy place, busy, with a couple of waiters dashing to and fro in a more or less comical, if random, dance. The walls were amber stone, broken by windows of etched glass. The furniture was bentwood and roughly elegant. At the back was a long zinc bar where Parisians sat and drank wine or coffee. There was, thankfully as far as Clora Lynne was concerned, no music.

They had already had their starters, and now Davison Ross tucked into a steak tartare while Clora Lynne picked at her veal chop. They were drinking a particularly fine Michel Lynch. The two actors seemed from a distance to be chatting amiably like old lovers.

Ross had left his bag in Clora Lynne's hotel room before they'd gone out for the evening. He was wearing a dark suit, with a white shirt open at the neck, like an orchestra leader gone AWOL. Clora Lynne wore a pair of black trousers and a blue silk blouse. She had washed.

Ross was well preserved for his sixty-four years. No longer the dashing young man that Clora Lynne remembered, but his face was still handsome, and his body, while overweight, still spoke of someone powerful and well fed. He had the appearance of a man who lived the good life. His accent, like hers, was RP, and seductive. No hint of his original Somerset remained. Perhaps he was putting it on.

After half an hour of reminiscing about actors they both knew, and dodging any real conversation, Ross said, "I can't believe I'm sitting here in a Paris restaurant with you."

"That," Clora Lynne said, picking up a piece of veal on her fork, "is because you never believe anything." She swallowed the veal.

"A lady of your years should not be living in seclusion like this."

"It's my choice now," Clora Lynne said. "At first, though, it was my only choice."

"Well," Ross said. "We all make mistakes."

She glared at him. He regarded her coolly.

"Remember Martin?" Ross asked, taking a sip from his wine.

"How's he doing?"

"He's playing King Lear at the Almeida."

"Bastard," Clora Lynne said.

"On our show, he couldn't string two words together."

"He was a drunk," she said. "A liar and a wanker."

"And a tart," Ross said, "though I suppose we all were."

"Only, you, Davison. You'd jump on anything. Male, female, dissenter."

"It's not my fault if I had a short attention span."

"How's your meat?"

"Raw."

"Unlike your performance in *Mother Goose*. Overcooked, apparently."

"You didn't see that, surely."

"I read about it on the web."

"From that little shit who destroyed you?" Ross's face went white.

Clora Lynne paused and looked him in the eye. "That was you, wasn't it?"

"I swear, Clora, on my mother's false teeth—"

"Nobody would ever dare to be *your* mother." Clora Lynne picked up her wineglass and emptied it.

"I suppose you're right."

"Anyway, that stuff is all in the past. I'm dying and it makes no difference."

"I'm really sorry to hear that," Ross said. "But tell me one thing. You never wanted me. You never did. You threw a glass of Liebfraumilch over me."

"It was Blue Nun. And of course I wanted you, but not like that. I didn't want to give in to your filthy little dick-brain."

"Oh, Clora," Ross said. "If only you had said yes. I would have left Johanna there and then. You and I—"

"Don't be an asshole, Davison. I want you now, and that's enough."

Two hours later, after a walk through the streets of Paris, during which they got increasingly romantic and sentimental, Clora Lynne and Davison Ross arrived back at her hotel. In her suite, they closed the door, turned on the lights and went into the master bedroom.

Clora Lynne had had champagne brought up. It was waiting for them, in a bucket on the dresser, beside two flutes. There was a note from Ribaud which said *Bonne Chance, Mme Lynne*.

"Open that," Clora Lynne said. "I'm going to the bathroom."

Ross looked at the champagne and smiled. "Don't be long," he said. "I'm horny."

In the bathroom, everything was as she wanted it. The staff had filled the bath with chocolate. This time, it was not drinking chocolate, but thick, viscous, with the consistency of treacle. She pulled her knickers down, sat on the toilet and urinated, then got up, flushed, stepped out of her knickers, and went to the sink where she splashed water on her face. Just as she returned to the bedroom, Ross popped the champagne and poured two glasses.

He handed one to her. "To Leonora," he said. "Empress of the Human Worlds, Lord Protector of the True Philosophy, High Admiral of All the Fleets, and Successor to the Glorious Founder."

As he spoke, a startled smile spread on Clora Lynne's face. "You remembered!" she beamed at him. "That's who I am!"

And Davison Ross indulged her with a smile. They clinked glasses, then drained them.

"Let's get into character," he said.

Clora Lynne put down her champagne glass and took off her blouse. She had been wearing no bra.

"My God," Ross said, "but you are old."

"So are you, ass-cream man," Clora Lynne said. "Now let's not spoil things." Then she took down her skirt and stepped out of it.

Davison Ross stared at her in wonder. He put down his own glass, went over to kiss her, but she backed away. "Go into the other room. Your bag's there. Come back in here as Raven."

"I brought the little leather costume from season four," he said. "You like that one."

Clora Lynne smiled. Ross went into the other room.

When he came back, she had changed into her black starburst dress with the collar. Ross was wearing his Raven costume. His jaw dropped. "You're…beautiful," he said. "Leonora."

"Raven," Clora Lynne said, channeling Leonora. "I have you in my power and nothing in the world can save you now."

They met in the middle of the floor and threw themselves into an awkward embrace. On the show, when they kissed, the rules were that their mouths never really connected. Now, there were no rules.

"Your friends are dead," Clora Lynne said, after she broke away from their kiss, "and your secret base is even now being overrun by my stormtroopers."

"I…" Ross said.

"That's where you're wrong," she prompted him.

"That's where you're wrong," Ross said. "Even now, the *Emancipator* is in orbit, ready to pluck me from this place. I'll not be your prisoner for long. But first…" he gripped her jaw in his right hand and threw her to the floor. She fell back, in an ecstasy of defeat.

"But first," Ross continued, "I have to kill you."

"You'll never do it!" Clora Lynne hissed, from the floor. "My guards will burst through that door any second now!"

Ross got on his knees and pounced between her legs. He took her starburst dress and tore the skirt, ripping it open. She grabbed his hair and buried his head in her pussy as though rubbing a dog's nose in its own mess. Then she pushed him away and said, "Not yet."

Ross backed off and knelt before her. "What do you mean, not yet?"

"I mean," Clora Lynne shouted, picking herself up off the floor, "that you are not worthy to ravish the Empress of the Human Worlds!"

Ross stood up. "Oh well," he said. "I have to go to the bathroom." And he went.

Clora Lynne, in the torn dress of Empress Leonora, sat on the bed, waiting for him. She expected him to cry out in surprise, but he did not. Instead, he calmly went about his business, then returned as though nothing was unusual.

Calmly, he said, "I see the bath is full of chocolate."

Clora Lynne nodded and got up.

"Well if that's the way you want it, Leonora," Ross said, gruffly, "then I'm going to have to cover you in Arcturian Love Paint before I fuck your brains out, Your Majesty."

Excitedly, Clora Lynne rushed to him and made to slap his face. As expected, he grabbed her wrist and once more threw her down, this time on the bed. He set to work, ripping the rest of the dress off her. In the wreckage of her Empress's gown, Clora Lynne gave in to him.

Ross lifted her up, not without difficulty, as neither of them was young, and carried her into the bathroom. All the way, Clora was swooning with delight. "Raven," she mouthed. "You have defeated me. My armies are yours. I... surrender."

In the bathroom, as gently as he could manage, Davison Ross lowered Clora Lynne into the bath of chocolate. Then he took off his clothes as if to join her.

"No," Clora Lynne said. "I want you naked, in the bedroom. Wait there for me."

So, bemused, he did.

For a few glorious moments, Clora Lynne wallowed in chocolate, thick as a mud bath, not watered down as she usually had it. This time, she would be caked in the stuff, absolutely brown. She did not make herself come. When she was done luxuriating, she got out of the bath and did not towel herself off. Covered in the gloopy substance, she went into the bedroom.

Stunned, Davison Ross watched as Clora Lynne lay down on the bed and raised her legs as though giving birth. She opened wide for him.

"I want you to lick me," Clora Lynne said. "Gently, just my pussy."

And down he went.

When it was over, when Clora Lynne had gushed, and when Davison Ross had licked her pussy clean, she pushed his head away. "Look at me," she said. "Stand up and look at me."

Ross did as he was told.

"You see the pink bit?" Clora Lynne asked him. "You see the pink bit in the middle, between my legs? And the rest of me covered in chocolate?"

Ross nodded.

"I'm Turkish Delight," Clora Lynne said.

Ross threw back his head, laughed like a maniac, and jumped on her again.

They made love five times that night. That is to say, Ross came once, prematurely, but his penis was not exactly the little trouper that, in his youth, had made entire chorus lines trip over themselves to get to him. Clora Lynne came five times. Once, when Ross had gone down on her that first time, and four more times, when, one by one, she had a Turkish Delight in her mouth as he pleasured her with his fingers.

In the morning, Ross was gone. There was a note in the bath-room, written in chocolate on the mirror.

Thank you, Leonora. I think I'd better get back to my wife now. Have a nice life, what's left of it. DR.

Clora Lynne sat on the toilet, naked, reading it. It was her turn to laugh.

Soon, she would have a shower. Then, she would call room service and get them to clean up the mess. She would leave them a very large tip. After that, went her plan, she would close up here and get on a flight to London.

Terrence Elliotte had been watching everything on her web-cam, and recording it. Soon, the video would go all around the Internet. At the very least, Ross would lose his marriage. She expected to see photos in the tabloids. She expected that Ross would become a laughingstock. She expected that the lump was benign. And she expected that perhaps, just perhaps, she would get her own reality show.

Half an hour later, as she stepped out of the shower and into a bathrobe, the telephone rang.

LEE UPTON

Bitter Chocolate

Lee Upton is the author of four books of poetry and four books of literary criticism, most recently, Defensive Measures. *Her fiction has appeared in* The Antioch Review, Ascent, Gargoyle, Glimmer Train, Northwest Review, *and* Shenandoah.

> *Give me my Romeo; and when he shall die,*
> *Take him and cut him out in little stars,*
> *And he will make the face of heaven so fine*
> *That all the world will be in love with night,*
> *And pay no worship to the garish sun;*
> *Oh, I have bought the mansion of a love,*
> *But not possessed it, and though I am sold,*
> *Not yet enjoyed.*
> —William Shakespeare

He has no rivals for her love. Not the two foil bunny boys three boxes beneath him, half her size and thus no competition. Not the sexless Peeps. And if a floor assistant with the crooked part in her auburn hair—if she would reach up and slide him over next to the goosegirl....

A man appears in the lingerie section to finger a chemise the size and consistency of a tablespoon of sugar. The cunningly arranged chocolates on their tower are there to drive a stake into some poor woman's heart. If lace doesn't melt her resistance, chocolate will. The man lifts the goosegirl bunny and turns her upside down. He turns her right side up and stares into her eyes.

She stares back, as blank-faced as a Golem. He puts her back where she came from.

The man has a jelly roll of fat at the back of his neck.

Buster breathes again.

He and the goosegirl should be grateful. They could have been available at the dollar store next to the turkey baster and the many-jointed Thanksgiving pilgrim. And the leprechaun figurine and the patriotic ponytail holder and the mesh scouring pads. But no. They are among the elite, in an upscale department store, among the inducements meant for passion. And they could lead a long life. They could last into the summer.

With satisfaction, Buster remembers shoppers' intake of breath upon seeing his price tag. Even after they have admired his quaint little trousers and his sweet little boots made of a pale blue substance resembling scuffed linoleum, they still can't get over how much he's worth.

Buster tries to catch the goosegirl's eye, and so at first he doesn't see that the man who had inspected her moments ago is coming back and pursing his lips in the goosegirl's direction. Huge and haired, with a gold knot below the knuckle, the man's hand reaches up for the goosegirl. The man brings the goosegirl down and holds her in front of his tie. She's the size of an Oscar, and he grips her at her waist as if he has won her before he walks away with her, right in front of Buster's eyes.

Buster is breathless. He's only a farmer with a watering can and a sugar carrot in his pocket. He's hollow. He's stiff. All his passion has come to nothing.

And now, as if all the world is making fun of him, the floor assistant is giggling with a salesman from the men's department. She trips on ahead of the salesman, setting up static electricity, swiveling past the snowy garment bins, drawing the fellow behind her as if he's her pull toy. Her hip catches at the second tier of the chocolate tower and the concussion sends Buster flying.

Buster's head bumps the thin prophylactic he's sheathed in. Stars and flames cloud the florescent lozenges of the ceiling lights.

A moment later his ear hangs off the side of his head.

When he wakes, Buster looks up to see the floor assistant putting the tower of chocolates together again. The nozzle of his watering can is still spinning beside him.

Just when he is sure he will be forgotten, Buster rises into the air. He is riding in the floor assistant's palms up to the cashier. He is purchased with a ten percent employee discount plus damage reduction.

As the air around him grows cold and the spring sky turns violet, Buster is held close to the woman's purse. And then he is tossed into the front seat of a Volvo.

What awaits him?

A brief stay on a glass coffee table only to witness the arrival of the menswear attendant for the long Easter weekend?

Or over time to dissemble slowly into cocoa dust—like a puff of ash from an underground mine, like crazed talc, like dusty bat guano?

Where is the goosegirl? he wonders. He grits his two teeth.

He supposes that with his ear gone he's not so good-looking anymore. It's like having a blow hole in his head.

What's the use anyway? He might be categorized as a farmland bunny, but he has never held a plow in his hands. Never took a horse its bucket or a chicken its feed.

Where oh where is the goosegirl?

Why have all his plans come to this?

When the young woman makes a left turn, Buster is thrust against the cup holder.

The heat in the car rises until Buster dreams of geese that whistle and volcanoes that spew and a shiny copper fondue pot assuming the shape of a foil sunshine reflector in a tanning booth. A giant hand emerges, with freckles like cinnamon on a café latte, and Buster's whole life passes through his dream backward until he's confronted with the most vivid image of a ladle.

No farmland anywhere, his nightmares shooting through him—and so why not be honest now. Tell the truth, tell us if you don't know him.

Good night, Buster, bound for drizzling atop a holiday panettone.

Good night, love without consequences.

RICHARD PEABODY, a prolific poet, fiction writer, and editor, is an experienced teacher and important activist in the Washington, D.C., community of letters. He is editor of Gargoyle Magazine *(founded in 1976), and has published a novella, two books of short stories, six books of poems, plus an e-book, and edited (or co-edited) eleven anthologies, including* Mondo Barbie, Mondo Elvis, Conversations with Gore Vidal, A Different Beat: Writings by Women of the Beat Generation, *and* Alice Redux: New Stories of Alice, Lewis, and Wonderland. *Peabody teaches fiction writing for the Johns Hopkins Advanced Studies Program. You can find out more about him at www.gargoylemagazine.com.*

LUCINDA EBERSOLE is the co-editor of several anthologies, including the infamous Mondo Barbie *and* Coming to Terms. *She is the author of numerous short stories, which have been published in* Yellow Silk, The Crescent Review, Barcelona Review, *and* American Letters and Commentary, *among others. She is the owner of Atticus Books, a virtual antiquarian bookstore in Shirley, West Virginia, where she lives. Her first novel,* Death in Equality, *was published by St. Martin's Press in 1997.*

Creative director DAVID PAUL WYATT PERKO delivered this astounding cover design via the graphic design company EdibleUmbrella. Perko is also a main brain behind Emperor Penguin Recordings. From a mountain (in hiding from unmentionable, vicious, and horrid forces) in Boise, Idaho, Perko continuously performs his endless array of duties in almost complete isolation. He shares his rare downtime with creative companions Indrid Cold, Mysterious Creature vocalist Curse Murphy, and musician Trevor Tanner (formerly of The Bolshoi). You can contact Mr. Perko at The Mysterious Creatures of OceanAstro's headquarters via info@embassygray.com (tell 'em Large Marge sent cha).